The Letters

The Art of Life,
Love, and Opera

Mary Ellen Cipolla
Grasso

WORD ASSOCIATION PUBLISHERS
www.wordassociation.com
1.800.827.7903

ISBN: 978-1-59571-879-2

Library of Congress Control Number: 2013903074

Designed and published by
Word Association Publishers
205 Fifth Avenue
Tarentum, Pennsylvania 15084

www.wordassociation.com

1.800.827.7903

The magic in my life still continues through my incredible family
Stephen and Lisa and their sons Brenton and Kyle
and
Susan and Joe and their sons Ford and Tucker.

Forward

In quiet moments, I sometimes refer to letters I have written and received. As I read through these snapshots, recalling a time long ago, I realize the importance of each moment and how every single event influences the next.

It isn't easy to grow up. Growing pains do not just refer to changes in height. Growing pains also refer to the changes in depth, in capacity, and in our ability to understand. This is important to remember when life is bleak. It is so much easier to say things worked out just the way they were supposed to ---- later. I have come to understand that the journey is important and should be cherished.

The book is not about letters but about the people who wrote them. The people I loved and adored ---- whether they deserved my affection or not. I learned a lot about myself by writing and receiving letters, an art that is lost today. When I read the letters now, the lessons seem obvious, but in the moment it is not quite easy to "see" or "understand" the message. Through the years I have learned to trust my instincts, to listen to that little voice inside me, to pay attention to every detail, every word, and to know that nothing happens by chance. There is indeed a reason for all things.

I hope the young women who read my book will see themselves, find hope, and be inspired to be fearless. Life is short, my dear friends. Live well. My book is set in another time, but feelings are timeless. Finding love, breaking up, and moving on are not easy. But they are the steps necessary for a full life as they open our hearts to our next great adventure.

The First Letters

My big independent adventures began after college. I didn't think I was pursuing big dreams. Rather, I was enjoying myself, *expecting* my life to be fine. Everything would work out like it should, and everyone would be happy. I expected to have a good life. My life had been without any great pain or loss, so I just thought that if I worked hard and did everything that was expected of me, nothing would ever go really wrong. I was fearless in my expectations and didn't even know it. I hadn't learned yet that sometimes the "failures" are the beginning of what is to come, what is supposed to be. I was a serious person and took everything to heart: my life, my feelings, and my future. I savored each experience and never allowed myself to think that people were anything other than who they said they were. I kept my heart open and allowed people and events to touch me.

I kept movie tickets, programs, photos, and especially letters: scraps of evidence saved to memorialize my life. I realize now that my life was punctuated by letters written to me by people I had met and loved, and those letters became catalysts that worked to change my life. I must have saved those letters, like one would save a photograph stored in a private place or in a box hidden on a closet shelf because they were too dear to part with as they represented places in time that had been cherished deeply but were now gone forever. A letter allows me to go back exactly to a place in time. Unlike a memory, a letter is physical evidence that feelings were true. Because the words are written in black on white stationery, I can always go back and see exactly what was said as many times as I wish to do so. I can touch the handwriting and

Mary Ellen Cipolla Grasso

envision the writer. I know now that each letter became a piece of a puzzle, telling the story of my life,that gave me direction, strength, and power although I was not aware of it at that time.

Perhaps at the time, I thought the letters might be important someday, but I didn't know why. I certainly did not have any burning desire to live in the past. I was certain I had destroyed them. Obviously, I hadn't. What made me keep them? Did I want tangible evidence of an unusual life for a woman at that time? Did I keep the letters because I never wanted to forget what emotions I felt at each exact moment? I loved every moment of my life—even those that ended in heartbreak. Those difficult times gave me capacity to enjoy the best ones with more intense feeling. Did I think the letters would be important some day for my children or because I wanted to understand the person I once was? Now, reading the letters today allows me to feel those same emotions I experienced long ago. I had forgotten I had saved those letters. When I found them, they transported me back in time, to a life filled with love and "opera."

Ah! The letters. How sweet it is to have had such delicious experiences and people to remember. The joy is in having had the experience and being able to remember them now in all their glory. What an incredible treasure to have a tangible connection to such delightful people, times, and places in your hands 52 years later. I envy you. I envy those tears that express how wonderful you have lived and have touched people put in your path.

Your life has been a brilliantly painted canvas, a moving composition, a kaleidoscope of events, people, and places. I feel so privileged to have enjoyed the stories of your escapades in Mexico during an adventurous time of your life, ending with the Ultimate Adventure with Orazio, The Wonderful.

---Mary DiStefano Diaz
Professor of English as a Second Language
Broward College
Davie, Florida

Finding the Letters

I don't know what it was that suddenly awakened me on October 11, 2008, at 2:30 a.m. I hadn't been dreaming. I wasn't having a nightmare, but I quickly sat up in bed wondering what it was that my former fiancé Ray had written in his letter of 1955, telling me the engagement was over and the marriage was off. Fifty-three years ago Ray gave me no reason for his change of heart. Why did I now want that letter after all those years? I got out of bed and began to look for his letters. I knew I had saved them, but I couldn't remember where they were. It had been years since I had seen those letters or even remembered about them. I knew from his obituary that Ray had died of cancer in 1996. Whatever made me think of Ray and that letter written so many years ago?

I looked in one of the dresser drawers. Ray's few letters weren't there. I checked the top shelf of my closet where I kept a box of mementos: programs, tickets to concerts, and other trifles. There were no letters from Ray. I went into the guest room, frantically looking for that one letter. All of the lights in the house were now blazing as I went from one room to another. I searched the cedar chest in the guest bedroom. No letter. I was wide-awake. I went back to my bedroom and decided to check the chest of drawers where I stored all of my sweaters. As I reached under the last neatly folded sweater, I found four stacks of letters written between 1955 and 1958 from four men I knew who lived in Mexico. The largest stack was from Memo (Guillermo Espinosa Sanchez), who worked for Mobil Oil, S.A. Two other stacks were from his friends: Guillermo Alvarez de la Cadena, an aspiring bullfighter, and Pepe, or Jose Delgado, Public Relations Director of Colgate

The Letters

Palmolive, S. A., a playwright, artist, novelist, and philosopher. All three men lived and worked in Mexico City. The last stack was from Pedro Alberto Pineda, an administrator at the *Gran Hotel Ancira* in Monterrey, where my friends, Carol and Dorothy, and I had stayed during a summer vacation in 1955.

I looked at the letters somewhat in disbelief that they still existed. I wanted to put them back into the drawer, but I couldn't. I fanned the letters on my bed, touching them. Did I want to read them? Did I want to remember the days of my youth in a country that I once had loved? Sadly, Mexico City is no longer like the one I remembered. On a vacation in 1982 with friends, Joyce and Gil Puissegur, and my late husband Orazio, I was disappointed to discover the Mexico I had loved disappeared. As I looked at the letters, still in shock that they existed, I decided to scan just a few, but that was a mistake.

Here were those old letters that brought me back to one of the most fascinating times of my life. I had forgotten all about those years--those wonderful, marvelous, delicious years when I had first escaped from heartbreak and later when I attended the University of Mexico in Mexico City. Reading some of those letters made me relive those days when I had not only fallen in love with the country but also with two men who fell in love with me. Finally, I stopped reading and put the letters away for another day. For weeks, however, feeling very nostalgic after finding those letters, especially the ones from Memo and Pedro, I wasn't able to sleep well. I was reliving those days, many of great joy and love and others of sadness and tears. Those days were some of the most incredible times of my life, and I couldn't get the images out of my mind of those men in Mexico and the memorable moments we had shared.

Broken Engagement

After earning both Bachelor's and Master's Degrees, becoming an educator, and my experience in the commercial sector, I once again taught at Arnold High School. I had first taught there when I graduated from college but left after a year and a half to enter the field of journalism as the Public Relations Director of The Pittsburgh Motor Club and then as the editor of *The Catholic Observer*, the newspaper for the Diocese of Pittsburgh. I was engaged and planning a summer wedding. Because the high school did not have a cafeteria, it was customary to go home for the hour-long lunch period. One day I was delighted to see a letter from my fiancé, Ray, lying on the kitchen table when I walked into the kitchen. We were in the last stages of planning the wedding, set for June 25, 1955, and he had gone to Florida searching for a job. I opened the letter with anticipation and joy, but then I couldn't believe what I was reading. It was a confusing letter, first telling me that he got a job working with a surveyor and then telling me our engagement was over and our marriage was off. I was heartbroken, especially when he wrote, "I still love you, but I can't marry you."

I didn't understand this since I had spoken with him the night before, long after this letter from him had been placed in the mail. At that time he told me that his sister Janet had his wedding guest list ready, and I should have her send it to me. He said this, all the time knowing that his letter from Florida was already in the mail. That action hurt me more than the letter itself. Never did he give me any indication that his feelings had changed or that he wanted to cancel the wedding. Perhaps I should not have been blindsided as I was. Always with Ray, I was guarded, never asking him too many questions about his past. Ray once said, "I wish I could trust you enough to tell you about myself." He never revealed himself to me. I knew from his parents that he had worked in New York before we met and for some reason left the job. I never knew whether he had been fired, forced to resign, or just left the job. I knew that he did have one job for a very short time during the months we were together, but he didn't seek another. I also knew that a department store in Pittsburgh telephoned my home because he had not paid his credit account. My mother spoke with someone in the credit department who wanted "to speak with his wife." My mother simply replied that he was not married, just engaged.

In hindsight, I should have realized that his telling me just hours before he would leave for Florida that he was going to look for a job was suspicious. We had gone to dinner in Pittsburgh as we had many times before. During dinner he said, "This is going to be a surprise for you, but I thought that after we married, we would move to Florida. I am leaving tonight by Greyhound Bus so that I can get a job and find an apartment for us." I was stunned. He kept reassuring me that since most of the wedding plans were completed, he felt comfortable knowing that I could complete the few that remained. Even though he had not been too involved in the wedding details, I had no reason not to believe him. I loved him unconditionally. In retrospect, I suppose his canceling the wedding probably saved me from more heartache, but it was difficult to feel that way when I read the letter.

I was heartbroken. I stopped eating to read the letter a second time and became hysterical. My mother couldn't calm me, and I knew I couldn't return to teach the afternoon classes, forcing my mother to call the principal, Dr. Joseph Pallone, to tell him that I had suddenly become ill. I recalled that Ray loved to see me wearing anything in blush pink, and I had ordered a beautiful gown in that color to please him. Kaufmann's department store in Pittsburgh had scheduled an appointment for my first fitting, and I had circled the date on my desk calendar. The cancelled dress-fitting date that year became a constant reminder of my sadness and disappointment. I would have to telephone the Bridal Department to cancel the appointment and the gown.

Back then most of my friends were married. A few married before they were twenty years old. Those who went to college married shortly after graduation. I did not. It was not for the lack of dates; I just never found the right man for me. I met Ray through his mother, Goldie Ronk, who shared a hospital room with my mother during the late spring of 1954. I had gone to the hospital one afternoon to visit my mother. She introduced me to her roommate who said, "You just missed my son. He left a few minutes ago. You probably got off the elevator as he as getting on. He was here visiting for quite a while." She wanted me to meet him and several months later she telephoned my mother to ask if it was all right if Ray and she came to visit. I was not home when they arrived. As director of the senior class play, I was at rehearsals until 9:30 or 10:00 p.m, but that evening I dismissed the cast early. My mother, Goldie, and Ray were in the kitchen having coffee and cake. While Goldie and my mother remained in the kitchen talking, Ray and I sat in the living room getting acquainted. He happened to see a Book of the Month selection I had been reading. He wanted to know if it was mine. I explained that the faculty at the high school where I taught had a book club, and each teacher who wanted to participate bought a book each month, read it, and then circulated it among the readers.

We started talking about books we were reading and other common interests, and I found Ray to be very personable. When his mother and he left, I had no reason to think that we would ever meet again, but a month later my parents and I were invited to an early afternoon barbecue at their home, about an hour and a half drive from Arnold. That day Ray and I spent much time together, even playing with one of his young nephews. He knew that I was attending the University of Pittsburgh on Saturday mornings, taking classes to earn a teaching certificate in Spanish, and he asked if we could meet in Pittsburgh, a halfway mark between his home and mine because he didn't have a car and had to travel by bus. We dated in this way about five months and then sometimes he drove home with me to Arnold on a weekend and stayed overnight at the home I shared with my parents.

On one of those Saturday afternoon dates in Pittsburgh, we had gone to a restaurant, and as we sat at the table talking and waiting for our lunch to be served, he suddenly reached across the table, held my hand, and proposed: "I should be saying this with flowers, a ring, and champagne, but there aren't any here. Will you marry me anyway?" I was already in love with him, and it was easy to answer, "Yes, I will."

I reached across the table to put my hands over his. "Ray, I've loved you for some time now, almost since the first time I met you."

He looked at me and said, "Why didn't you ever tell me?"

All I could answer was "I couldn't. I didn't know how you felt. I didn't want to be hurt."

His reply? "I will never hurt you. Trust me."

Because I was scheduled to chaperone a school dance, I telephoned home to tell my mother that I would be late and to telephone the co-advisor, Bill Hajel, to let him know. I told her that Ray had just proposed to me. I was so excited that I must have sped all the way home. Ray had borrowed his father's car, and he had to return it that evening. He would not be coming home with me. Never did I believe the ending would not be as we had planned it. We were engaged in December, two weeks before Christmas, when Ray surprised me with a ring. Ray and I set a date for the wedding and began to take Marriage Preparation classes at my Catholic church, Mount Saint Peter.

After my marriage plans with Ray failed, everyone knew. I lived in a small town in western Pennsylvania, where everyone knew everyone else. I had a large extended family who were all delighted when I became engaged. I taught in the local high school, the same one from which I had graduated. My family was prominent, and it seemed as though everyone kept asking, "What happened?" I couldn't answer because I didn't know the reason. I heard students whispering when they noticed I no longer wore the engagement ring. I felt confused, rejected, and depressed. For more than six weeks I just taught my classes and continued taking a few classes at the university, putting one foot in front of the other, getting by, but not really living. It was all I could do to get out of bed in the morning. I was so distraught that for the first time in my life, I earned an "F." It was in Spanish grammar. I just couldn't concentrate. I really didn't care anymore. I found it difficult to talk with my parents or siblings. I just withdrew. I almost never ate dinner with my parents and my brother Ron but chose to remain in my room grading papers or developing curriculum. I felt very dejected, and sometimes I just wept until I fell asleep.

My family worried about me. I remember one morning on my way to work, my mother's cousin, Anita, who cleaned and ironed for us, said, "Mary Ellen, you only mourn for the dead three days. So get over it." She meant the formal visitations of the deceased and the funeral, which lasted traditionally three days. I realized that she was right, but I felt humiliated. I didn't know what I was going to do, only that I had to keep moving. I just needed to get away.

Leaving America

It was then that two friends and I decided that we needed to get out of the country for a while. We couldn't afford to travel to Europe, so we decided on Monterrey, Mexico, for a summer vacation, just far enough away from the United States. Since my Uncle Jimmy and Aunt Marye lived in New Orleans, I suggested that we could stop there for two days and see the French Quarter. There were two of us who just wanted to get away from the men who had betrayed us. Dorothy was to have been married June 18, a week before my June 25 wedding. I knew only that Dorothy's fiancé had been in the Navy, but I did not know why the relationship ended. Carol saw the trip as an opportunity to vacation in Mexico and was delighted that we were going. We took turns driving my 1951 Ford Sedan, which I had named *The Green Hornet*.

Those were the days of no air-conditioners in automobiles. One day we decided to stop in Biloxi, Mississippi, to go swimming because of the heat. Dorothy and I did a lot of crying while traveling on the road. Some song on the radio made one of us cry, either "our song" or "that song was going to be for our first dance." After driving a number of miles, we dried our tears, which we all shared, and decided just to stop and try to have a good time on the beach in Biloxi. We swam and sun bathed. Two men, also swimming, decided to sit with us on the beach. Carol and Dorothy chatted with them. I was still feeling sad and depressed, and after a short time I went to the dressing room to shower, get dressed, and be ready to travel again. As I showered, I noticed that my shoulders, arms, and legs were a bright red.

Little did I know that what I thought was just a sunburn was really a bad case of sun poisoning.

We arrived at my Uncle Jimmy and Aunt Marye's home planning to go to the French Quarter that night. I was excited to see everyone, but I felt miserable, and I remember that Dorothy and Carol chose not to go to the French Quarter that evening without me. We were sure that we could go the next day. In the middle of the night, I spiked a high fever, and my uncle called his doctor, who came about 3:00 a.m. I had sun poisoning. He gave me an antibiotic and an ointment and advised me not to travel the next day. By the next afternoon I felt a bit better and wanted to go to the French Quarter, but Uncle Jimmy thought it was unwise since I still had a fever. Dorothy and Carol wouldn't go without me, and I felt guilty about ruining their vacation. We left the next morning for Mexico, but I was still suffering from that severe sunburn. Carol and Dorothy drove while I slept on the back seat, stopping along the road for cold watermelon. Still feeling guilty about their not touring the French Quarter, I suggested we stop to visit The Alamo.

Mexico Adventures

We believed the trip to Monterrey would be uneventful. It was anything but that. Driving along the mountainous roads in Mexico, we noticed that the car was overheating. We stopped the car on a shoulder of the road, opened the hood, and looked in. There we were--three women alone in Mexico on the side of a lonely road with little mechanical knowledge, if any, peering inside, under the hood of the car. None of us knew exactly what to do. We thought the radiator cap was about to blow. At least we knew not to try to remove the cap. We were completely unprepared and had no tools to help us. Our brilliant idea was to get a motorist to stop and help us, but most of the vehicles traveling on the road had Mexican license plates, and their drivers just whizzed by. Finally, we spied a car with a Texas license plate. Great! Our fellow Americans would stop and help us. The three men in the car did slow down, stop for a second, look at us, and then just drive by. Disappointed, we thought about removing the radiator cap, which we believed was now cool, but we didn't even have a rag to help us unscrew the cap, a container of water to put into the radiator, or a bucket to fill with water if we found any nearby. We didn't even have an empty gallon bottle. It was looking pretty bleak, and we still had miles to drive.

In the distance we saw a truck coming down the road. The driver stopped, and we noticed the truck was from the Carta Blanca Beer Company. The driver who spoke as much English as we spoke Spanish was able to remove the cap and put water into the radiator. He kept saying, "*Pobres senioritas.*" He then told us to look for the signs along the road that read "*Agua.*" Before he left, he gave us a small bucket for water and reminded us again to stop, and stop we did at every possible hut, farm, or well we saw that had a sign. We were amazed at how helpful those Mexicans along the road were. They opened the hood, took off the cap, and poured water into the radiator. We offered to tip them, but they refused. After many stops, the *Green Hornet* finally got us to Monterrey without any other problems although we did have the car checked at a service station recommended by the hotel during the next week.

We arrived at our destination happy, tired, and a little less sad. After our road challenges, we felt powerful and ready for anything. We were staying at the *Gran Hotel Ancira* and that evening chose to walk to a nearby restaurant. *The Green Hornet* was tired and needed a rest, so we parked the car in the hotel garage. The truth was that we just wanted to be "out on the town." We found a very nice restaurant, went in, sat down, and ordered wine. With the help of the waiter, who described some of the entrees for us, we made our selections. From the menu that was all in Spanish, we found the service in that Mexican restaurant to be quite slow, but then we had had no experience with restaurants south of the border. We were sure that we had ordered just three glasses of wine, but the waiter, instead, set a large bottle of wine on the table with three glasses. We tried to refuse the bottle, but there was a lack of communication. The waiter poured the wine, took the bottle, and left. While we waited for our dinners, we were served yet another three glasses of wine. We never ordered more than one alcoholic drink each, and we were told that the three men sitting across the room had ordered them for us. We turned to look at the men, and they waved. We smiled and waved back.

We then asked the waiter to thank the men. Suddenly, a violinist seemed to have come out of nowhere and appeared at our table. We thought he was just wandering around, playing romantic tunes for tips. We looked at each other not sure what to tip him, but the three men were just behind him, and they took care of the tip since they had asked him to serenade us. The men had already finished their dinner and asked if they could sit with us while we finished ours. Feeling a bit flirtatious, we said yes. There was small talk. One of them was an engineer, another had a leather shop, and I don't recall what the third did. They asked us the usual questions: "Where do you live? What do you do? Are you attending the college in Monterrey?" After a while, they asked if we had seen Monterrey at night, especially the mountains of the two lovers. Of course, we hadn't. We had just arrived that afternoon.

They said that they "would be most happy to take us sightseeing" because their car was parked outside. We felt comfortable and safe talking with those men. After all, there were three of us. They spoke English fluently, and feeling adventuresome, we agreed. The trip around the city and its outskirts was quite enjoyable. The men knew the history of the sites and were better than any tour guide I had in the States. A couple of hours later, they dropped us off at the hotel, said "Good night," and I never saw them again. Perhaps the other two did. Would we do that today? Go sightseeing with three strangers we had just met? NO! Of course not. But that was a different period of time. We were in our twenties and had been working for some years. We felt perfectly secure accepting their invitation and riding with them.

Several days later Pedro, an administrator of the *Gran Hotel Ancira* who always made a point of conversing with me when I stopped at the desk to drop off my room key, asked me out to dinner and a movie. After all, I reasoned, "What harm is there in going to a movie?" Little did I know. What I did know was that Pedro and I had an instant connection when we first met, and that was the reason I had accepted his invitation and not for the reason I gave him that "I have never seen a Mexican movie." Besides, I wanted to get to know him better.

At the movie theater, he chose to sit in the upper balcony. We sat down, and he held my hand. Then he leaned over and kissed me. I asked him not to do so, but he continued. I wasn't as reluctant the second time. Two days later he invited me to visit one of the historical museums. We walked and talked, nothing personal, just about the exhibits and the city's landmarks. Later, we sat on a park bench and just continued talking. He kissed me again, and I felt butterflies in my stomach. I was attracted to him and he to me. Here I was trying to take a break from men, and I found myself being attracted to one. However, I did become concerned when he started to notice when I came and left the hotel. For the remainder of our stay, I took my room key with me. I didn't want him to know whether I was in or out. If Carol, Dorothy, and I were out, we didn't always leave or return to the hotel together because I was still quite sunburned and blistered. In short, some days I felt miserable, and the Mexican sun didn't help. Furthermore, I did not want Pedro to keep tabs on me, which I learned he had.

Pedro told me that he was originally from Spain, but when he was a boy during the Spanish Civil War, his parents sent him to Italy with many other Spanish children. He lived in Italy with a foster Italian family until the end of the Civil War, but I am not sure how and when he got to Mexico. I found him to be extremely well educated, speaking English, Spanish, and Italian fluently. The fact that he was tall and quite handsome was an attraction of its own. He was very intelligent, very cultured, and very charismatic. He even encouraged me to speak Spanish. Still, I had only less than a two-week vacation, and I did not want to get involved because I had made the trip to get over a heartbreak.

The Letters

So, I avoided Pedro as much as possible. The night before it was time to return home, we were sitting in the lobby talking. No one else was there. He leaned over and kissed me again. My emotions were in chaos. I was glad that we were leaving the next day, and I had no thought of ever returning to Monterrey. Why start a relationship now? It was futile. "That kiss was just a moment in time," I told myself. The trip helped Dorothy and me cope with whatever heartbreak we had suffered, but my emotional response to Pedro made me want to continue studying Spanish.

Duke University

The summer before my trip to Monterrey, I had studied Spanish at Duke University on a scholarship to attend a session at Duke's School of Languages. I was scheduled to teach Spanish at the high school where I was employed. After my summer trip, I knew I couldn't return for another summer session at Duke because a scholarship was not available, and I couldn't afford the tuition, room, and board. I thought I might like to attend a university in Mexico to continue working on a Master's Degree in Spanish. I liked the idea that at Duke we were required to speak only Spanish. I reasoned that attending a university in Mexico would give me greater opportunity to speak the language most of the time because I would be immersed in it.

At Duke in the summer of 1954, I had met a Brazilian resident doctor from Duke Hospital at a Fourth of July party sponsored by some of the students attending the School of Languages. I began to date Berto, as I called him, instead of using his name Humberto that everyone else used. I enjoyed being with Berto, and I found him to be very pleasant, but I considered him to be just a good friend. I know now that Spanish men don't always want to be "good friends." I discovered that on our last date.

We had gone to dinner and a movie at Chapel Hill and were returning to Duke University. As he drove back to campus, he took one hand off the wheel and drew me closer to him, trying to kiss me while he was driving. I resisted his attempt. I wasn't thinking of him in that way. He lost control of the car, missed the road, and landed in a deep ravine. I hit my forehead on the windshield and suffered a gash. Blood ran down my forehead and face and on my dress, but he was more concerned about the damage to his car-- especially the windshield, not me. I was worried about the School of Languages getting a demerit because I had missed curfew, and the director was proud of the fact that the School had never received a demerit, emphasizing that at orientation.

Doors were locked from the outside, and only the campus police had keys. According to campus rules then, I had to go to the campus police to report in. I didn't know until later that the director had planned to cover up my late arrival by opening the door for me from the inside. He took pride in the fact that the School of Languages had never received a demerit. Instead of returning at midnight, the curfew, I returned about 1:30 in the morning because Berto and I had to wait until someone driving along the same road happened by chance to see the car in the ravine. There was almost no traffic on that road, but a driver who stopped promised to call the police when he got home, which he did. A tow truck pulled the car out of the ravine, and we were able to continue driving. The gash on my forehead was superficial, and I chose not to go to Duke Hospital. However, I did report to the campus police who took me to the School of Languages, and the school got a demerit because I had missed curfew. However, once everyone learned about the accident, saw the blood and the gash on my forehead, the demerit was removed. At the School's annual farewell dinner held at the end of the summer term, I was given a policeman's whistle from the Campus Police with a note: "Use this the next time." I was embarrassed by the attention, but everyone else laughed. I stopped dating Berto after the accident, but he still telephoned me.

The accident wasn't the only problem I had that summer that worried the director. One eventful evening I had gone to the infirmary because of a severe toothache, but because the student infirmary was closed, I was sent to the emergency room. Just as I arrived, a patient who had been stabbed and slashed by her husband was wheeled in accompanied by two police officers. I was just a student with a toothache. One of the doctors had checked me and asked the nurse on duty to give me pain pills. I was instructed to take one every four hours and see the oral surgeon the next morning. The following morning, I could barely walk. I was holding onto the walls of the corridor and stumbling just as one of the other students, Libby, grabbed my arm and insisted that I go to the cafeteria with her for something to eat. The cafeteria was closed, but I was offered a large glass of grape juice. Libby insisted that I return to the emergency room.

I remember very little. Libby did explain to a nurse that I was to see the oral surgeon that morning. I do know that I was refused entrance to the hospital's emergency room because I was a student, so I was sent to the students' infirmary where I was placed on a gurney. Libby placed a large piece of cardboard on my chest with my name printed on it and left for class. I do recall actually sitting in the surgeon's dental chair, and I do remember giving him the yellow envelope with the remainder of the pills. He started to check my mouth; then he suddenly started to shake me: "Wake up! Wake up! Stay awake! Look at me!" When I didn't respond as quickly as he wanted, he unbuttoned my blouse to check my heartbeat with his stethoscope. Then he ran to the telephone. The last thing I remembered was his voice: "I have a student here who has overdosed on pain medication and may die."

I didn't remember anything else until I found myself in a hospital cubicle. An intern was with me, and I just exploded grape juice everywhere: on the walls, on me, on him, on the floor, on the bed. After several hours, I was transferred to my dormitory room, and an aide was sent with me. I slept for nearly two days because the doctors had no knowledge of exactly what pills I had been given.

The Letters

With all the excitement surrounding the victim who had been stabbed and slashed and was critical, the nurse in the emergency room failed to record the name of the medication on my chart or on the envelope with the pills.

When I finally awakened a day and a half later, I saw that my room was filled with revolving fans of various sizes. The students had collected and donated them because there was no central air conditioning at that time, and the rooms in the dormitory became very hot. I could never thank those faceless students enough, and I have never forgotten their kindness. Berto telephoned me, apologizing for the accident. This time he was genuinely concerned about me. Had it not been for my embarrassment for the incident at Duke Hospital when he was with me, I might have seen him again. However, I never did despite his wanting to date me.

In addition to worrying my director, I learned a lot about men that summer at Duke, even through one of my professors, Senor (Sr.) Jose Amor, who taught Mexican history (in Spanish) and who always scheduled his students' oral final examinations in his office over a three-day period. My appointment was for the last day, and I was the last student to take the exam. I had studied for days. Usually in class Sr. Amor always asked me questions concerning historical events such as the dates and outcomes of the wars and treaties signed, so I decided to focus on those parts of the text and the class lectures. Before entering Sr. Amor's office, one of the students asked me to take a cold glass of lemonade to our professor because he had been testing students all morning and hadn't had a break. When I walked into the office and gave him the lemonade, the first question Sr. Amor asked me was, "How do you like the new air conditioner in the cafeteria?" I muddled through that one because of all of the technical terms. Then he asked me about the movie I had seen the night before. My habit was never to cram before an exam but to relax by seeing a movie the night before the test. For nearly forty-five minutes, we just chatted about current events, the classes I had taken, and my opinion about them. I had heard from the other students who had already taken the exam that it lasted no more than twenty minutes, and it covered the class lectures as well as the textbook. He didn't ask me one question that dealt with the history class, and I kept waiting for that difficult academic question from the text or the class lectures. Instead, he suddenly just dismissed me. I was puzzled and worried. What was that test all about?

That evening after dinner we students were all in the lounge comparing notes about the exam, when I heard Sr. Amor say to the director, "I got so bored asking the same questions that I decided to have some fun with Senorita Cipolla. I knew that she could answer the questions from the text and the lectures, so I just decided to just talk with her. Poor girl."

Since I had heard him, I walked over and said, "Sr. Amor, that wasn't fair. Do you know how worried I've been?"

"I was bored. You gave me some laughs. It was the best oral exam I have ever given."

I thought, "He was bored, so he had fun with me because he knew he could." I didn't receive an *A*, but I did earn a *B+*. It must have been those darn technical terms.

University of Mexico

Attending the School of Languages at Duke University the summer of 1954 was the catalyst that made me want to attend a university in Mexico. But it was my experiences with Berto at Duke and Pedro in Monterrey that made me want to immerse myself in the language and culture of a foreign country. After I returned from that fateful summer in Monterrey, Mexico, I began to research colleges and universities there. I was intrigued by the information I read concerning Mexico City, and I decided on the University of Mexico. The little I had seen of Mexico I loved, and I wanted to return if I could find a scholarship to help pay expenses. I learned that the H.C. Frick Educational Commission in Pittsburgh awarded scholarships for students who wanted to study outside of the United States. I applied in the winter of 1955 and was awarded one for the summer of 1956. All expenses-- transportation, tuition, field trips, room, board, and even some spending money--were included in the scholarship. I just had to pay for personal items such as cosmetics, laundry, entertainment, and out-of-class trips if I went beyond what the scholarship allowed. The summer session began in June, but I began making plans immediately. I wanted to save money so I would be able not only to buy gifts for my family but also to have extra spending money.

Several weeks after arriving home from Monterrey, that despondent summer of 1955, I received a postcard with a huge question mark as the message. The card was from the *Hotel Ancira,* and I assumed it was from Pedro. I didn't reply, but a month later he telephoned and asked me to write to him. I did and told him about my going to Mexico City the following summer. He wanted me to visit Monterrey first, promising he could help me find a good but inexpensive hotel in Mexico City through his connections until the Student Housing Department from the university found me either a room or an apartment. He said that he wanted to see me again. I made flight arrangements to stop in Monterrey for four days before I was due to attend the University of Mexico. We continued to correspond, but he preferred to telephone me. I sensed that his emotional connection was deeper than mine, but I did want to see him again.

Meanwhile, Ray telephoned me in August of 1955 after I had returned from the Monterrey trip with Dorothy and Carol.

"It's good to hear your voice again. I've missed you," he said.

He wanted to come that weekend to visit me, but I was modeling for the Junior Women's Club's fall fashion show, and I told him to call me the following week. I wanted to meet him in Pittsburgh, but my parents were still angry about his treatment of me and suggested that he come to our home instead. My dad left early, but my mother remained at home. Ray and I sat in the kitchen while my mother made coffee. My mother did most of the talking, asking about his mother and father, because I hardly knew what to say to him. I could barely look at him. After a while, she left to watch television in the living room.

I asked, "Ray, I just want to know why?"

What he said didn't make any sense to me: "I kept thinking what if you get sick? What if we have a child and something is wrong?"

Little he said made much sense to me. I replied that he could never understand the hurt and humiliation I had endured. We spoke for perhaps a half hour before he left.

While he was leaving, he said, "I wish we could start the relationship all over again."

I knew I couldn't. I could never trust him again, not with my heart, not with my emotions. I was not really satisfied with his explanations. Besides, my brother Bud and my dad were still furious with him, and I knew they would never accept him. Most of my love for him was gone. My heart had started to heal, and I was beginning to date again.

I was dating Sandy. I had dated him before ever becoming involved with Ray. When he learned that my engagement was broken, we started to date again. Sandy's father was district director of the Lions Club, and my dad was president of the Club in Arnold. I had met Sandy at one of the parties sponsored by the Club, and we had dated off and on for a couple of years or more, but with him I never knew where I stood other than we were great friends. When he knew that I was going to attend the University of Mexico the summer of 1956, he asked me to get his mother a teacup because she collected them. I had a Mexican craftsman make her one. I returned from the University of Mexico that first summer, and we continued to date. I enjoyed being with him, but I had no idea what our relationship was or could be.

I remember that he picked me up at a wedding reception for a friend who taught in the same high school.

Walking to the car, he asked, "When are we going to do that?"

Did he mean "we" together or "we" as individuals? I was not sure of his question. I should have answered, "When someone asks us."

We sat in the car in the parking lot talking, and the question of religion came up. I said I was Catholic. Sandy said he was not. I mentioned that while I could not change religions, I was not adverse to mixed religious ceremonies. Sandy was reared in a family in which his father and mother were of different Christian religions. Sandy replied that he would not marry in a mixed religious ceremony. It was always difficult on religious holidays choosing which church he would attend. He had decided that he would become a Protestant like his father and eventually join the Shriners. We continued dating off and on for the next year or so, and then the relationship just slipped away.

At the same time, I was corresponding with Pedro, wanting to see him once more. He telephoned several times during that year, and he was always happy to talk with me. I knew that he was as attracted to me as I was to him. Stopping in Monterrey the summer of 1956 was a mistake because I had allowed that relationship to continue and flourish, knowing that it might not endure despite our affection for one another. One of us was going to be hurt. Unfortunately, Pedro and I reconnected when I stopped in Monterrey in June on my way to the University of Mexico. By now, I was emotionally involved with Pedro, not knowing how involved he was with me. I was free from all of the heartache I had suffered with Ray, but I was vulnerable. I just didn't know it.

It was then that Pedro surprised me by telling me he was divorced, even showing me a snapshot of his ex-wife and two daughters who were living in the United States. He revealed that he had lost everything when he divorced, especially the house

33

that he proudly declared had two bedrooms for the girls. How did I get myself into such a predicament? When he kissed me goodnight, I had butterflies again. He said, "Please be good for me." I had trouble sleeping that night.

Before I left Monterrey, Pedro gave me all the information I would need for my reservation at the hotel in Mexico City and also gave me the telephone number of a friend of his who might be able to find me a small apartment. When I got to the hotel in Mexico City, I found that I had been placed in a small suite. In the sitting room, there was a very large basket of fruit and a beautiful arrangement of flowers floating in a large bowl. There was a card in the basket that read, "Welcome to Mexico City." I called the desk to tell the manager that I must be in the wrong room. I explained that I was a student on a limited budget. I just needed a small bedroom. He said, "No, you're in the right room because we have no single bedrooms left. We are not charging extra for the suite." I really didn't believe him. I wondered what Pedro had said to him.

I ate dinner that night in the hotel dining room because I didn't want to venture out alone. While I was eating, a three-man Mariachi band came over to my table to serenade me. I reached in my purse for the tip, but I was told by one of the members of the band that they had already been paid by a man sitting at the bar. He pointed out the man who had turned his stool around to catch my attention. He had been looking through the mirror above the bar. I just lowered my head, finished eating, signed the bill, and went to my room. I didn't even acknowledge him by saying, "*Gracias*" or waving. Was he the manager, perhaps checking up on me for Pedro, or had he singled me out because of my short honey-blond hair and the fact that I was American? I was sure that Mexican men had a lot of practice prowling in

Mary Ellen Cipolla Grasso

bars and restaurants, flirting with the American students. If that was his reason, he just wasn't lucky that night.

The next morning I went to the university to get my student identification card, schedule four classes with my advisor, and pay my tuition. I was also given a schedule of all of the social events for international students. I took a class in Mexican music, one in rural education, one in Mexican culture and folklore, and one in advanced Spanish grammar and conversation. I had to return the next day to the Housing Department to find a room. Since I had time that afternoon, I called Pedro's friend. He asked me to come to his office at five that afternoon. I was naïve. I should have insisted I meet him in the lobby, not in the office. I couldn't suggest a restaurant for coffee because I didn't know any nearby. I was so trustworthy.

When I went into the rather large office complex, he was totally alone. I suddenly became frightened, but I tried not to show it. As he got closer to me, I backed away. I could read his face, and I knew what was on his mind, and I warned him, "You have the wrong girl, and I'm sure that Pedro would not like to hear of your behavior. I'm leaving, but he will know about you because he does telephone me frequently." I was near the door, so I fled. I didn't even wait for the elevator. The next time Pedro called, I was infuriated with him. I told him what happened and then yelled, "Don't ever call me again!" He was shocked about his friend's behavior and kept apologizing. I was just angry. Had he set me up? What was he trying to prove?

I was at the hotel three days before I could get student housing. I was sent to a private home near the national bullring. The landlady showed me the accommodations and told me that the room was listed at $90 for the summer. It had a double bed, a chest of drawers, and a small closet. Breakfast was ten cents and dinner, fifty cents if I chose to eat at the house. But there was a restaurant nearby, and I preferred to buy typical Mexican dinners for fifty-six cents each because I had a choice of different entrees. At first, I was pleased with what I had been shown and told about the accommodations by the owner. I had to share a bathroom with a "few other students" who were living there, but I didn't mind. I could do laundry on the roof since there was a cold-water faucet as well as a large galvanized tub provided for students to wash their clothes by hand, of course. Those provisions I understood and accepted. There were, also, clotheslines on which to hang the wash. The landlady showed me the attic, which happened to be the two maids' bedroom where an ironing board and iron were provided for the students' use. After touring the house, I was satisfied with the accommodations.

But two days later I discovered that I had three roommates, each of us paying $90 and all three of us sharing the double bed, sleeping on the width of the bed, not the length. There was no room in the closet for four girls to store their clothes. By snooping around, I discovered that there were about twelve other students living there, beyond what was permitted by the university for that size of the home and the available bedrooms and bathrooms. I returned to the director of student housing to complain. I wanted to leave, but I also wanted my money returned. I needed the money in order to rent something else. One of the other girls in the room, Theresa Davila, also wanted to leave, but the landlady refused to refund our money. Because the university couldn't help me, I went to the American Embassy. No one there seemed to be able or want to help me. Frustrated, I wrote to the congressman in my district in Pennsylvania who advised me to go to the Office of Tourism, which I did. I spoke with the director who said there was nothing he could do. In short, I was ignored. I tried another tactic.

I wrote four letters, mailed one to the university's housing department and one to the American Embassy. I held two: one to the director of the Office of Tourism and the other letter would be sent to a major newspaper in my area, *The Pittsburgh Post Gazette*. I walked into the Office of Tourism, handed one of the letters to the receptionist, and announced that I was notifying the United States Government about the treatment of American students in Mexico, and I would be sending a letter to a newspaper in the United States. The receptionist asked me to speak first to the director, whom I had spoken to before. The director said that he had already spoken "that very morning" with someone in the American Embassy, and he "would be more than happy" to take care of my problem, which he "didn't understand" the first time I had spoken with him. Of course, he would take care of my request. The Mexican Government didn't want a problem with the American Government since many American students attended the various colleges and universities in Mexico. It was all about money. Much to my surprise, I was given a check immediately as was Theresa. I was astonished when I was refunded the entire $90. The house where I had been staying was put on notice,; and after an investigation, some of the students were placed elsewhere.

Theresa and I checked the newspaper classifieds and found a suitable furnished apartment on *98 Calle Shakespeare*. We split the $75 rent for the apartment that included water, electricity, and the laundering of the sheets and towels. It was a large three-room apartment: a bedroom with twin beds, a kitchen, a combination living and dining room, and a bathroom. The custodian for the building would do our personal laundry for extra money if we so wished, but I chose to have the Chinese laundry down the street launder those clothes that I couldn't launder by hand. The only other expense was for the telephone. I had finally settled into my classes and finding my way throughout the city by using the bus system.

During those years in Mexico City, there was an expansive network of city buses rated by class: first, second, and third. The first class buses were the most expensive to ride, but they were the most deluxe. Those buses were newer, very comfortable, and mechanically safer. When I first arrived in the city, I took the first class buses to the university because they made fewer stops and took the shortest routes to the university or any other destination. The second-class buses were more economical, but they were slower and usually traveled secondary routes. They were often crowded and made many stops, but they didn't always reach their destinations on time. I recall a day I was a passenger on one of those buses, and we came upon an accident that had occurred between two other vehicles traveling on the other side of the street, just ahead of us. The two drivers were out of their cars arguing rather loudly. One even punched the other. Suddenly our bus driver, along with a number of passengers, got out of the bus and entered into the argument deciding who was to blame. The driver and those passengers believed they were witnesses. I'm not sure they all saw what had happened. It wasn't until the police came that the passengers and the driver returned to the bus, but they carried on the argument among themselves. There was no reason that the bus had to stop. Our way was clear. There was no apology by the bus driver even though I missed my first period class.

The third class buses intrigued me, and I did travel many times to the university on those buses not only because they were the least expensive, but also because they had the most atmosphere. The buses were very crowded, very cramped, and in need of repair. Because they traveled the more rural routes and the neighborhoods of the poor, they made many frequent stops.

As a student, I had to make sure I had ample time because I couldn't depend on the bus schedule. On one of those trips I held the baby of one of the peasant women. I offered her my seat, but she refused even though she was carrying some packages. Those buses were very old, and often the seats were very uncomfortable. Sometimes a window could not be raised so air could circulate. There was always an unpleasant odor because passengers were permitted to transport small animals such as birds or baby goats or lambs as well as poultry and baskets of vegetables and fruit. Third class buses were not as safe as the other two, and there was a possibility of theft if a student passenger flashed money. However, students only rode this class if no other bus was available or if it was absolutely necessary for budget purposes. As I rode the bus system, I was beginning to notice the various classes in Mexico and their lifestyles.

I loved visiting the museums, the art galleries, and the various antique buildings. I also began to make friends from the university. Since a few of us did not eat lunch at midday because of our schedules, we often ate late in the afternoon. We frequented one restaurant that featured a Caesar salad. I always ordered that, but then everyone else helped me eat it. The other students always ordered some other entrees from the menu but just wanted to "taste" the salad, just a "bite" they would say. Many times the owner and the cook sat with us, and I noticed that the salad was getting bigger and bigger each visit. I think the owner noticed that we poor students were sharing what was becoming a part of "everyone's dinner." Usually the restaurant was empty because no one ate lunch or dinner at that time of the day. We all practiced conversing in Spanish with the owner, and the cook practiced speaking English with the students. The owner already spoke fluent English. Those were memorable afternoons of discussing politics, comparing our classes and the field trips we had taken, and exchanging information about Mexican culture, folklore, and art.

Our apartment was rather far from a bus stop, but Theresa and I always enjoyed the walk. It was on one of those trips back to our apartment that we met two men. We had been walking for some time and were tired. We noticed a cream colored car following us, but we thought that the men in the car were students who were asking for directions for this side of the city. They weren't. Both were Mexicans. The driver, quite handsome, had blond wavy hair and green eyes. The other had more Indian features. The car stopped and the driver called us. He said something about the fact that we must be students because of the books we were carrying and asked us where we were going.

We said, "Home."

"Where's home?" he asked.

"98 Calle Shakespeare."

"That's really far. Let me drive you home."

We were tired, and after a few minutes of talking with them, we were assured they were all right, and we got into the car. They introduced themselves. The driver introduced himself as Memo (Guillermo Espinosa Sanchez) and his friend, Guillermo Alvarez de la Cadena. We gave them our names. We chatted, made small talk. Memo spoke English, but Guillermo didn't.

They dropped us off at the apartment, only to return several hours later to ask us to dinner. We had already eaten late that afternoon as was our custom, and we refused their offer. They stayed; we talked; we laughed. Memo called me "Picola," a name that remained between Memo and me as well as from Guillermo who occasionally addressed me as *"Picola"* in his letters of 1957 and 1958, long after Memo stopped writing. Memo did have two other pet names for me, *"Chuleta"* and *"Chulita,"* which he sometimes called me or wrote in his letters. I didn't know where the name Picola came from unless it was a modification of my last name, Cipolla, but the other two names were variations for the translation of "cutlet" and "pretty" or "funny girl," which were used as regional terms of endearment. He never used my given name.

There was a vendor outside hawking baked sweet potatoes. The men hadn't had dinner, so they went outside and bought four sweet potatoes, and I had my first taste of those delicious baked sweet potatoes. The night ended with Memo trying to kiss me. He chased me, but I blocked him with the dining room chairs. We all sat down in fits of laughter when Memo failed to catch me. Guillermo said that Memo wasn't used to hearing "No."

For a day or two both Memo and Guillermo stopped during the evening to visit. Then one evening Memo came alone. He wanted to go dancing, and we did. That was the first time I met Marcos, his friend. That was also the first time Memo kissed me goodnight. This time, I decided I was not going to get emotionally involved. I was never going to return to Mexico City after the summer session at the university. I couldn't afford the trip without another scholarship. Still, Memo and I saw each other nearly every evening. A week later, while we were getting ready to go out one Saturday morning, he remarked that I reminded him of Josephine when Napoleon asked her one night for the shortest distance to her bedroom, and she replied, "Through the Chapel." We both laughed so hard that tears came to our eyes.

The Letters

That was the start of an exceptionally adventurous, memorable summer with Memo and the beginning of all those letters I had saved and found 52 years later. I don't know why I had ever saved them. Or maybe I do. I know now that I can't destroy them. They are too much a part of my life-- two seasons of much joy, much love, and some heartache --seasons that now define and validate who I am. Until now, no one has known that part of my life: Not my friends, not my parents or siblings, not my husband, not my children.

I hadn't forgotten Pedro and the way I felt when he kissed me. But I was now infatuated with Memo. Pedro had no idea that I had moved or where. I didn't know if I could trust him especially after that encounter with his friend and an incident that occurred the last time I saw him in Monterrey. We had been walking for about a half hour just talking. He asked me if I trusted him. I believed I could. We got into a taxi that took us to a rather small motel. I wasn't sure what Pedro had in mind until I realized when the taxi stopped that the rooms were rented by the hour. I refused to get out of the taxi, but Pedro insisted that he just wanted to talk. I warned him that if he had any other ideas, I was the wrong girl, and I would scream. I did get out, and we sat in that room for about a half hour. He sat on the edge of the bed, and I sat in the chair across the room from him feeling uneasy. He sensed that and made no attempt to get near me or kiss me. We did just talk, but I was angry with him for bringing me there.

When the taxi returned, the driver just honked. Embarrassed, I kept my head lowered as we walked to the taxi. When I got back into the taxi, I told him that I was humiliated.

"Pedro, how could you do this to me? You know me well enough, or is this another test?"

His reply was that no one knew me except him so it didn't make any difference what the taxi driver thought, but it did to me. He apologized several times, trying to explain that he just wanted to get out of the heat, and he couldn't take me to his apartment because he would be embarrassed by where and how he lived. Neither could he just sit in some other hotel lobby because he was well known. Eventually that day I did forgive him, but I didn't telephone or write to Pedro during the entire summer.

I became involved in my classes, especially the folklore one. I went on every trip that was offered, especially the one to Acapulco by a plane the university had chartered. I particularly enjoyed the one field trip that was part of the class on rural education. It was a summer of immersing myself in a new culture, meeting new people, having study sessions at the apartment, and experiencing some "marvelous moments." Theresa was Mexican, and she did not have the same reactions as I, but for me everything was new and exciting: trips to Cuernavaca, Vista Hermosa, and Xochimilco with Memo, as well as Saturday drives around the countryside.

Cuernavaca, about fifty miles south of Mexico City, was more than I could have ever imagined. Traveling on a mountain highway, I began to see beautiful trees and lush foliage. The flowers were spectacular. Twice I made Memo stop the car just so I could enjoy the scenery and take photographs. Memo and I walked around the city where I stopped to buy a silver cuff bracelet. I couldn't get enough of the sights and sounds of this colonial town. The first time I went to Vista Hermosa, about 25 minutes from Cuernavaca, I was in awe of the grounds, which were stunning. There was a large swimming pool, filled with sparkling blue water. In the pool were aqueducts that had been built in 1529. When I was there in 1956, Vista Hermosa was for the young elite of Mexico City whose families usually went to

Cuernavaca to enjoy the weather. I wasn't the strong swimmer that Memo was, but I did dive into the pool after a bit of coaxing and the lure of the crystal blue water. That day is now one of those "memorable moments" Memo wrote about in a letter, and I have never forgotten.

That afternoon Memo wanted me to see the Hacienda Vista Hermosa that had been built by Hernan Cortez during the conquest of Mexico in the Seventeenth Century. We walked through the Hacienda, and I, typical tourist, wanted to see and touch everything. The rooms were very rustic with high ceilings and furniture from the Colonial Period. There were candles everywhere, giving off a soft glow, making the Hacienda a perfect place for a romantic day. I wondered how many nights or weekends Memo had spent there. He knew a lot about the rooms, especially the bedrooms, and as we walked through several of them, he mentioned how romantic they looked at night, only lit by candles. I had no illusions. Obviously he had spent a few weekends in one of those rooms. The Hacienda had, of course, deteriorated over the years when the Cortez heirs still owned it, but when I was there, it had been restored in the Twentieth Century by the government, and I saw it at its best, in all its glory. I may have forgotten other cities I had toured, but I can still see in my mind's eye the beauty of Vista Hermosa, especially with Memo at my side.

I went to Xochimilco twice, the first time alone with Memo. Memo and I went a second time in 1957 with Patty, a student of mine from Arnold High School who also was enrolled with me at the University of Mexico, and Jerry, my best friend from home, who was on vacation in Mexico City. Xochimilco was about an hour's drive from Mexico City. It was outside the city, and the scenery was spectacular. Memo and I drove there one Saturday morning that summer in '56. Usually, Memo had some destination planned for Saturday or Sunday or for both days. Seldom did he tell me where we were going, but even if he had, I wouldn't have been familiar with the place anyway. At that time Xochimilco was called the "floating gardens" because the boats, pushed along a network of canals by a pilot, were brightly decorated with flowers. I was awed when I first saw the *tranjineras* (boats) decorated with those floral arrangements.

The round trip on the boat ride was about three hours long. According to the guide's information, Xochimilco dated back to the time of the Aztecs. The ride was very relaxing, and Memo, at his wittiest, always had something amusing to add to my questions. The trip was also the most romantic. It was far too easy to be infatuated with him. That day he was at his best. He was one of the first men that I felt comfortable with talking about myself. Unlike Ray, Memo was completely open, and we were seeing each other frequently. Had he not written these romantic, passionate letters after I left Mexico that summer asking me to marry him, I might never have applied for a second scholarship. Memo and I could have remained just friends as I was with Reuben, a random pen pal from Argentina. Reuben and I exchanged letters for about forty years, sharing information about our families and our lives, never meeting, just corresponding by mail.

But there was more to Mexico for me than just the beautiful scenery. The national bullring also caught my attention. I had passed it every day walking from the bus stop to the first home where I stayed. Whenever I could, I went to the bullfights at the national arena. Usually, the summer events featured the young bullfighters that were just beginning their careers, not the famous *toreadors*. I even bought a book about bullfighting so I could learn as much about it as possible, but it was the opportunity I had with Guillermo, an aspiring bullfighter, to tour the facilities at the bullring that made me develop a passion for the bullfights. I tried to go to as many of them as I could afford. When the procession and the music started, my heart raced, and during the fight, I began to yell, "*Ole, Toro*" with everyone else. At times the bulls were much braver than the bullfighters.

My interests were wide and varied. I was a fan of the movies and always wanted to visit a movie studio. I didn't believe I would ever travel to Hollywood, but I thought I might be able to go to the *Estudios Churubusco*, a movie studio in Mexico City. One of my dad's friends, Mr. Bart Datolla, who owned a movie theater in my town, made arrangements for me to visit the studio. I had the red carpet treatment. Cantinflas, Mexico's famous comedian at that time, was shooting a movie the day I visited the studios, and I was allowed to be on the set. I met the director who asked that I wait outside until the scene with the children in the schoolroom had finished their take and were dismissed.

I remember the next take very well. Cantinflas' character was that of an adult student taking a class in the elementary school. He had deliberately missed defining the types of water so that the teacher, whom he had a crush on, could keep him in the classroom during recess to tutor him. Cantinflas kept flubbing his line, and each time he did, the director called, "*Corta*!" Immediately, make-up was at the actor's side, touching him up with a powder puff, while Cantinflas' diction coach had Cantinflas review his lines. The only line the actress had to say was "*Siquela*." There were many takes because Cantinflas kept making a mistake at different points in the dialogue. During one take, the actress said, "*Continua*." The director was infuriated. He yelled at her so loudly that I backed up a few steps. That was my introduction to a celebrity. Cantinflas could do no wrong. Finally, everyone was dismissed for lunch.

That day I had a studio escort who had an itinerary for me and took me to the commissary for lunch. He introduced me to a few people who also worked at the studio.

After lunch, I visited the editing department, which I enjoyed immensely. The editors were very patient while explaining everything to me. I couldn't keep up with how fast the editors were able to cut scenes, but I marveled at the process. I had the run of the studio: costumes, props, scenery, and construction. I particularly enjoyed the set that had been constructed for an outdoor scene for the production of *The Three Musketeers*. I had to touch the "stone" columns, the steps, the street. At a distance, everything looked real to me.

I next went onto a set constructed for a movie about Henry the Eighth. A long banquet table was set with "gold" dishes. As I got closer, I realized that the dishes were not made of china but were cardboard and painted gold. I had to touch them. I was a charter member of the New Kensington Civic Theater in my hometown and familiar with stage productions, but I had never seen a set for a movie, and standing on one of those sets gave me a new perspective of set construction for movies: just an expensive illusion. My favorite place to visit that day was Properties, a warehouse filled with any article that one could imagine that could be used in multiple movies. I picked up a sword. It was heavier than I thought it would be. That day I was like a child in a penny candy store.

A few days later, touring the country again, I visited the pyramids at Teotihuacan, about 30 miles from Mexico City, on a field trip with one of my classes. I was fascinated by the Aztec culture. I started to climb the rather steep, narrow steps, but I was not aware that I had agoraphobia. It was the professor who noticed that I was breathless and the last of my classmates climbing the steps. He stopped me after the first two sections and did not allow me to climb above that very narrow landing. I was so frightened. I knew that I couldn't walk down the steps. With his help, I was able to sit down on one of the steps and go down the stairway the way a toddler does, one step at a time. The professor said that he noticed that I had turned gray, and he was afraid I was going to lose my balance. He came down the steps with me, holding my hand and urging me just to look ahead, not down and literally talked me down those steps. Still, I was disappointed that I could not go to the top to see where the human sacrifices were held.

A week later, through my rural education class, I found myself engulfed in the culture of another class of Mexicans when we got to visit a very poor family who lived on a mountain. Their home was a "two-room" dirt dugout. One so-called room was for the family and the other one was for the chickens, roosters, and goats. The living quarters were nothing more than a pile of blankets in one corner of the dugout. The professor explained that the blankets were used for sleeping. No mats were available. A large wood fire was in the middle of the room. Over the fire was an iron fixture with a large kettle hanging on it. Some of us were invited to look in the pot to see what was the family's dinner; only beans and corn were cooking, but the dinner smelled delicious. The area where the animals roamed had a distinct pungent smell. I wanted to cover my nose, but I didn't. The father made and sold brushes, and I bought several. I had never seen anything like that dugout, and I felt such compassion for the family of seven. I took slides of the family and their "dwelling" after asking permission. The children smiled as I snapped their pictures.

On this field trip, I remembered the family I had stumbled upon living under a footbridge near the bullring. I had stopped on the bridge to rest after walking a mile from the bus stop. Looking below, I was shocked to see a family living there. I just thought at first they were vagrants. Somewhat embarrassed, I quickly turned away from the scene, not knowing how to respond, especially when the children looked up at me. I just said, "Hello." I realized after that field trip they weren't vagrants. They were poor and homeless. That experience at the footbridge in Mexico City and the one in the mountains were the first real knowledge I had of poverty in Mexico.

On another field trip, our class also went to the Teacher's College for both the academic and vocational education of students who wished to become teachers in the rural areas. Students who had their academic classes in the morning had carpentry, farming, and other vocational classes in the afternoon. The students who started the day with vocational classes had their academic classes in the afternoon. We visited several vocational classes. In one class students were making tables, chairs, stools, and bed frames: furniture that was to be used in the classrooms in the elementary schools as well as in the one-room living quarters of the teachers. In another class, students were making lamps or other electrical fixtures. The college also had a working farm, and students were learning all about the care of animals and the planting and harvesting of crops.

During our field trip of the college, we attended some of the academic classes. A few of us went to a history class. We noticed that there were no textbooks for the students. Instead, the students copied the information as the teacher read from the only available copy of the textbook. In the English grammar class, students worked from old American magazines such as *The Ladies' Home Journal*. The day we visited, the students were studying verbals, but no one had the same magazine, so it was quite difficult for the students to interact. Several of us were asked to help tutor the students. I noticed that they were eager to learn.

The college students also taught the children who attended the elementary school on the grounds of the college. Usually there were at least two elementary classes in one small room with only a movable slate board to separate them. We were able to visit the classrooms, and I noticed that most of those second and third grade students were barefoot and dirty, yet they were well prepared for the day's lessons, and they all participated. We were told that they had walked several miles just to attend school. For them it was a privilege.

Students selected for the college did not pay tuition. They did, however, have to sign a contract that they would teach for a minimum of five years in a school in one of the rural areas.

Just before leaving the college, the director of the school asked us please to send any books written in English to the school because they had none. He said that after every field trip he makes the same request, but no one who has ever visited had sent books. I had been to their library, and other than the magazines I saw, there were no books written in English. I took him at his word, and when I returned to my high school that fall in 1956, I spoke with the new principal, Alex Tannas, and found that old classroom sets of books, dictionaries, and encyclopedias were just being thrown away. With the help of student service organizations, we mailed about forty or fifty cartons of books. Many were classroom sets of English grammar, literature, geography, science, and history texts. Sets of encyclopedias were also sent. Many parents, as well as service clubs in the town, donated money for postage after I was invited to give several lectures, along with a slide presentation, of my trip.

I later learned through the professor of English at the Teachers' College that the English section of the library had been named after me. The English professor had sent me the students' first research papers written in English, along with beautifully written thank you notes from the students. The professor wrote that having classroom sets of English textbooks made teaching much easier and doubled the time for teaching the subject matter. I was humbled by his letter. Oh, I wished I had saved those student papers and personally written notes!

But my summer of 1956 in Mexico City did not end with that trip to the Teachers' College. I kept close company with Memo, and he enlarged my social circle that summer when he introduced me to a close friend of his, Pepe Delgado, public relations director of an American company, Colgate-Palmolive. I really liked Pepe. He was a novelist, poet, playwright, and artist. I remember visiting him and touring the factory where he worked. When I left that afternoon, Pepe gave me a huge gift basket of products that I appreciated and used. Pepe also invited Memo and me to his home for lunch on another day. Like very close friends, Memo and I saw each other nearly all of the time. Still, he never forgot to kiss me when he came into the apartment or kiss me before leaving. Being Italian myself, I figured that was just the custom in Mexico as it was in Italy and Spain. He was very affectionate, very sweet, and very likeable. I was falling in love, but I told myself it was just a "summer romance." After all, I had no plans to return to Mexico after this summer, and I didn't want him to know how I felt. Besides, unlike Pedro, he never told me how he felt. For Memo, I didn't believe I was exclusive, and I didn't expect to be.

But there was more to that summer than only dating Memo. I was there to study Spanish, and participating in my four classes and completing the assignments were a priority. I loved all my classes, especially the music class taught by a full-blooded Aztec professor who after the final exam invited his students for dinner at his home. The home was magnificent, a palace filled with treasures from his ancestors. He showed us the feathered headdress that belonged to one of his grandfathers. It was beyond anything I had ever seen in any museum--such workmanship! During one of his class lectures, he told the class that he had never attended a public or parochial school in Mexico. His father, a famed conductor, built a private school in their home for his children and the children of other full-blooded Aztecs to attend so they would not have to integrate with other Mexicans, which he always referred to as *Mestizos*. The professor mentioned that when he had to attend the university, he felt very uncomfortable, especially when one of his classmates touched him on his arm or shoulder. He was pure Aztec; his classmates were not. He may have been pure Aztec and believed that Aztecs were a superior race, but we students always had to connect the phonograph and slide projector because he never could. Doing so was too complicated for him. During that evening at his home, I realized that despite his shortcomings, I would hate leaving the university and Mexico City when the semester was over.

Living in Mexico City

There were evenings when Memo did not come to pick me up and afternoons when I skipped that late lunch. On those afternoons I spent time in the university library doing research for a special project. Those times Theresa and I cooked dinner at the apartment, but we always had a lot of food left over. We knew that the custodian had four beautiful children because we had met them and often played with them. We asked her if she would like the leftovers for the children. She was very gracious and thanked us for thinking about her family. We didn't ever see a husband, so we thought she was a single parent. Sometimes we would buy a loaf of sliced bread, use four slices, and then give the loaf to her. Sometimes it was a box of cereal or half of a roasted chicken dinner. We never knew on any given day whether we would be eating at a restaurant or at home. I was lucky to find such a compatible roommate as Theresa, and I feel blessed to have had her all these years as part of my life through Christmas cards and letters.

Nowadays, when I think of Theresa and our days in Mexico that first summer, I remember the custodian's youngest child Kiko, an adorable four-year-old boy not yet in school. Whenever he saw us at home, he usually came to visit. If Theresa and I happened to come home early, we would block off the street with wooden boxes we found behind our apartment and play either baseball or football with children from the neighborhood. There was almost no traffic in that area during the afternoons, and no one complained about the games. I had bought a bat, a baseball, and a glove, and everyone took turns using them. We didn't have a football, but we used a large ball that one of the boys had. We called the game "touch football." No one was allowed to tackle a player, just touch him.

Theresa's schedule was different from mine, so we weren't always together. She had friends who lived in Mexico City, and often times she met them. We did, however, find time to visit historical sites such as the Museum of National History. I remember a time Memo wanted to go to Vista Hermosa to swim. Because I had not brought a bathing suit with me, I needed to buy one. The day I brought it home, Theresa liked it so well that she asked if she could try it on. She did and then wore it the entire day in the apartment. I didn't mind. Theresa was my friend.

We usually had a lot of snacks left over from the study sessions at our apartment that students just left with us, and after those improvised games, we shared them with the neighborhood players. They devoured them. However, after a couple of weeks, Kiko's mother asked us not to bring food to her apartment anymore and not to give the children snacks. She explained that once we left, the children might start stealing or her daughter might prostitute herself. She could not afford the food that we bought. Sometimes the children would walk with me to the grocery store, hoping I would buy treats, which I wouldn't do. They would correct me if I used the wrong Spanish word, giggling at the same time, and I taught them some English, which they practiced every day just to delight me.

I remember Kiko coming to our apartment claiming, "I have a bad sore throat. If I had some potato chips it would go away." I hated to say that we didn't have any, especially when he looked at us with those sad brown eyes, but I knew I had to do so. Kiko and his siblings ate sliced bread as though it were cake and baked chicken, pork chops, and cold cuts as gourmet foods. They even liked the spaghetti and meatballs I made. From that time on, Theresa and I rarely cooked or bought loaves of white sliced bread. Many times I just ate a late lunch in an inexpensive restaurant. Besides, I was so busy with homework and field trips that I never seemed to have time to eat. Sometimes I made myself deliberately busy. I was becoming too emotionally involved with Memo, always looking forward to being with him, to having him hold me, kissing me.

Some afternoons the university presented a typical Mexican musical show given in the university's theater. There was usually a different Mariachi band along with the *Folklorica Dancers*. I enjoyed the shows and never missed one, unless I was on a field trip. Those programs became the highlight of my time at the university. I had really immersed myself in the Mexican culture. One afternoon while exploring the neighborhood, I discovered a girl sitting on a street corner with a small table. She repaired runs in nylon hosiery using a unique tool, something I had never seen. I happened by chance to see her on one of my walking trips. Instead of buying new hosiery, I took them to her to be repaired. What a way for me to save money while at the same time the girl had a job. Why didn't we have that tool in the United States? I always meant to buy one at a department store in Mexico City, but I never did.

I felt very comfortable living in Mexico City. I shopped at the local stores and outdoor markets. I had my hair cut at a Mexican salon, not at one that catered to Americans. I went to a neighborhood church although I sometimes had to stand for Mass. I remember going to the Church of the Virgin of Guadalupe. I stood in line with everyone else, held a candle, and wept. I knew one version of the history of how the image came to be on Juan Diego's tilma (a cloak fastened on one shoulder by a knot). According to the story, on December 15, 1531, Juan was walking along a road when he saw a vision of the Virgin who asked him to persuade the Spanish bishop to build a church on Tepeyac Hill. The bishop wanted a miraculous sign to prove Juan's claim. The next time the Virgin came to him, she asked him to gather the flowers on top of the hill, which she helped arrange them in his tilma. When he went to the bishop and emptied his cloak, the Castilian roses spilled out, and the image of the Virgin of Guadalupe was imprinted on the tilma. Because it was winter, there would have been no roses growing. Convinced, the bishop had the church built by Tepeyac Hill. I became overcome with emotion as I looked at the image of the Virgin of Guadalupe. I was surrounded by people in wheelchairs and on crutches. There were children being carried by their parents, many hoping for a miracle from the Virgin. I lit my candle and said a prayer for all those hoping for that miracle. I even climbed the hill where the rose bush grew and bought a bottle of holy water from a young priest.

I ate many of the Mexican dishes although I was warned that I might get sick, but I never did. My favorite was capretto (young goat) roasted on a spit. The first time I ate an avocado was in Mexico. At first, I wasn't sure I would like the taste, but I discovered that I did. I usually had a waiter describe the food first if I wasn't sure what it was, but I never turned down a dish. At least I tried it. I did, however, avoid drinking the water.

I was truly busy absorbing all the smells, sights, and sounds and enjoying my time with Memo. Two of my classes at the university were in Spanish and two in both English and Spanish. Those in Spanish were only difficult because I found myself translating the lectures and writing notes in English as the professor spoke. I didn't trust my written Spanish. My favorite class, a combination of Mexican folklore and its arts and crafts, was the one taught by Patricia Fent Ross. I still have the textbook, Made in Mexico, in which she had inscribed, "For Mary Ellen / With sincere good wishes and my friendship." Her class was standing-room-only.

Usually I could make it to the upper floor in five minutes, but sometimes I couldn't, so I sat on the floor, where I couldn't see the screen, or I stood. It seemed as though everyone wanted that class. I had registered early so that I was on the official roll. Getting there on time so I could get a seat was my problem.

I began to see Memo nearly every day, and I eagerly looked forward to seeing him when he finished work. I tried to accept the fact that I would be leaving at the end of the summer, but when he knocked on the door, my heart raced. I was remember one specific evening when he came to the apartment, and someone from his family telephoned to remind him that it was his mother's birthday and that the family was waiting for him so that the cake could be cut. He asked if I was invited and if he could take me. I understood from his side of the conversation that they had refused, and I heard him say he would not be there. I urged him to go home, honor his mother, and be with his family for the celebration. He left, but he was back within less than an hour. He told me that he had stayed only long enough to eat a piece of cake. I hoped that his family had not blamed me. I was well aware of the fact that most Mexican parents did not want to meet the American girls their sons were dating, and I understood their reasons for doing so.

I'm sure Memo's family did not approve of me or my dating him, for I remember the evening we went to his aunt's home to pick up his cousin Javier and Javier's girlfriend Monica because we four were going to a movie. Memo's aunt was making candied apples in the kitchen while we chatted in the living room with Memo's cousins. At one point, the aunt called her daughter into the kitchen to get the tray of apples. I was sitting on the sofa next to Monica, who took an apple. I was ignored, not even offered one. Seeing this, Memo and Javier each refused one. The aunt had never even greeted or acknowledged me when we first came into the house even though Memo had introduced me. I was invisible.

Was I hurt? No, I was embarrassed. I knew that American girls going to the university did not have a stellar reputation. We were considered girls of loose morals. Because I was over 25, I was not required to attend a special lecture by the Dean of Women for International Students concerning American girls' behavior in Mexico. I didn't attend, but the next day the lecture was the gossip of the day. It seemed that one of the students, following a date to a bar with a Mexican resident, had been raped. The university, as well as the police department, became involved, and the last thing that the administrators wanted was a questionable relationship between the American Embassy and the summer school administration. The Mexican summer schools attracted hundreds of American students, some as young as 16. American girls were considered wild. Even then, many had a reputation for sleeping around. The behavior of the American girls was considered worse than "spring break" in the United States, and according to many other international students, "It's always the Americans." I wasn't sure it was. The other students, especially from Italy, France, and Spain, were also part of the campus gossip.

Because I understood too well why Memo's aunt had ignored me, I couldn't focus on the movie that night we went. I kept wondering, "What kind of girl does his family think I am?" Memo knew better, and he respected my code of morals and ethics. Sex was never a part of our relationship. I was committed to abstinence until marriage, not unusual for the 1950's. There were days when Memo and I did not see each other, and I never questioned what he did on those days. We had no commitment. Other girls were not as careful, like Peggy, a student at the university who often took the same bus as I and usually sat next to me. Peggy's conversations were peppered with tales of Luis, her boyfriend. I assumed they were engaged because she told me that she was at his parents' home frequently. Peggy also had begun shopping for a wedding gown and even pointed out the shop to me as we rode by, describing a dress she had tried on. She was quite excited. According to her, she and Luis were planning to marry during the fall of that year. About two weeks before the end of the summer term, I found Peggy sitting on the bus with red, swollen eyes. She was very distraught and crying.

Between sobs, she told me that she had mentioned to Luis's mother that her parents wanted to meet Luis and his family before she and Luis married. Luis's parents did not approve of the marriage and simply told her that there would be no marriage with their son. His mother said, "You're not the kind of girl we want Luis to marry. You sat on the sofa next to him, holding his hand, showing too much affection. You even came here one evening in shorts."

Much worse, Peggy told me, Luis had never actually proposed to her, but she felt they "had an understanding." She was humiliated that evening because he defended his parents. I wondered what he might have said to his parents when they questioned him. What was Peggy's "understanding" based on? Did he tell his parents that she was just a *"pasatiempo?"* I never saw her after that episode, and rumor was that she had returned to the United States before the term was over.

For me, that summer was one filled with joyful adventures and magical moments. The summer school ended with a semi-formal dance at one of the hotels. I had brought a new semi-formal dress, hoping I would have an occasion to wear it. It was an off-the-shoulder silk dress. A large bow was attached to the shoulder of the dress. It was quite striking: white with a small black design running through it. The skirt was flared, and, according to the fashion of the day, I needed to wear a crinoline underneath the dress. When Memo came to take me to the dance, all he could say was, "You look as though you have stepped out of a fashion magazine."

I just smiled. When we arrived at the dance, he ordered drinks, and before they were served, he wanted to dance. While dancing, he stopped in the middle of the dance floor to kiss me, more than once. I was embarrassed because people were looking at us. I recognized some of the students, so I whispered, "Not on the dance floor." He just looked at me. He didn't care. He just kissed me again. That dance was another one of those "marvelous moments" he wrote about weeks later. It was a wonderful evening, but I was afraid that I was in for another heartache.

When I left Mexico City in August, I had no plans to return. I knew that it was impossible to be awarded a second scholarship because the H. C. Frick Educational Commission would do so only after an interim of three years. Memo and Guillermo drove me to the airport, and Memo promised that he would mail to my home the carton of books that I had used for my classes. I had left the box in Memo's car because he felt that I had too much luggage to handle. We stood on the tarmac waiting for the plane, just laughing and recalling some of his escapades, like the time he stopped his car on the road to chase a bull that was grazing in a field. I had grabbed my camera to take a picture just as he was jumping the fence to get back into the car. I still have that slide.

We said, "Goodbye, *Adios*." He asked me to write to him when I got home so that he would know I had gotten home safely. I considered that the "summer romance" was over. At that time I wasn't even thinking of corresponding with him long term. I knew that I would miss him terribly, but I would get on with my life: teaching and directing the class plays at the high school, acting in the Civic Theater, and working with organizations such as

Mary Ellen Cipolla Grasso

Gay Ladies, volunteering for the Red Cross and the Junior Women's Club.

When I arrived home, I did write to tell him the trip was fine. When the carton of books arrived, I wrote to thank him for his trouble. He replied, and that was the beginning of how those letters came to be. He wrote almost every week, long letters that he usually typed. He wrote that when I left Mexico he had no idea that he would miss me as much as he did. He said that he loved me and thought about me constantly. I addressed my next letter to "Dear Don Juan." He replied that he was sincere, and I wanted to believe him. Those letters were some of the most romantic, passionate letters I had ever received. He was becoming more emotionally involved. Was it more than a summer romance for him?

I dated now and then, but the letters kept coming, keeping me in an emotional turmoil. If he didn't receive a letter from me in ten days, he was worried. Had I forgotten him? I knew that I wanted to return to the University of Mexico, but I also knew that I wanted to see him again, especially when he began to write about marriage. Meanwhile, I submitted my required report to the H. C. Frick Educational Commission and applied for a second scholarship, which I knew they never gave, but I thought I would try. I didn't have enough money saved that would allow me to return for another summer session. Much to my surprise, Mary H. Kolb, the executive secretary wrote a post card acknowledging the receipt of the scholarship report: "What a fascinating report you do write. When are you going to consider our summer conference at Wilson College? Your enthusiasm would be an asset!" Later, she wrote that "the board had read my report in its entirety, which it rarely did, enjoyed it very much, and felt that not only had I immersed myself in the culture, but also had spent the Commission's money wisely." She also wrote that most of the time, the members of the board just receive an itinerary of the trip. The Board decided to give me a second scholarship based on my written report. Lucky me! The Frick Scholarship was a first rate one.

Memo wrote often. Each letter filled with his endearments. Letter after letter he talked about wanting to marry me, about my being his wife. Then in one specific letter he asked me if I would marry him. Now I was getting very emotionally involved, but I did not answer that question when next I wrote to him. Instead, I wrote that I did not want ever again to be hurt; I could not answer his question about my marrying him and that his writing, "I love you" a zillion times didn't make it so. He wrote back that he had always had "*amantes*" and "*pasatiempos*," but he never before had told any other girl that he loved her. He also wrote that he was a fool not to tell me he was in love with me when I was there and before I left. I don't remember whether I believed him or not. I did know through Guillermo, who also wrote to me, that when he met Memo on the street, Memo was always with a different girl. I remembered the time he did use the apartment one weekend when Theresa and I were in Acapulco. He had asked if he could have the key so that he could check on the apartment when we were gone because of all the children who lived nearby. But when Theresa and I returned, there were traces of someone other than Memo's being there. I never questioned him about it. I should have.

Memo continued writing letters, all filled with plans for the future, full of excitement. He said he was counting the days until I returned. There were so many plans he had envisioned, but we needed to be together to talk about them. He fantasized about how he could make me happy, about what kind of life we could have, about just holding me. He wanted me near him. He wondered if I could live in Mexico on his salary. Now and then, Pedro would telephone me or send a postcard, but I never told him that

I was returning to Mexico. He wanted me to return to Monterrey. I knew that if I saw him again I would become emotionally involved with him. I wasn't sure of Memo's sincerity because I still remembered my relationship with Ray, and a later from Pepe who said, "Love built on passion burns out quickly."

However, I was sure of Pedro's sincerity. Pedro had touched my heart and left an imprint, but I knew that there were too many obstacles to overcome. Still, I couldn't let him go. Was I in love with two men at the same time? Was it just infatuation? Perhaps I would find out the truth when I returned to Mexico City.

Then Memo wrote that he had found an apartment for me. June of 1957, I returned to Mexico City. Accompanying me was one of my high school Spanish students, Patty, whose father had once been the principal of the high school. Patty was excited. As we were flying to Mexico City, I made a mistake and told her about Memo and that he was one of the reasons I wanted to return to the university. Memo met us at the airport. I sensed almost immediately that there was a change in him, but he had written that when he would meet me at the airport, he would hardly be able to speak when he saw me. I believed that was the reason for the change. He first took us to his friend Karen's home for lunch before taking Patty and me to the apartment he had found for us. Karen, an American, was married to Carlos, a pilot and one of Memo's Mexican friends.

During lunch, Karen asked me if I had ever received the Christmas gift, a desk set, Memo supposedly had sent to me. I hadn't. Memo had written to me that Carlos had mailed it from Texas on one of his flights there to make sure I would receive it because Memo did not want the gift to go through customs. I had even checked during December with our local post office when I did not receive it. When I wrote to Memo that I had not received the gift, he claimed in one of his letters "it must be lost," but that afternoon I discovered that wasn't true. Karen told me that he had never given it to Carlos to mail in Texas.

She told Memo, "Give it to her now. You still have it."

I wanted him to give it to me. I told him I didn't have one for my desk, and I would really love to have it, but he said, "No, it's not much of a gift." I would have appreciated anything as long as he had bought it for me. For only an instant a thought crossed my mind, "What else that he wrote about in his letters to me wasn't true?"

We finished lunch, and Memo was eager to take us to the apartment, a lovely one on *Avenida Insurgentes*, located in a far more elegant area from the one where we lived the summer before. Just beneath our apartment lived four men we met as we walked into the building. Memo introduced Patty and me to them, and I wondered how he seemed to know them so well. They told us they also were students, and we spoke for a few minutes, getting acquainted. We were on the second floor. Our apartment had two bedrooms, each with a set of twin beds; a large combination living and dining room; a kitchen; and a large bathroom. This apartment, far more luxurious than the apartment Theresa and I had at *98 Calle Shakespeare*, was beautifully furnished with all of the necessities. Because the apartment was located near a bus stop, I knew that Patty and I would have no problem getting to the university.

As Memo walked us through the apartment there was something about him that made me feel insecure: he did not appear to me to be the Memo from the summer before, the Memo I knew and loved through his letters, but I didn't notice anything tangible other than the sparkle seemed to be gone from his eyes when he looked at me. Was that feeling just my imagination? His letters were always filled with expressions of love for me and proposals of marriage.

I thought the unexpected change was because Patty was with me. When I didn't think I could be awarded a second scholarship, I considered taking a group of students on a tour to Mexico City. I had written to him about the plan, but he didn't want me to take students with me. He said we could never be alone if I did that. I knew he was right, but Patty was an exception. She was not only my student but also a "little sister."

For the next few days, Memo came to the apartment to check on Patty and me and drive us through that section of the city where we lived to acquaint us with the area. I was responsible for Patty, so I didn't want to leave her in the apartment alone and spend my time only with Memo. Besides, Memo really liked her, and he was protective of Patty, especially from the men who lived downstairs. Patty and I were busy the next week registering for classes, buying textbooks, and shopping for a few groceries. Memo continued to come now and then just to take us sightseeing. Then one day, perhaps a week and a half later, when just Memo and I were out together on some adventure or another, he drove me home early that Saturday afternoon. That was an unusual act for him. He walked me to the door of the apartment and announced that I should not expect him to be with me as he was the summer before. He would not be seeing me again. There was no explanation. He was cold and distant. I was stunned. Tears welled in my eyes. I didn't know what to say. I just turned around, unlocked the door to the apartment, and walked in. Patty was out with friends, but the student who had rented the second bedroom from Patty and me until she could find her own apartment was at home and asked me what was wrong. I didn't know what to say. I fell on my bed in a fetal position and began to sob. It was Ray all over again.

The Letters

One would have thought that I had already learned my lesson through Ray, but obviously I hadn't. I sobbed and sobbed, and I couldn't tell her what was wrong. I wish I had now, but at that time I was closing down, and I trusted no one. Here I was in a country far from home, a country I loved, with no one to support me, no one I could talk with.

I'm sure Memo must have heard me crying because the windows and French doors facing the street were open. I felt that once more I had become a victim. What had I done? How could he have changed so rapidly, within less than two weeks? Why had he written those passionate letters declaring love for me? Why had he proposed to me, more than once? Why had his sister Maria Rosa sent me pictures of the family? Had he never written those letters, I would not have returned with any expectations. I would have just attended the university with Patty and gone on with my life. The summer of 1956 would have just become sweet memories for me to remember, and Memo and I could have been just life-long friends though we lived miles apart. We could have shared news of our families, our joys, and our griefs. I would have wanted, at least, that relationship with Memo, and we could have had it were it not for his letters.

I couldn't stay a minute more in that apartment. I was thankful that Patty was out with friends. I just started to walk and walk -- to the park, to the church, just anywhere. I couldn't stop crying. I noticed a bench at a bus stop and sat down. I was exhausted, still trying to make sense of Memo and still sobbing. I supposed that Memo, meanwhile, had returned to the apartment to find me, but our roommate must have told him that I had left. He may have driven around the area looking for me because I saw him slowly drive his car twice around the block, but he didn't see me.

Then, when he finally saw me, he stopped driving, parked at the curb, and honked the horn. "Hey, *Picola*, come here. Get in the car."

I just started walking again. He followed me, driving slowly and honking the horn. He stopped the car again and ran to me. He caught me by the arm, walked me to the car as I tried to resist him, but he sat me down on the passenger's side. He apologized, tried to comfort me, told me he was afraid, confused, said that nothing had changed between us except that he had been going out with "bad company, getting drunk, and coming home late."

He had written in one of his letters that he had gotten into a couple of fights. While I tried, between tears, to talk to him, he also told me about a girl he had met, had been dating before I returned that summer, and had been intimate with her. He assured me that she had returned home to the United States, but I didn't believe him. I also wondered if she was one of his *amantes* or *pasatiempos*. I wasn't surprised about those episodes. He did mention that she was "very petite," something I knew I wasn't.

We drove around and talked, stopped for a sandwich, and talked some more. The hurt was still there. Did he realize how much he had hurt me? For me the magic was gone. What was I to believe? Were all men alike? I was heartbroken by the events that day. The worst part was that I had fallen in love with him during that year of his letter writing, his declarations of love, his marriage proposals. Was this the man who wrote that he adored me? Had it just been a game to him? Patty was still not at the apartment when I returned, and I did not tell her what had happened when she returned. She liked Memo, but I was the adult, trying to set boundaries for her. I was still her teacher.

The Letters

That night I couldn't sleep. I tossed and turned. I thought about those letters. Did I miss the signs? I remembered some doodling on a letter he had sent me, written while he was attending an English class. He wrote that he was bored and was just drawing some sketches. There was a sketch of his professor lecturing and one of me. My sketch had dollar signs coming out of my nose. Did the Christmas gift of the cashmere sweater I gave him have anything to do with that sketch? He didn't realize that I was by nature a very generous person with family and friends. I did reply in the next letter that I wrote him that school teachers in the United States did not make a lot of money and without the scholarship I could not return to the university. He never replied to that statement.

I also remember he asked me to send him a photograph of myself. I did and asked him for one in return. He wrote that he kept my photo on his bureau because it was the "last thing he saw at night and the first thing he saw in the morning." He claimed that he had taken a studio portrait, but the proofs were so bad that he didn't choose one to be developed. I knew that was a lie even when he wrote it in his letter. That man couldn't take a bad picture if he tried. He was too handsome. He was take-your-breath-away handsome. Besides, I'm certain the photographer would have taken another set.

Weeks later I received a wallet-sized studio photograph of him. He had written on the bottom of the photo: "*Para Picola con todo mi amor. Memo.*" It was dated "15/4/57." I misplaced that photo, and in all these years I never knew what had happened to it because it was not in any of my albums. Shortly after I found the letters, I found that photo in a small picture frame that had snapshots of his sister Maria Rosa's children. The frame was in a box with postcards from Mexico that had been sent to me by his other sister, Yolanda. I also found a cardboard fan that Memo had given me one afternoon when it was very hot. On the back was an advertisement of a jewelry shop:

Hernandez y Gusman
S. DE R. L.
Guadalajara
Fabricantes de Joyeria en Plato Ora
Guadalajara, JAL.

I did know that Memo frequently stopped at the store to see Guillermo, who worked in his sister's Mexico City jewelry shop. All these years, I believed that Memo had picked up the fan from the counter when he was visiting Guillermo or that Guillermo had given it to him for me the summer before. Later, reading again one of Guillermo's letters, I noticed that he had used an envelope with the return address of his sister's store. I know now that the fan in my album came from another jewelry store, one in Guadalajara. I received the fan, but someone else must have received the jewelry.

I was determined to play out the summer. I would enjoy my four new classes, go on field trips, show Patty Mexico City, go to Acapulco with her, and make sure that we would visit as many historical sites and landmarks as possible. I knew that my friend Jerry was coming during the middle of the summer session for her vacation and that Memo had promised to pick her up from the airport, and I was certain that he still would. I simply had to cope with the situation as it was although my heart hurt. Memo and I did not see each other for the next few days. One evening, I knew that Memo was in the downstairs apartment because his car was parked outside my balcony. I hadn't been invited, but I didn't expect to be. Were these men the "bad company" Memo had written me about in his letters?

The Letters

I had two visitors that evening: two men from my hometown. When I had returned home from Mexico after the first summer session, Pete and Mike told me that they had planned to go to Mexico City to attend school, also. That evening was only the second time that I had seen the men since my arrival. Pete said something that confirmed my doubts about my relationship with Memo. During a conversation about Memo, he said, "You don't want to know what he said about you when I gave him your Christmas present, the black cashmere sweater." I hadn't wanted to mail it because I was afraid that Memo would never receive it. I begged Pete to tell me, but he refused. Obviously, it was something very hurtful. Neither one wanted to tell me. Did he say that I was just a "*pasatiempo con dinero?*"

The two men wanted me to go bar hopping with them. We hadn't seen each other for weeks. I remember that I was wearing black slacks and a black sweater because the evenings usually got cold. It was an outfit that I never wore outside of the apartment. I wanted to change, but the men said that we didn't have enough time and that no one knew me anyway. I don't remember how we eventually ended up at a bar for gay men, but the men seemed to know the area quite well, and I wondered if they had been there before. I felt certain they had. Did they want me to wear that outfit because I would have been out of place wearing feminine attire? The two men ordered drinks, but I had just a Coke. We didn't stay long, but long enough for one of the patrons sitting at the bar to come over to our table to ask me to dance. With my short blond hair and my outfit, he couldn't tell whether I was male or female. I refused, and Pete suggested that he and I dance. Now I felt uncomfortable. We left the bar after one dance and went to several heterosexual spots. That was the last day I ever saw either one in Mexico or back home in Pennsylvania. I had often wondered about their relationship. I didn't really know them that well.

Memo came now and then to the apartment, and we still dated, but not as frequently as we had before. When we did go out, he was always attentive, very charming, very affectionate. Still, with Memo I never knew when he would make an unplanned appearance.

One particular night Patty and I were sound asleep. It was long after midnight, when Patty heard a horn honking. She awakened me and said that Memo was outside parked under the balcony and wanted to talk with me. There was also a police car next to his. I got dressed and went down to the street to see what the problem was. When I got there, Memo told me that he had been speeding and that the police stopped him. According to Memo, he didn't have enough money on him to negotiate a bribe rather than receive a ticket or be taken to jail as the two officers had threatened. He also didn't want to go home to ask his father to help him because he knew his father would be very angry.

I wasn't surprised about his getting a ticket for speeding. He liked to drive fast. He had written in a couple of his letters that he had borrowed his friends' cars, a BMW and a Jaguar and enjoyed driving as fast as possible. He asked me if I could go to the station with him in the police car, and during the ride, he would determine if they would take a bribe. Of course they would. That was the whole point. There has always been a lot of corruption in Mexico. At first the officers wanted $20.00, which I did not have. Except for a $10.00 Travelers Cheque in my wallet, I had no other cash with me. I had deliberately left my book of Travelers Cheques in the apartment when Memo asked me to take my purse with me. The police finally settled for $10.00, which I paid. They drove Memo and me back to my apartment where his car was parked. I hardly spoke with him. I was angrier with myself than with him. I thought of the sketch with the dollar signs coming out of my nose. Was he using me? Did he think I was some rich American girl or was I a friend he could count on? I will never know. What I do know about myself is that I will always help a friend. In this case I wasn't sure what I meant to Memo, but I did consider myself, at least, a friend.

I tried to distance myself from Memo by not always being available, but that was difficult for me. I couldn't stop loving him. During the time I was attending classes at the university, I became friends with one of the students. Jim was from Seattle, and we met at the university cafeteria one morning. We spent a few afternoons also there drinking coffee and just talking. He was a great distraction for me, and I enjoyed my time with him.

I seldom saw Memo for any length of time although he would stop frequently at the apartment to see if Patty and I were all right or needed anything. He was always very pleasant, inquisitive about what I was doing and where I had been. He was eager to share news about our friends, Pepe and Guillermo. Sometimes I wasn't home, and when I was elsewhere, I missed him terribly.

One Saturday evening Jim invited me to a stringed instrument concert and a late dinner at a restaurant that he frequented but one that I had not been to. That evening he ordered the specialty of the house: Welsh Rarebit over chicken with a side salad and toast points. Since I had never eaten Walsh Rarebit, I decided to try it. It was quite good, and I knew that I would order it again at some other time. When we arrived at my apartment about 12:30 that night, we stayed in the car and continued talking. I noticed Memo's car across the street. I assumed that he was upstairs talking with Patty or downstairs partying again. He wasn't. He was just sitting in the car. He honked. I ignored it. Jim finally noticed the Mexican license plate and asked me if I knew the driver. He wanted to be sure he wasn't a stranger. I just said that the driver was someone I had dated but didn't care to see. I had no idea what Jim must have thought of me, but he did walk me to the door. Memo was still not out of his car. After that night I never saw Jim again in the cafeteria. He must have thought, "Well, she is one of those American girls that everyone talks about."

When Jim drove away, Memo followed me to the doorway and asked me more than a few questions. I told him that Jim was a classmate, and we had gone out to a concert and dinner. I had no idea why Memo was just sitting in his car and how long he had been parked there. He told me that he just wanted to ask me about Jerry's flight number, the time and date of her arrival. He still planned to go to the airport with me. Since she wasn't coming that soon, I figured that was his excuse when he realized that I wasn't home that evening. He was going to stay outside in his car until I did get home, wondering where I was. He wanted to go for a drive, but I refused. It was late. He walked me upstairs, kissed me lightly, and left.

From that time on, Memo seemed to be his old self. He even checked on Patty when she had the flu, and I was attending classes. I hadn't asked him to do so. According to Patty, he performed some healing ritual with candles on the bed. Obviously, it worked. Patty got well very soon. Unfortunately, the day Patty became ill I was supposed to visit the school where I had sent so many books. A party had been planned in my honor, and I was to travel with the class now taking rural education. I did want to see the professor of English and a few of his students, as well as the section of the library with my name on a brass plate. I didn't want to ask Memo to stay with her until I would get home about 5:30 that afternoon. He was working, and I didn't want to take advantage of him. Besides, I needed to be back to make her some chicken soup for dinner. I was still responsible for her. She was just sixteen years old. Memo was still at the apartment when I returned.

The Letters

I thanked him, and he said, "I would do anything for you, *Picola*. Don't you know that?"

Memo left and said that if we needed anything to call him. He would be home, but Patty was soon well and attending her classes again. We were back to normal activities. Patty and I always slept with the windows and French doors slightly open because we preferred to sleep having cool air come into the bedroom. It was on one of those nights when I heard the sounds of a Mariachi band. I awakened Patty. I thought at first we had left the radio on, but the sound was coming from outside. Still half asleep, I thought it was a car radio playing the music. We got out of bed and looked outside. We didn't believe that a band was serenading us although it was playing beneath our balcony. At first glance, we didn't see anyone except the band members. Then just to the left of the band was Memo, just standing there grinning. The Mariachi were playing and singing some of the most romantic love songs I had ever heard. I didn't know about Patty, but I was lost in one of those enchanting moments I had experienced the summer before with Memo. I had seen and heard those serenades only in movies, and here Patty and I were in the early morning hours standing on a balcony being serenaded. What was I to make of this? Was this a gesture of friendship for Patty and me? Was it a gesture of love for me? I was hoping that he was not toying with my emotions. I was still very fragile when it came to Memo and his relationship with me. Yet, that night was one of those magical, spectacular moments that took my breath away-- a moment in time that will always be a part of my life.

The next time Memo and I were together, it was quite different. Guillermo was scheduled to fight his first bullfight, and his sister was having a *Traje de Luces* party at her penthouse in celebration of the occasion. I learned much later that Guillermo's sister was married to a very wealthy American from Texas. Memo invited me to go with him. The scene in the lobby was spectacular. In the center was a very large palm tree. Only the trunk of the tree was in the lobby. I looked up and noticed that the tree went all the way through a very large hole in the ceiling, continuing through the floors of all other apartments. Lights flooded the lobby and the trunk of the tree. We took the elevator that went directly to the penthouse. As we waited at the door to have Memo's invitation checked, I saw that the top branches of the tree ended in a hole in the center of the living room floor, a breath-taking scene with colored lights twinkling everywhere. A bar and a buffet table with finger food circled the tree. It seemed as though I was the only American there, and the doorman confirmed it when we entered. Memo led me to a sofa. I sat down and he sat next to me. He stood up to introduce me to a friend of his who took his place on the sofa as Memo went to the bar to get us drinks. I noticed that quite a few people, especially the women, stopped to greet him affectionately and talk with him. He was enjoying the attention. Obviously, he was well known. He brought me the drink and said, "Just sit here on the sofa" and then began circulating. What was I supposed to do?

Guillermo came to talk with me. He was so excited about the party and the fight on Sunday. Out of courtesy, he asked me if I wanted to see his Suit of Lights, but I knew that no one other than those who dressed him ever saw a bullfighter's suit before he entered the ring. It was supposed to be bad luck.

"Thank you very much for the honor, Guillermo, but not to-night." I added, "I'm sure that you will look very handsome in it. Good luck." I told him that I would say a prayer for him. Guill-ermo stayed just a short while, excused himself, and left -- to bed I supposed.

Meanwhile, Memo just circulated and circulated, coming to talk with me at times. He never asked me to stay with him, though. He appeared to be the life of the party. I didn't circulate, but Memo did keep a watchful eye on me. If I stood up to talk with someone, he was next to me for a few minutes. I knew very few people there, and making small talk in Spanish was a bit difficult. My tongue got tied. I am shy at first in a crowd of people I don't know. I did feel self-conscious when anyone asked me if I was a student at the university. I didn't know what to make of the evening -- a new cultural experience? The guest of honor may have gone to bed, but the party continued until 1:30 in the morning. I had no idea why Memo wanted me to go with him that evening, other than Guillermo may have asked him to do so. I wasn't sure.

Memo did escort me to the buffet tables for some food and introduced me to some of the guests, who were very cordial. Most of the guests just drank, nibbled on the food, and circulated. I walked around, looked at the paintings, and spoke with a few people who were curious about me, the American. One curious guest asked me whom I had come with because he said, "You seem to be alone." When I said that I had come with Memo, someone replied, "Hmmm, Memo? How do you know him?"

I replied that I knew Memo and Guillermo from the previous summer and that we were friends. I made sure that I told them I was a teacher in the United States, I was of Italian descent, the university was excellent, Mexico was beautiful, and it was for the last two reasons that I had returned for another summer session at the university. I knew they were trying to figure out if I were one of Memo's "*pasatiempos*" or an "*amante.*" I was glad when Memo decided it was time to go. Driving home he was fine, talkative, attentive, and affectionate as ever. He hoped that I had enjoyed myself. Actually in a way I had. It was, after all, a new episode in my life and one I have never forgotten.

Mary Ellen Cipolla Grasso

I was surprised a few days later when Memo told me that he was anxious for me to meet his parents, but advised me that I should not feel hurt if "they just greet you, talk for a minute, and then go about their way. It's a signal that they do not approve of you. If they ask you to dinner, you will know that they have accepted you."

I thought, "Accept me for what? What have you told them about me?"

Yet, I wanted to meet them. I wanted them to meet me, to talk with me, to learn something about me, and to see that I was not one of the wild, sleep-with-anyone, stereotypical American girls most Mexican parents thought we all were, especially those of us who went to the university. His parents were not at home at the time we arrived. At his home were his brother Oswaldo, Oswaldo's wife, and their young son, who was sleeping. Every time we heard footsteps, it was "Mama, Papa." I tried not to show I was nervous, but I was. Finally, his parents came, a lovely couple that reminded me of my own parents. Senor (Sr.) Espinosa spoke English, having lived in California at one time. Senora (Sra.) Espinosa came from Spain, I think, but spoke no English, at least not to me; however, she was smiling and was very pleasant to me. We spoke Spanish for a while. Suddenly, Sr. Espinosa said, "When can you come to dinner?" I answered, "Whenever you wish." Everyone was smiling, and I finally relaxed.

As Sr. Espinosa and I talked, he suddenly said with a twinkle in his eye, "When are you two going to Niagara Falls?"

"Niagara Falls?" I answered. Then I realized what he meant. For him it was a honeymoon destination. I quickly changed the topic by telling him that I had an aunt, uncle, and seven cousins who lived there; that I had seen Niagara Falls on many occasions; and that the falls were indeed beautiful.

Several days later I was at Memo's parents' home for a delicious Mexican dinner of *tamales*, a dish I had not eaten before. These were very large rolls of corn meal and bits of meat wrapped in what resembled grape leaves, but these leaves weren't edible. One was all I could eat, but with persuasion I had another. The evening was very pleasant, and I really liked his family. I remember that the last advice Memo's father gave him as we were leaving was, "If that girl as much as trips on the sidewalk, I will hold you responsible. Be careful."

Memo was pleasant, charming, and affectionate with his family and me that evening. He was the Memo of the summer of 1956 and the Memo from the letters he wrote in 1956 and 1957. I had no idea what he had said to his family before they agreed to meet me. Memo had certainly not discussed marriage with me during that summer.

Despite meeting his family and having dinner with them, Memo and I still did not see each other every day. I was busy with classes, especially an archeology class I had taken on the advice of my academic counselor. The first day of class I realized I was completely out of my element when the professor asked us to stand and introduce ourselves, giving our name, our occupation, the country we lived in, and the reason why we were enrolled in the class. I probably was the youngest student there. The first student, from the Philadelphia Historical Museum, had been working on trying to decipher Mayan hieroglyphics for a dozen years or more. The second one was from Washington, D.C., and he worked for the Smithsonian. He had been working on the Mayan Culture for twenty-five years. He added that archeologists could read the symbols for all the numbers but not necessarily for the alphabet.

Mary Ellen Cipolla Grasso

All of the other students had also been working with the Mayan culture. I was last. I could barely say anything. I choked a whisper, "I teach Spanish and English in a senior high school in Arnold, Pennsylvania. I have no experience working with Mayan hieroglyphics." I felt quite small. What was I doing in this class? At the end of the session, I spoke with the professor and asked him to withdraw me from that class, but many of the other students standing around the professor's desk encouraged me to stay. They said they would help me.

So they did. I learned a lot, but I never knew the difference between og or grog or whatever the names of the numeric hieroglyphics were. A few of the other students would say, "Look at the chin lines. See how they are different?" They looked the same to me; many of the symbols did.

But, oh, what a thrill it was to go on those field trips underground. I was fascinated. There were the murals, those that I had seen only in books. The men patiently taught me how to lift the hieroglyphics to paper. The first few times I had trouble holding the chalk correctly, but then I got so that I did not need anyone to help me. I remember the first time I felt secure enough to have one of those tracings taped to the slate board in front of the room. The professor even praised my work.

I spent hours, nevertheless, studying for the tests. Still when the grades were posted, mine were always the lowest. I never got discouraged, though. I just kept trying. At the end of the term, I received a "C." I'm sure that the professor gave me that grade for effort. I received "A's" in my other three classes, so I wasn't concerned about my grade average. I was grateful to those other students who had encouraged me to remain in the archeology class. Attending that archeology class did have an effect on me and played a roll in my life.

The Letters

Two years later when I did marry someone else, my husband, an Italian national, had an artist design a three-quarter inch wide heavy gold wedding band that has four hieroglyphics in relief around the outside of the band: ring, man, woman, death. (With this ring man marries this woman until death.) He knew how much I had enjoyed studying in Mexico. I remember that during the marriage ceremony, the priest stopped to ask about the rings that had just been handed to him by the Best Man. Father Fusco remarked that the rings were very unusual, and he asked about them. I thought he was disapproving of the rings because of the pagan symbols, but he wasn't. He just blessed the rings and continued with the ceremony.

Patty, also, had taken a class in Mayan culture and archeology. Hers, however, was in English and did not include field trips. My class was in Spanish and English. Our class schedules were nearly at the same time, so we always traveled by bus together. Patty and I usually took a second-class bus to the university, but we both preferred the third-class ones. One morning we were too late to get a seat on the second-class bus, but the third-class one was available. We paid our fares, looked for seats, but there were none. We both had to stand in the center of the aisle with no pole to hang onto, just squished in the middle of many other passengers, also standing. The bus was so crowded that there was no fear of losing our balance. There was no room to fall if we had. Patty was standing in front of me, facing a young woman carrying a large plastic bag of cornmeal dough. The bus was incredibly hot. Our attention was drawn to the woman carrying the dough. We noticed that the bag was expanding and expanding. There was no space for Patty to move back even a few steps. Suddenly the bag between Patty and the woman exploded. There was flour with sticky dough all over Patty's outfit, and Patty and the woman were stuck together like conjoined twins.

No one could even help Patty or the woman, and no one on the bus laughed. The woman got to her stop first, and she and Patty tried to pull themselves apart. A few others helped, but there was no way for Patty to clean her outfit before going to class. We started to walk into the entrance of the university, and there was Patty with flour and bits of dough on her. We tried to clean her outfit, but it was impossible. The sun seemed to be "cooking" the dough. It was only then when we were walking into the building that we started to laugh, but no one laughed harder than Memo when we told him the story that evening. However, that incident didn't stop us from riding third-class buses.

Despite my studies and the many field trips I took, as time went on, Memo and I did see each other more frequently than before. Sometimes he was very affectionate; sometimes he wasn't. I still couldn't stop loving him, and I kept telling myself that I was just a dear friend. I so desperately didn't want to get hurt again. Often I would walk through Chapultepec Park, to think about the emotional situation I was in. It was and still is the largest park in the city, soit was always possible to meet some student I knew, and we would sit on a bench and just talk. There was always a museum or the castle I could visit to distract me, but at times I preferred to go shopping, knowing that I could always find a bus nearby.

I remember one morning walking through the park on my way to a bus stop just to get away from the traffic. As I walked, an elderly man sitting on a bench called me over. I assumed he was homeless, lonely, or pandering for money. I was ready to give him a few pesos. Instead he said, "Do you know that many, many years ago that there were *chapulines* (grasshoppers) all over the woods here?

"Strange conversation," I thought, but then he asked me what my name was, and I answered, *"Marie Elena."* The next sentence was even stranger: "Would you like to marry me? I have a little bit of money saved."

I replied, "Ah, but I'm looking for much more money," as I quickly walked away. That must have been his standard line to any of the girls walking by. Ah, those Mexican men. They never stopped womanizing.

When Memo and I did see each other again, the relationship was not as intense as it once had been, when we were never apart and when he wrote those many love letters. I was puzzled. Why did he frequent the apartment downstairs? Did he know those men before I came? Did he select that specific apartment in order to keep an eye on Patty and me or because he enjoyed being with those particular friends? I do remember Pepe's writing and warning me that Memo had changed: "He's not the sweet boy you knew from the previous summer." I did know that they had a falling out because Memo resented any advice from Pepe.

I noticed the change first-hand one specific evening. I was home alone doing homework. Patty was gone for the evening. She enjoyed going to the *Zocalo*, the main plaza of the city, considered to be the historical center where many young people gathered for the night. I went there frequently, also. In fact, I had silver cuff links made for the men in my family and a pair for me designed by one of the jewelers who had a shop there. The cuff links were the initials of each person receiving them. I also bought two sterling silver cuff bracelets. I didn't know where Memo was that evening until there was a knock on the door. He was holding a large bowl. "*Picola*, I'm downstairs, and we ran out of ice. Can you fill this bowl with ice cubes?"

While I filled the bowl, he kept insisting that I go downstairs with him. He didn't want me to be alone. I knew most of the people there, not all I liked. At first I refused because I was working on a school project and because I was wearing lounging pajamas. He wouldn't take "no" for an answer, and he wouldn't leave until I went with him, as I was dressed. He didn't even give me time to change clothes.

There was a lively discussion going on downstairs, and I joined in. It soon became a debate, reminding me of the study sessions at the apartment on *Calle Shakespeare*. We were all laughing about one thing or another. I didn't pay any attention to what Memo was doing at the other end of the room other than a glance at him. He hadn't joined in the debate, but he was drinking. Suddenly I heard, "Hey, *Picola*." I turned towards him and saw a revolver pointed at me.

I am terrified of guns, and he knew that. I was hysterical. I was screaming. I tried to leave. I made a dash for the door, but it was blocked by an overflow of guests who were standing in the entrance hall of the building. My heart was pounding. A few people yelled at him to put down the gun. Someone caught me as I struggled to leave and said, "He's just kidding." I started to cry.

One of the men said, "That's not a real gun." I didn't know whether it was or not. It looked very real to me. How could I love this man who serenades me one evening and terrifies me another?

This was not the Memo I knew, the Memo who wanted me to meet his parents the Memo who promised he would never hurt me, who only wanted to make me happy, who had asked me multiple times to marry him. The one who wrote, "I know my parents will love you as though you were another one of their children, and you will learn to love my family after we marry." Was this the Memo who had seen the Mexican movie *Feliz Ano Nuevo, Mi Amor* and wrote that he wished I had been with him?

The Letters

Someone took the gun from Memo and put it away. I was still crying when Memo came over and said, "*Picola*, I was just teasing. Why are you crying? It was all in fun." It wasn't fun for me. I left shortly after his remark along with a few other guests, but Memo remained. The party continued. The next morning there were feathers all over the hallway. That must have been some party.

I should have walked away from him, but I couldn't. I still remembered that sweet, loveable man from the past summer and all of his love letters to me. I also recalled that in one of Memo's letters he wrote about the bad company he was keeping and the type of life he was now living. I must have written that he needed to change his so-called friends. He replied that I was right, that he was going to change his lifestyle of drinking, getting into fights, coming home late, and driving hard and fast. Instead he would go back to his former lifestyle, the "one of boredom, without fun." Hadn't I had heard those words before: "fun" and "boredom"? That evening I realized Memo had changed. Had I missed the signs in his letters? Was I that much in love with him? Had I learned nothing about relationships with men? Memo's letters, filled with love, passion, and marriage proposals, were aimed at my heart, not my head.

Patty came home that night with several men she had met, and I had to deal with that situation. I wasn't very pleasant. According to Patty, she had met the men in the city, at the *Zocalo* and invited them to come home with her to ask permission to go out with them that evening. She was impressed by the fact that they were all wearing suit jackets. I could tell they were older than she. Patty was upset by my attitude, and the men tried to convince me that they were honorable young men. I held my ground. I told them that she was just sixteen years old, and she could not go out with them that evening or any other evening. I had no idea who these men were. I only knew that someone named Antonio did most of the talking. I was thinking that I had had enough of honorable men that evening.

When the men left, I explained to Patty that there had been an incident the previous year with a university student who had been raped. Young Mexican men were always flirting with the American girls, especially those attending the university, and they had little respect for them. Patty was still upset. I didn't tell her about the episode that had happened downstairs. I was sure that Memo had been drinking too much and had been showing off. He was, I realized, self-centered. What happened to him between those many months that he wrote me such sweet, loving letters, full of promises for the future and anxiously awaiting my return to Mexico City? I had to stop thinking about my problems because Jerry was arriving soon, and I had to focus on planning events and sightseeing tours for her.

Jerry arrived on July 28, 1957, and Memo and I did go to the airport to get her as he had promised. He was very pleasant, very engaging, even suggesting some places we could all go together, such as Xochimilco. Because it was late and Jerry wanted to get settled, Memo left, and she started unpacking her suitcases as I sat on the bed talking with her. All of a sudden the bed seemed to be sliding back and forth. I thought I was dizzy. Then I heard the china cabinet in the dining room slide back and forth. I ran to hold it so the dishes wouldn't break.

I yelled to the men downstairs who were standing in the outside hallway of the building. "Hey guys! What's happening?"

One of them answered, "Nothing. It's just a tremor."

Jerry and went to the balcony but did not step outside. We noticed that the apartment complex across the street seemed to be swaying. Cars had stopped on *Avenida Insurgentes* with some passengers standing outside of their vehicles. Never having been in an earthquake, we didn't realize that we were in the midst of one; Jerry, Patty, and I were frightened. What do we do? The tremors were over very quickly. We waited for about five minutes; then we began to put the furniture back in place. We slid the china cabinet against the dining room wall, cleaned up some of the broken glass that lay on one of the shelves and on the floor. Very few pieces had broken, and we were glad about that. It seemed as though the earthquake was over in minutes.

We all went to bed, convinced it was over. The cars that had stopped were gone. Everything seemed to be quiet. We didn't know until early the next morning when I got up to make breakfast that our butane gas tank on the back porch had pulled away from the wall and the pipes were twisted. The pilot light in the range was out, and there was no gas. Before I could even react, I heard noises on the back porch, just behind the kitchen. The superintendent had sent his maintenance men to check the tanks. All six tanks for the complex were on our porch just behind the kitchen, and all had been torn away from the wall. Thank heavens that the tanks had not blown up during the night. We were told that we would not have gas for a few days because all of the tanks had to be removed and new ones installed.

Since it seemed that the earthquake was over, Jerry and I decided to walk to church for the Sunday morning Mass. The church was not too far away, maybe a mile. When we left our complex and made a right hand turn in the direction of the church, nothing seemed out of the ordinary. There were some young men playing soccer in a field, and a few people were walking on the sidewalk. Jerry did notice that there were not a lot of parishioners in church, but even that wasn't too unusual for me. Most Sundays the church wasn't filled. Not until we returned to our apartment did we notice that the complex to the right of ours had been damaged. The further we walked past our complex, the more damage we saw. Our building was untouched.

We had just gotten back to our apartment when Memo ran in shouting, "The Angel fell! The Angel fell!" At first we couldn't figure out what angel he was talking about until he explained that it was the *Monumento de la Independencia* (the Monument of Independence). It was and is still considered to be the number one landmark in Mexico City. Many times we had driven past it. It sat on the top of a tall column in the center of one of the city's roundabouts. The statue was a gilded angel that most people just referred to as "*El Angel.*" We got into Memo's car and drove around to see how much destruction there was. The Angel had a lot of damage. The business center was hit hard, as well as the movie theaters and the retail establishments. Everyone was grateful that the earthquake happened in the middle of the night when there were very few people in any of those building. The Hilton Hotel, however, had damage. The building had separated at the point where the new extension was joined with the old during the renovation of the hotel. The old part was not damaged, but the new one was. Many Americans stayed there, and the first report was that no one had been killed. What was amazing was the fact that the tallest building in the city, The Tower of Latin America, had no damage. That building, according to reports, just swayed. We thought about volunteering at the Red Cross, but when we went to the location and saw bodies lined on the sidewalk, we changed our minds. We had been told that we might have to help move them to the morgue. We just continued driving around the city.

I learned a few days later that my parents were watching the news on television Sunday morning and heard about the aftermath of the earthquake in Mexico City. They tried telephoning me, but the lines were down. They were frantic. My dad called the local Red Cross chairman who told him that there was no initial report of Americans killed or injured, but he would check and call later. It wasn't until later in the afternoon that my dad was told that no American students were involved. I tried telephoning or sending a telegram to my parents but that was impossible. I had to rely on just writing a letter. However, my parents were able to telegram me. I still have the telegram, and in the envelope are two very small pieces of the building that was near the one in which I lived and had been damaged by the earthquake.

Classes were in session on Monday as usually, and the university scheduled its last trip to Acapulco for the coming weekend. There were still small tremors, but Jerry, Patty, and I decided it would be all right to take the trip. This would be the only weekend Jerry could come with us since she had just a one-week vacation. Memo offered to drive us to Acapulco. The roads were dangerous, and it seemed as though we would never get to our destination. When we arrived, we settled into the hotel that was usually reserved for university students. However, I don't remember Memo's staying at the same hotel, but he may have stayed with friends, either who lived there or were there for the weekend. His letters always mentioned meeting friends in Acapulco on his frequent trips there.

I remember, also, sitting on one of the balconies of the hotel where Jerry, Patty, and I were staying, along with a number of other students. Some of us were standing on the balcony or sitting in chairs enjoying the sights of the clear blue sky over the enticing waters of the Pacific Ocean. I was sitting in one the chairs, bracing my feet on the balcony railing when suddenly there were a few strong tremors. Someone standing behind me grabbed my swimming suit straps with one hand and the chair with the other and pulled me back before I was pitched over the railing. I didn't know who it was; I just yelled, "Thanks!" That was the last time

I sat out on the balcony that weekend. I had no idea that there could be tremors for days after an earthquake.

Memo was with us most of the time, the Memo I knew from the previous summer: witty, sensitive, warm, and loveable. Patty did know a little about the relationship between Memo and me, but Jerry did not. That weekend he was the Memo I knew and loved, but I tried to keep my distance. I was so afraid of being near him, of touching him. I didn't want Jerry or Patty to know how I really felt about him. They only knew we had a wonderful friendship. We all swam and sunbathed. We saw the remarkable cliff high divers at night while having dinner at one of the restaurants high above the cliffs. The following day we rented a small motorboat to take a ride on the coastal waters of the Pacific Ocean, just off one of the beaches. I was in awe of the beautiful scenery, the clear blue water, wishing I didn't have to leave Sunday evening because I knew this was the last time I would go to Acapulco. We all were having fun. At one time, I climbed out of the boat and went into the water. I paddled around, soaking in the sights and sounds. Memo seemed to be his old self. He hadn't been drinking, at least not around us. He was charming, and we all enjoyed those few days, but deep in my heart, I knew that he could be one way today and another way tomorrow. Yet for me this weekend would be one to be remembered and cherished.

I hated to see Jerry leave for home because we had had such an enjoyable time. I still recall the trouble she had the first time we ate at a restaurant trying to select an entrée from the menu. Anything I suggested was not to her liking. She finally asked for a grilled cheese sandwich. The waiter told her that it was not on the menu. She then asked for a ham sandwich, and that wasn't available. I just chuckled, but we both finally settled on *Arroz Con Pollo Sin Picante* that was on the menu. She did like the chicken and rice dish that was not spicy. It was an experience for her to try some of the Mexican dishes. She did eventually find entrees she enjoyed eating at the restaurants that catered to Americans. It was just that I preferred eating Mexican food and usually avoided those "Americanized" restaurants. Jerry, Patty, and I did enjoy all of the various side trips we took, as well as the entertainment provided for the students in the university's theater.

After Jerry left, Patty and I began to make plans for our return trip to Pennsylvania. We had about two weeks more of school, and there were places I still wanted her to see. I recall the Saturday afternoon that Antonio, one of those young men she had met that I did not approve of earlier, asked if he and his friend could take Patty swimming at Vista Hermosa on Sunday. Originally, I refused. "Two men?" I questioned to myself. I didn't trust them, but Patty really wanted to go. I decided I would go as their chaperone. I had no plans with Memo because he seldom made any. He would just show up at will. While we were gone, Pepe had stopped at our apartment to invite us to his sister's ranch, some kilometers away, for a Mexican Fiesta she was having. Pepe hadn't telephoned ahead of time, believing we would be home because he learned my relationship with Memo had cooled. When I learned the next day of his invitation, I really felt bad. I would have preferred attending the Fiesta, a new experience for me and spending the day with Pepe, as well as meeting his sister.

Besides, the day at Vista Hermosa was a total loss for me. I didn't want to swim, and I didn't want to interact. All I could think of was the time that I had been there with Memo when we had toured the Hacienda. I now lay on the beach and recalled seeing all those rooms without electricity, just candles. I remembered one of the bedrooms to be quite a romantic scene, but that was because Memo was with me. I thought about that day and realized that Memo must have been there many times before. That day with Patty I imagined I saw him lying next to me on the sand, putting my silver ring on his finger so that he "could keep me always close to him." I felt very weepy, but I had to make sure that I kept my eyes on Patty and the young men. I kept in mind that I was still Patty's teacher.

The following Saturday, Memo wanted me to go horseback riding with him. In one of his letters he had mentioned that he enjoyed the sport. We had a pleasant ride and an enjoyable afternoon. I was rather surprised, however, that he asked me to pay for the rental of the horses. He said he would take care of lunch. Who could make sense out of this relationship? Why couldn't I just walk away from him? I knew that I would never return to Mexico City, but I couldn't walk away. I was too emotionally involved, and he wouldn't stay away. We went somewhere for lunch and then spent the rest of the day together. I asked him if he again would mail my box of books when I left. He said he would take care of it. I gave him Patty's and my flight plans and told him that I would confirm them. He said, "Fine." The summer before, he had insisted on confirming my flight plans. He always took care of me.

About a week before we were to leave, Memo came to the apartment. He knocked, and I opened the door. He didn't come in as he usually did but just stood on the landing and asked me to take a drive with him. We spent the afternoon together like old times. When we went back to the apartment, he didn't come in. He just stood on the landing again. He suddenly suggested that Patty and I cash in our return tickets. He thought it would be a great idea if he and Guillermo would drive us home to Pennsylvania. I had never seen Guillermo drive, and I didn't think that Memo would have allowed him to drive his car. He mentioned that he wanted to meet my family, but I didn't think that was the reason. I told him that I was responsible for Patty and that she would have to get permission from her parents before I would even consider such a trip.

Much to my surprise, Patty said that they gave her their permission. In a letter from Pepe months later, he wrote that it was "incredible that you would have allowed Memo to drive you home. Why?" How could I explain rationally to Pepe that I was still uncertain about Memo's feelings for me, or was it my feelings for him? The summer had been so difficult for me. I knew that Memo and I would eventually have to say goodbye. Why prolong it? I thought an extra two weeks would help us put closure on our relationship, whether it was a life-long friendship or marriage. Maybe without all the distractions in Mexico City, Memo would finally make a decision, one way or another, and we could both go on with our individual lives as difficult as that would be for me. I didn't know whether Guillermo had money for the round trip, but I assumed that Memo did. He was the one with the job. However, I understood that Patty and I would use the money that was refunded from the tickets for our personal expenses and for all car expenses. Was having Memo drive us home the right decision? I would find out later.

The next week Memo helped us pack souvenirs that we had bought and our textbooks. He was excited about making the trip. I was anxious to leave. The morning we left, both Memo and Guillermo packed the car. It was so filled that we had to put some small boxes and bags on the floor of the back seat. I even had a stone sculpture of some Mexican god that had caught my eye, and I had impulsively bought. It was quite heavy, but I didn't want to leave it behind. In fact, I still have it today standing in a corner near my front door. In addition to the sculpture there was a very large floor vase that Patty must have bought. Memo and I planned to take turns driving. He would drive in Mexico, and once we passed the border in Brownsville, I would drive in the States.

Mary Ellen Cipolla Grasso

Driving north, the road was not always paved. While we were still in Mexico, the car broke down. We stopped at a repair shop, and after examining the car, the mechanic said that it was a minor repair and would take about an hour that actually took about two hours. While Memo and the mechanic talked, Patty and I walked around the shop. Hanging in the repair shop was a machete that I took a fancy to and wanted to buy. Memo bargained with the owner, who sold it to me for $2.00. No one could figure out why I wanted it. I just liked it, and I thought that I could show it to my students. I had the machete until 1999 when I moved to Gainesville, Florida, a year after my husband Orazio's death.

I paid for the car repair with the money from the refunded tickets, but I had expected to do so. I had become the unofficial treasurer. Because of the time we had spent getting the car repaired, it began to get later and darker than we had expected. Memo drove until he believed that it was no longer safe to drive on those roads. We tried to find a motel for the night, but it was impossible. There weren't any available. It was quite late, nearing ten o'clock at night, and Memo could no longer chance trying to continue driving in what I believed to be uncharted territory. There were no lights along the unpaved, dangerous roads. There were mountains with roads for only two vehicles and steep ravines on both sides with no barriers to prevent a car from going over. We all were very tired and sleepy. We were hot and dirty. The men suggested we pull off the road when we could, go into a nearby field, and sleep in the car. Memo and I were sleeping in the front; I slept with my head on his shoulder. Patty and Guillermo slept sprawled in the back.

Although I was not sleeping soundly, when several men on horseback came to the car, I found that I couldn't even move. It was as though I was paralyzed. I tried to call Memo, but I couldn't speak. The men, dressed in white and wearing sombreros, rode around the car several times while peering inside. We had opened all four doors of the car so that we could have the cooler night air. I couldn't understand what the men were saying, but they soon left. I was frightened, yet I still couldn't move or utter a word other than making a gargling sound. Perhaps the men noticed the Mexican license plates, saw four young people in the car, and decided we weren't dead or American tourists. I'll never know whether they were police officers or highwaymen. Our guardian angels must have been watching over us.

The next morning when we all awakened with the bright sun on us, I asked the others if they had heard anything. They hadn't. I told Memo that I tried to awaken him, but I felt paralyzed, and I just groaned. He thought that the men, perhaps, were farmers who lived nearby, saw the car in their field, and came to investigate. I wasn't sure because they had rifles hanging from the sides of the saddles. We all agreed that we would stop early that day so we could get two adjacent motel rooms. We knew that we would arrive at the Brownsville border later that morning. We were all sweaty, dirty, and hungry, but there was no way to get washed until we found a place to eat that had an available bathroom with a sink--something we couldn't find easily on our current road.

We were certain, however, that other restaurants would be available the further north we drove, perhaps near the border, and there were. Patty and I found paper towels that were only in the women's rest room. Sharing the towels with the men, we all sort of made ourselves presentable before going into the restaurant to eat. We thought that soon we would be in Brownsville and find more suitable accommodations and thought once we got through Customs in Brownsville, which we believed wouldn't take more than fifteen minutes, we could continue driving to Texarkana, about 650 miles away. With two of us taking turns driving, we planned to drive at least ten hours that day, if not more.

But Customs at the United States border in Brownsville had another idea. We were stopped, asked to pull off the road. The officers took our visas and other documents, such as driver's licenses and other identification cards, and took them into the office to check them before returning all of the documents to us. We were asked a few questions and then told to empty our car out completely, open all suitcases, all boxes and every bag, regardless of the size. Then the car was searched: inside, outside, and under. Every piece of luggage, every box, and every bag was searched thoroughly. Clothes were taken out and just piled on a wooden table. I didn't notice any other driver being asked to stop so that the contents of the car could be searched. We must have looked suspicious. That stop took over two hours because repacking the luggage, the bags, and the boxes before putting them into the car was not easy. In one of the towns in Texas, we stopped to eat lunch and to browse in a nearby souvenir store. The men wanted to buy a few postcards to send home to their family. Memo bought about six, but Guillermo was buying many more. I suddenly heard Memo whisper, "*Recuerdo quien paga.*" Hmm, "Remember who's paying." I paid the bill for all four of us at the souvenir shop, but the phase lingered in my mind. Now I understood. I realized that I, the treasurer, had also paid for our lunch. I thought that perhaps the men were saving their money for their trip back home. When it came to Memo, I made excuses.

Once in the United States, I breathed a sigh of relief. We found a gas station, filled our tank, and continued driving. We had a great time. We sang, laughed, and played games, such as finding items on the road using the alphabet. We also kept changing places in the car. When I drove, Memo would sleep in the back seat, and Patty or Guillermo would sit in the front. When he drove, I slept in the back. We wanted to drive as many miles as we could that day so that we would only have to stay one night at a motel. We didn't stop early in the afternoon as we had planned because I noticed that there were a lot of vacancy signs along the way, and roads in Texas were excellent.

I don't remember there being a speeding limit or a lot of traffic. I only remember how hot it was in the car without having air-conditioning and how fast we dove. We finally found a motel with two adjacent rooms available later that night. The price was reasonable, and there was a restaurant nearby. When we came back to the motel after dinner, I let Patty shower first. She was exhausted, and I was afraid she would fall asleep if I showered first. The next morning, realizing that we were near the Arkansas border, Memo and I decided we would try to drive straight through to western Pennsylvania without making any unnecessary stops, but we couldn't. We hadn't counted on our having to stay another night on the road, but we all were exhausted, especially Memo and I. We had to find another inexpensive motel, but I no longer remember what state we were in.

Pennsylvania

I do recall that when we arrived in Pennsylvania later the next morning, we first dropped Patty off at her home and stayed just long enough to introduce the two men to her parents. We three then went to my parents' home in Lower Burrell. I had no idea what my parents thought of the men, especially Memo. They were aware of the many letters I had received from him, and my mother often knew the contents, especially those letters when he asked me to marry him. Neither my mother nor my father had asked me any questions when I wrote to them that Memo and Guillermo would be guests at our home. They welcomed both of the men the morning we had arrived, and during that stay, my parents treated the men as though they were members of the family. My youngest brother Ron, home from Bucknell University for the summer, did not interact much with Memo and Guillermo though my brother Buddy and his wife Mary did meet them and thought the men were very pleasant. Mary thought Memo was "charming and very attractive."

Although we didn't see Patty, her parents had invited us to dinner one evening. Memo couldn't have been more engaging, more charismatic. Guillermo followed the conversations as well as he could; still seemed to be enjoying himself. He was very amusing that evening, really making an effort to use English. We did visit Jerry one evening, and a few other evenings the men chose to just stay at home, sitting on the swing in the backyard talking, spending an evening with my family, or just watching television. One of Memo's earlier letters described a similar scene he wanted to have with me when I returned for the second summer session. But we never had those moments together in Mexico. Memo, Guillermo, and I toured the Allegheny Valley and went to some nightspots we had nearby. We drove to Pittsburgh to shop at the large department stores. I wanted to purchase some toys for Memo's nieces and nephews, so we went to a toy store that fascinated both men, but I no longer remember what Guillermo bought for his family, if anything. However, I did purchase a few items for his sisters. I was certain now that Guillermo had no money. Another day we went to Kennywood Park outside of Pittsburgh. It is known even today for its wooden roller coasters. Memo and Guillermo especially enjoyed the Haunted House. We had a wonderful day, riding the roller coaster and going on all the other rides. It was cotton candy, ICEE's, hot dogs, hamburgers, and colas. Memo and I were like two young people who had just discovered each other. The sparkle was back in his eyes, and we were laughing and holding hands as we went from one ride to another.

The night before Memo and Guillermo left, we three had gone out for a short time to the Rustic Inn for coffee and conversation. Patty's parents had telephoned to say they would visit that evening about nine o'clock to say goodbye and to thank Memo for taking care of Patty when she was ill in Mexico. We promised we would be back before that time. We were, but the Pallone family came early. Guillermo went inside, but Memo and I stayed in the car for what we thought would a few minutes. I said, "The summer is over. I have to say goodbye. We won't ever be seeing each other again." I barely got the words out when I started to cry. We both cried. We just cried and cried. I didn't know what he was thinking, but he said something strange. "I love you, but before I marry, I want to buy a BMW." Like a fool, I answered, "We could sell both of our cars eventually and get the BMW." I had no idea how much his salary was or how much a BMW would cost.

Then he said something that really must have been on his mind for a long time. I realized for the first time that he didn't love me unconditionally because he said he wanted me to start going to a physical fitness gym with him when we did marry. At that time I wore a size 10 or 12, depending on the style. I realized it was over. What was he thinking? Why hadn't he been honest with me? Why did he really take this trip? Was it to meet my parents as he said? Pepe had seen that trip to Pennsylvania in a different way as I had and didn't believe the reason Memo had given me for wanting to drive us home: to meet my family. In a letter Pepe wrote to me a few months later, he saw driving me home as a selfish act by Memo. He wrote, "For Memo it was a cashmere sweater and a free vacation." Those words stung me. Could Memo have been so callous?

But that evening, Memo and I sat in the car for maybe a half hour, both crying, trying to make sense of our relationship. Did Memo finally realize what he had done to me? Is this why he was crying and not because he would miss me as he said? My heart was breaking. We just held on to each other and cried. I could hardly catch my breath. I noticed my mother looking out the window. It was nearly ten o'clock, and it was obvious when we walked into the house that we had been crying. I simply said, "It's hard trying to say goodbye." I went into the bathroom to wash my face and compose myself. I wasn't sure before that evening what the Pallones knew through Patty about my relationship with Memo, but now I was sure they did. They stayed about a half hour and then left. Memo and Guillermo had to get up early, so we all went to bed. I didn't even say, "Good night."

I didn't know about Memo, but I couldn't sleep. I realized that the money from our refunded tickets had paid for the entire trip. Was it a free vacation for Memo and Guillermo? All Memo had contributed was the use of his car. I assumed that they had very little money with them. I didn't want them stranded on the road so I gave Memo the remainder of the refunded ticket money and an extra $50.00 I had withdrawn earlier that week from my bank account for the two of them to get home safely. The next morning Memo asked me to accompany them to the entrance of the Turnpike. He wasn't sure of what road to take. I did accompany them, but driving alone was difficult. Memo and I stopped our cars at the side of the road before coming to the first toll booth. We got out of our cars to say goodbye. I said, "Drive safely and let me know when you get home. Don't speed." I didn't want him to touch me, but he hugged and kissed me. He looked at me, held my face in his hands, and just said, "*Adorada Picola.*" I quickly got in my car because I knew I would cry. I waved, and that was the last time I ever saw him.

The Breakup

I got a postcard from Memo when he was in Kentucky, telling me that all was well, but he was tired because he was the only one doing the driving. He telephoned me from somewhere in Texas to say that they had trouble being served in a restaurant because he and Guillermo were Mexican and were speaking Spanish. Only Memo spoke English. When he returned home, both of his sisters wrote me letters. They thanked me for the gifts I had sent to the children. Silvia wrote telling me that Memo was the favored one of the family, and everyone loved him. Maria Rosa wrote that Memo never got tired of talking about my family or me, and the only word he kept saying about my family was *"Fantasticos. Fantasticos."* She also wrote that I "should ask God for the two of us [Memo and me] to realize and finalize our plans of marriage." This was something that he wrote about only in his letters. "What plans?" I thought. "We never even had the talk about marriage. He only wrote about that in his letters. His parents, he once wrote, wanted us to marry, believing that I was the perfect girl to be his wife.

I did hear again from Memo. The first letter was a very long one about his trip back to Mexico. All the endearments of the past were in that letter. He addressed me as his *"Adorada Picola."* I read the letter and was confused. I must have written a reply, but what it was I no longer remember. The second letter said that he couldn't get married for six or seven months. In fact, he wanted me to understand why marriage might be difficult. All summer we had never talked about marriage. I don't know what he ever said to his family when there was no marriage even discussed. He probably blamed me. At any rate, he wrote that he had promised his parents that he would help them pay for their new home and that he couldn't be a good husband if he first couldn't be a good son. He also wrote that his dad had lost his job, which I didn't believe because I thought the Asphalt Company belonged to his father and brother. Memo felt that he could not make enough money in the United States to continue to support his parents, and he would have to keep his job in Mexico. He was determined to accept responsibility for them. How much of that was true? According to Pepe, Memo always had unlimited amounts of money. Memo also didn't know whether I could make the cultural transfer to Mexico, living on his salary alone. I still had no idea how much money he made.

Two days later I received a third letter, asking me not to blame or hate him but to try to understand. He also wrote that the treatment Guillermo and he received by my parents was "undeserved." He added that if any of my family or I ever went to Mexico "we would be treated like kings by him and his family." He also wrote he would always remember "those marvelous moments we had spent together." He ended the letter by writing, "Please don't stop loving me because I will never stop loving you. Please forgive me. When you have time, write to me." Instead of signing his letters as he always did, *"Tuyo Memo,"* he signed his last letter "Memo" and wrote a line of X's below his name. It was over. Memo had made his decision.

In a letter Guillermo wrote to me months later, he mentioned that he had seen Memo, who said, "I miss *Picola.*"

A month later, sometime in October, Memo telephoned. At first, he called Patty's telephone number, but her mother told him that he had the wrong number. He then telephoned me. My mother, sitting near the telephone, answered and told me that it was

Memo. I had no idea why he was telephoning me. He asked me if I could find hotel accommodations for his parents because he wanted to come to Pennsylvania to get married. He sounded sincere. He was happy to hear my voice. He missed me. All I could say was, "Let me know when." I wondered for an instant if he might have been drinking. Patty's mom called my mother to ask whether or not Memo had called me. She wanted to know what he had to say. My mom just told her that he wanted to talk with me, nothing important. What had he said to Mrs. Pallone?

I never heard from Memo again, but Guillermo wrote to me and said that he couldn't understand "why two people who had such a beautiful relationship didn't write or speak ever again." Guillermo felt that our not continuing the relationship was "because of fear, but fear of what? Only you know the reason why." Guillermo also wrote that he couldn't believe I would not ever return to the university or Mexico City and wanted to know why.

I answered, "Ask Memo. He knows why."

Many days while I was driving to or from work, the lyrics from the song "I Could Have Told You So" by Carl Sigman and John Von Heusen played in my mind, but I usually changed some of the lyrics to suit my situation:

> *I could have told you he'd hurt you*
> *Love you a while then desert you*
> *If only you'd asked I could have told you so.*
> *I could have saved you some crying*
> *I could have told you he's lying*
> *[But you were in love] and didn't want to know*
> *I see him now as I toss and turn and try to sleep*
> *I hear him now making promises he'll never keep.*
> *And so it's over and done with*

The Letters

[He'll] find someone new to have fun with
If only you'd asked I could have told you so

There were days I couldn't erase the lyrics from my mind. I blamed myself. I never asked anyone for advice, and when I did, it was too late. I should have asked Pepe. He would have told me the truth.

But I did ask someone else, a friend of mine, Louis Cianco, a well-known handwriting analyst in the Pittsburgh area. Louis was on a retainer for a large manufacturing company to read applications and analyze the handwriting on applications for executive positions. All applicants were asked to write a proposal for some project during the personal interview. I had sent Louis several of Memo's handwritten letters to analyze. Louis analyzed the letters and did write that he "doubted Memo's sincerity, that he had a dual personality." He was "one person to one group of people and another to a different group." He was "tender and loveable," but he could be "cold, distant, and selfish." Louis analyzed that what Memo said "one day, may not be the same the next."

Louis was right. I had seen all of those signs the second summer. Memo was, as Louis wrote, "mercurial. Indecision plagues him, and courage fails him many times." Memo did have difficulty making up his mind, and he was deeply emotional but not emotionally mature. Louis wrote that Memo "was able to reach you through your emotional nature" and that you have "allowed your heart to rule instead of your head." He said, "Many people [like Memo] often proved to be unfaithful and failures in marriages."

I was also corresponding with Pepe because I needed to have a shoulder to cry on. I knew that it would take me sometime to try to understand what had happened and to be able to cope with this new heartbreak. Pepe knew Memo better than his own family did. Pepe did try to advise me indirectly when he once said to me in Mexico City that second summer: "I am worried about your marrying Memo." I had never told Pepe that Memo had proposed to me. Maybe Memo told him. Memo was torn between his heart and his mind, his duty and his desire. He tried to tell me that in one of his last letters. Was I a fool or just in love and "didn't want to know" the truth?

Often I would sing the lyrics of that song and just cry, but I never shared my feelings with anyone else, not even my closest friends. I didn't want them to feel sorry for me. I didn't want them to say, "Not again. What's wrong with her?" My mother, who was my dearest friend, only asked me once about him. "Why did he stop writing? What happened?" I couldn't even say he was just a friend because friends would have still corresponded. I just told her, "I don't really know." She finally said that my dad and she thought he was a "wonderful young man." I never answered her. I couldn't. I was also glad that Patty and Jerry never asked about him.

Both Pepe and Guillermo kept up a correspondence with me for the next year and a half, but I must have gotten involved with work and friends, and either they or I stopped writing in 1958. However, Pedro and I had been corresponding from 1955 to 1958, trying to make sense out of that relationship. I was tempted to return to Monterrey many times, and I might have if he had made just one trip to my home. I was making a valiant attempt to put my life in order again. Unlike the heartbreak with Ray, this time there was no way to escape my problems. There was no Mexico to run to. I had to keep busy, to become involved in new projects.

My high school graduation class was planning a reunion with the class that had graduated the year before us. I decided to work on the planning committee. One of the men, also on the committee, asked me to go for out for coffee after one of the meetings. I did, and for seven or eight months we dated. We went to dinners, operas, concerts, off-Broadway shows, charity balls, and movies. He even helped me chaperone my students when I took them to an opera. He was safe. I knew that there would be no emotional involvement. We were just friends. I had decided that I needed time to heal. I think I might have been a cover for him. There were rumors that he was gay, but we had a lot in common, and I could just relax when we were out together. We stopped dating suddenly when he wrote to me while I was on a two-week educational retreat that it would be a good idea for us not to see each other anymore. Silently I agreed. I was finally ready to get on with my life. I always wondered why my principal had nominated me for that retreat. Most of the participants were much older than I and had been teaching for years longer. I learned much later that the principal, a friend of mine, was very concerned about me and thought that the retreat would help me get through the past difficult year and a half I had had with Memo.

In the days after Memo and I had stopped communicating, I wondered, "Was I just a victim of 'emotional fraud,' as Pepe once suggested to me, or was I just a young naïve girl in love, trying to figure out relationships and men?" Memo had given me an unbelievable amount of joy, laughter, and love. The love was real, even if it was only for an "instant" in both of our lifetimes. I have no doubt that he once loved me. In his letter he wrote, "If you ever talk about me, never say that I didn't love you. Just say that you were too good for me." We also shared a beautiful friendship that neither one of us chose to continue. I do recall the greeting card I sent him, on his birthday, June 25, 1958. He was still on my mind, so much a part of my life. He sent a postcard back asking if I wanted him to write to me again. I replied, "I don't think so; unless you really want to." He never wrote again, and I always regretted that we did not remain friends

Pepe was right when he wrote that he was always worried about the possibility that Memo and I would marry. He worried about me, and he wrote, "Marriage (with Memo) for you would be a conquest, but it would come as too high a price for you, one of disaster and pain." I thought, "Probably for Memo, also." He was really not ready to settle down, to give up the life of a bachelor, to commit himself to one woman. Guillermo wrote that every time he saw Memo, he was with a different girl. Did his parents really think that if he married he would settle down?

Strange as it may seem, I never forgot Pedro. How could I love two very different, exceptional men at the same time: one who broke my heart and the other whose heart I broke. I often think of a beautiful ballad, "I Fall in Love Too Easily," sung by Frank Sinatra in the 1945 movie, *Anchors Aweigh.* I have seen the movie on television many times since that year. Jule Styne wrote the music for the song, but it is the lyrics, written by Sammy Cahn, that suited me in those days:

> *I fall in love too easily*
> *I fall in love too fast*
> *I fall in love too terribly hard*
> *For love to ever last*
> *My heart should be well schooled*
> *'Cause I've been fooled in the past*
> *But still I fall in love too easily*
> *I fall in love too fast.*

Those lyrics define me. They are a reflection of my relationships with men and a reflection of me. It took me a long time before I could ever trust anyone with my heart. I had locked it away. From the time I first met Pedro, he left an imprint on my heart. He was the one I first trusted, the man who had brought love into my life after the episode with Ray. He had all the qualities I admired in a man. I knew he loved me and would be an excellent husband and father, but there were too many obstacles to overcome. He painted a depressing picture when he wrote that I could not expect a wedding in a church or a reception after the marriage. There would be no honeymoon because he claimed that he had lost everything and had just his salary to live on. We would have to save every penny because we would need it. He claimed that he could not give me the conveniences I enjoyed in the United States. He would never leave his beloved Mexico, and I could not leave my family without his knowing them. I wondered that if money was an issue, would I ever be able to visit my family? Was there no hope in the future for a successful and happy marriage?

Pedro and I met at the wrong time of our lives and in the wrong place. He once asked me why I wasn't married and if I were ashamed of what had passed between us. Nothing had ever happened that I would be ashamed of except the fact that I couldn't give up a secure life in the States, but at the same time, I couldn't give him up. It took me nearly another year and a half to realize that. Because I loved him, I had to be honest with him, to let him go. I wanted him to find happiness. I did tell him that I had never married because I hadn't found the right man for me. He would never have wanted me to work even though I had always believed that a wife should also work, and it should not be only the husband's responsibility to earn money. I always hoped that he had married and was happy. I don't think he ever knew how sad it was for me to give him up, especially when I received a telegram from him that said, "You will never know how much your letters have meant to me."

Now that I have reread all of the letters, I realize that each of those men came into my life for a reason. Memo and Pedro made me feel wanted, loved, and adored at a time when I felt rejected and unloved. Memo was young, not ready for marriage, despite the many times he proposed to me. Pedro, who was ready for marriage, had personal problems that love alone could not overcome. How could I marry a man who would not or could not come to visit my family? He wanted me, instead, to return to Monterrey for a while, without any commitment on the part of either of us, to see how he lived.

Pepe was the broad shoulder to cry on, a voice of reason to warn and advise me. He was a philosopher who gave me much to ponder. I'm sorry that we never continued writing to each other. Guillermo was a friend who tried to understand what had happened between Memo and me since he, too, was having a similar problem with an American girl named Jane. He was in love with her and believed they would marry, but she just slipped away, and he never heard from her again.

I am grateful to those men who touched my life in some way, who gave me emotional support when I needed it the most. They taught me about relationships, about what men value in themselves, in women, and in friends. They taught me that love could be but a moment in time or a lifetime of marvelous moments. My relationships with them, brief as they were, led me finally to unconditional love, marriage, and children; but this time love did not come too easily. I had been fooled more than once.

Enter Orazio

I thought I was done with finding old letters with those of the men who lived in Mexico, but on December 20, 2008, I found 53 letters, or they found me, written by my late husband, Orazio, between August 21, 1959, and March 1, 1960, I didn't know they still existed. For weeks I had been feeling very nostalgic after finding those other letters, especially from Memo and Pedro. I hadn't been able to sleep well since reading them and reliving those days, many of great joy and love and others of sadness and tears. Those days were some of the most incredible times of my life, and I couldn't get the images out of my mind of those men in Mexico and the memorable moments we had shared.

I seemed to have no holiday spirit that December, and I kept praying that I could forget about the past that just cluttered my mind. Some mornings I would awaken at two o'clock, not being able to fall asleep again. I wondered if anyone else had the same experience. Memories from my distant past played in the darkness of the room like scenes from a movie. After several sleepless nights, I decided one morning to go shopping. Perhaps, seeing others in a happier mood while they shopped at the Oaks Mall would raise my spirits, but it didn't. At first, I just sat on a bench near the scene with Santa Claus, watching the children standing in line, excited to talk with Santa. I thought, "I should stop moping and start shopping." I walked around the mall and did manage to purchase a few gifts. When I returned home, I wanted to wrap the gifts I had purchased. I needed the ribbons, bows, gift tags, and wrapping paper that were stored in two large plastic boxes on a closet shelf in my home office.

For the past nine years, I have climbed on a step stool to take down those two boxes without any problem. The boxes this year seemed to be wedged against the back wall of the shelf. I tugged and pulled to get at least one box out, but instead, a small cranberry-colored cardboard box fell down, landing on my head. The box, tucked in the corner against the wall of the closet, had never fallen out before that day. I climbed down and suddenly recognized the box that had once held the invitations to my wedding. Inside were the letters Orazio had once written to me: 31 from Milwaukee, Wisconsin, before we got married, and 21 from Chicago, Illinois, shortly after our wedding. I held the letters in my hand and thought, "Our marriage was a giant leap of faith." I had forgotten about those years, but rereading those letters made me realize that I had married the right man. I'm sure God might have thought, "That idiot has no sense when it comes to falling in love. I'll make the choice." So He threw Orazio Grimaldi Grasso into the mix. It has been eleven years since Orazio's untimely and unexpected death, and just recently I had written in my journal, "I miss him more today than all the yesterdays."

I took the letters out of the box, flipping through the envelopes. I must have at one time numbered them according to the dates they were written. I forgot about wrapping the gifts and decided to read those letters. Some were handwritten in a style that was definitely a foreign script. The later ones were typed because I couldn't always understand what he had written although I was sure at that time that I didn't want to understand those early love letters from a man I knew only six days. I stopped after reading about a dozen letters and glanced around my office. There he was in a photograph with Dr. George Young, Vice President of Student Affairs of Broward Community College (BCC), now Broward College, where George and I both worked. George, his wife Dawn, Orazio, and I were friends as well as neighbors. I looked at the photograph. There Orazio was smiling broadly, those dark eyes always squinting when he smiled or laughed. Peeking out from his suit jacket was one of those many suspenders he always wore when he became middle aged. Belts were for the young as far as he was concerned. According to Orazio, the older, more sophisticated man wore suspenders. He was a man of independent thought and action.

I never realized how many photos are displayed of him. They were everywhere. As I turned to my right, I saw a photograph of a cover of a Luciano Pavorotti album, *Rigoletto Highlights*, on the top of a small curio cabinet. A photographer friend had superimposed a photo of Orazio sitting next to Pavarotti, the internationally known Italian tenor. Below the singer's name the inscription read, "*Luciano Pavarotti con il suo amico Orazio.*" The album and the photo were birthday gifts because Orazio always fancied himself capable of singing duets with Pavarotti when he played songs from any of the tenor's albums, and so he was featured on the fake cover as "*Luciano Pavrarotto with his friend Orazio*" although Orazio's friends knew otherwise. In truth Orazio was tone deaf, but he loved to sing arias from operas. When his friends complained, he simply said, "There's something wrong with your ears," or "You don't know opera. Be quiet when we sing."

I left the den to look at the other framed pictures in the living room. There he was with one of his young soccer players. He was known as "Coach" by the hundreds of boys he coached in the Plantation, Florida area. For years he had tried to get members of city councils wherever we lived to approve the sport of soccer for their Recreation Department, but he was always turned down. When we moved to Plantation, Florida, in 1969 he tried to convince the Mayor and City Council that "soccer was a great sport to participate in whether you were five or 50." Eventually he was given a plot of land behind the Plantation Park Elementary School. He and his friend Larry Bunin organized the Plantation Soccer Club (PSC), a rival to the Plantation Athletic League (PAL). Since they had little money for equipment, Orazio made the goals, which he stored in our backyard.

He attended classes at Miami-Dade Community College to become a certified coach before becoming the "Pied Piper" of so many youngsters of five to 16 who registered for the club. Orazio's five to eight-year-olds won the Florida State Pepsi trophy because players didn't just kick the ball or run up and down the fields; they learned how to play properly. There were no tryouts. Anyone who wanted to play soccer, including girls, got on the team. No one sat on the bench, and everyone got a chance to play at least once or twice during the game, even the boy who had cerebral palsy. Since Orazio had played soccer in Italy, he insisted that the boys learn the proper way to kick, run, and make goals. It was about the players having fun, getting exercise, being part of a team, and wearing a soccer uniform.

Memories flashed before my eyes as I read Orazio's letters, and it took me a day and a half to read all of them. Yet, it was as though the events and sentiments written in those letters were not written to me but to some other person: a young feisty girl, a maverick, out of sync with her generation, who thought and acted independently. I looked at the letters in my hand as tears began to fill my eyes. My life was punctuated with a series of letters written to me by people I met and loved, and these letters became catalysts that worked to change my life. All the events happened for a reason. I saved these letters like one would save special photographs - stored in a private place or in a box hidden somewhere in the house because the letters were too dear to part with since they represented a place in time that had been cherished deeply but was gone forever.

Left: Christmas 1954. Ray Ronk and Mary Ellen during happier times. The wedding date was set for June 25, 1955, but it was cancelled two months before the wedding

Right: Carol, Mary Ellen, and Dorothy on our way to Mexico, June 1955. We got as far as Monterrey, Mexico, when my car overheated and needed to have the radiator repaired.

The Hotel Ancira in Monterrey where I met Pedro.

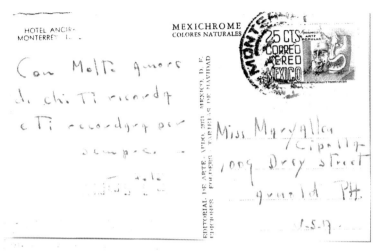

Top: One of the many notes, postcards, and letters sent to me by Pedro, one of the administrators at the hotel. Translation: *"With much love from the one who remembers you and will remember you forever."* He usually signed "Pete". Not Pedro.

Bottom: Hanging out with the professors at Duke University. Since the students were adults, professors and students roomed together - segregated, of course, by gender.

Left: Orazio and Dr. George Young. The sophisticated man wore suspenders, not belts.

Right: Identification card for the University of Mexico, 1956.

Left: Identification card for the University of Mexico, 1957.

Right: The birthday gift given to Orazio by his photographer friend.

Left: My roommate in 1956, Theresa Davila, when we shared an apartment on Calle Shakespeare in Mexico City.

Bottom: *"Take our picture, please."* Two of the children I met while walking home from the university.

Top: The six children of the couple who lived in a cave-like home in the mountains. I bought home-made brushes from the father during a field trip for my class on Rural Mexico.

Left: A typical Mexican Indian woman living in Saltillo, making hemp to earn her livelihood. It was part of our field trip on June 26, 1955.

Left: Guillermo (Memo) Espinosa Sanchez. Our meeting in Mexico City was the beginning of more than just a summer romance.

Bottom: Jerry Vairo, Memo, Patty Pallone, and me on our last trip to Acapulco before leaving for home.

MEMo ESpinosA   1957

Top: Memo in front of the garage that was across the street. We stopped to have his car repaired on our way to the United States.

Right: Memo's sister, Maria Rosa Sevilla, began to send family pictures to me when she thought that Memo and I were going to marry. Sra. Espinosa is with two of her grandchildren, Paty (Spanish spelling) and one of her brothers, Oswaldo.

122

Left: Maria Rosa in September 1960 with Paty and two of her brothers, Kiko and Oswaldo at the Baptism of Martha Patricia Cabello, the daughter of Yolanda, Maria Rosa's sister.

Right: Milwaukee Clipper photo of Orazio and me.

Top: Zia Marietta, Fina, and Mamma Elvira in Naples, Italy to get the documents Orazio needed to get married in the United States.

Left: Orazio and Mary Ellen several weeks before the wedding.

Left: A photo Orazio slipped in my purse Labor Day weekend when he came to visit me in Pennsylvania. I found it weeks later.

Bottom: The winds of November 21, 1959, delayed the wedding by ten minutes at St. Peter Church while the train of the dress, caught on the car door, tore and had to be repaired by my mom.

Top: Afraid I would shove the slice of cake in Orazio's mouth, he held my left hand down.

Bottom: The Honeymoon Basket passed from one friend to another. Mary Ellen, Orazio, Clara Jo Sakaluk, Vera Ginnochi, Tony Ginnochi, Lucille Latagliatta, and Mary Farinelli.

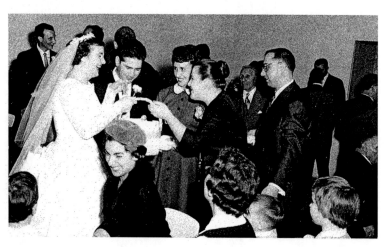

Top: The Wedding Party: Front Row: Dorothy Marinucci, Lisa Perino, Connie Perino, Mary Ellen, Orazio, Jerry Vario, and Mary Cipolla. Second Row: Bob Cipolla, Dom Perino, Ronald Cipolla, and Buddy Cipolla.

Right: Bob and Ron, wearing the Arnold Firemen's Band Uniform, with Mary Ellen in front of the 1009 Drey Street home in Arnold.

Jay, Lisa, Connie, and Dom celebrating Christmas with us in 1959 in Milwaukee.

Meeting Orazio

We had a strange beginning. I met Orazio on a blind date on August 15, 1959. My eight-year-old nephew Jay, who lived in Milwaukee, Wisconsin, had been vacationing that summer with his grandparents and me in Lower Burrell, Pennsylvania, where we lived, when we moved from Arnold. He decided that he did not want to return home, wanting, instead, to remain with us and attend the elementary school in Lower Burrell because all summer he had been pampered. His Uncle Buddy, my oldest brother, took him fishing at the reservoir where fish were bred and raised. Buddy would pay the breeders some money so that Jay could catch several fish. Aunt Mary, Buddy's wife, would take him to her boutique some days to "help" her run the store. Grandpa took him to the woods to train the hunting dogs and to sight the guns. Grandma cooked his favorite food, and I played board games with Jay and took him to the park and the movies.

School would be starting soon, and it was time for Jay to return home. I, along with my mother, would drive him home to Milwaukee and invited Jerry to come along for a week's vacation. Jerry and I would share the driving to Milwaukee and do some sightseeing in Wisconsin, but my mother planned to remain for a month with my sister Connie, Jay's mother. We planned to leave at nine o'clock the morning of August 14. It was a ten-hour drive, and I wanted to arrive in Milwaukee before it got too dark. Jay refused to come with us that morning. He even had a temper tantrum, and no coaxing or bribing would change his mind. He wasn't leaving. He cried for hours. As a result of such drama, we didn't leave until two o'clock in the afternoon. Because I was not familiar with Milwaukee, finding Connie's home at night was difficult. We finally arrived about one o'clock in the morning.

Connie had been waiting for us, afraid that we may have had an accident. She was anxious to tell us that she and her husband Dom had purchased four tickets to attend a presentation of an old-fashioned, audience-participation melodrama.

"Our friend Bernice and her family are moving to Israel, and there is a bon voyage party this evening, so Dom and I can't attend the play, but I've invited two men to escort Jerry and you," she said. "One of the men is a professor of chemistry at the University of Wisconsin in Milwaukee; the other is an Italian national that I met through my Italian class at the university."

She explained that Professor Anna Dunst had invited her Italian class from the University of Wisconsin and a few Italian nationals to a luncheon at her home so that the students could practice speaking the language. The luncheon also served as a review for the final oral exam. Connie added that she had also invited the two men to dinner so we could get acquainted, and our mom was going to prepare the meal. Those plans upset me even more, but I couldn't tell Connie why.

I had stopped dating after the episodes with Memo and Pedro, and I no longer wanted to date anyone. I didn't think I could ever fall in love again with any other man. I wasn't even sure that I wanted to. Some of the men I knew were players, but I no longer wanted to play their games. I just gave up on dating. Being in love for me hurt too much. I wondered, "Could I ever connect with or trust any man again?" In fact, I had gone to talk with my parish priest, Father Nicola Fusco. I was, at one time, managing editor of *The Catholic Observer* in Pittsburgh, and I was familiar with several mother superiors when I wrote articles about their orders.

I thought that I wanted to be a nun. Maybe that vocation was my destiny. Father Fusco said, "Mary Ellen, the convent is not for you. You would upset the entire order. You would be trying to change everything, and more importantly, you wouldn't be obedient because you would always want to finish whatever task you had started when you were called for prayer. Besides you can't escape from life. Why not think about going on a retreat, even for a few days. There is one in two weeks." Father explained that it was a silent retreat, and because it was, the retreat appealed to me, and I decided to register for that specific one. I didn't want to share my feelings talking with anyone else there. It was after that weekend of praying, meditating, and talking with no one that I decided not to date, at least for a year. As a result of that vow, I asked Connie to give us the four tickets, and we would go alone. I told her that I would try to sell the two unused ones or return them to the box office.

"You can't," she replied, "I've already made plans with Bob and Orazio."

Later that morning, Jerry and I and drove to New Glarus, the home of "Little Switzerland" in Southern Wisconsin. The Alpine architecture of chalet-style homes and shops was excellent. The old churches and their cemeteries fascinated us, and we spent a lot of time reading the inscriptions and epitaphs on all of the tombstones. There were museums and shops to visit and a small Swiss restaurant where we ate lunch. We spent even more time looking at artifacts, sometimes twice. Jerry kept reminding me of the time. Finally I told Jerry that that I didn't want to go out that evening, but she said, "I'm a guest in Connie and Dom's home, and I don't want to disappoint them or appear ungrateful." Because I didn't want to explain my reasons about not wanting to go out on any date, arranged or not, and didn't want Jerry to know about my personal vow, I reluctantly agreed to go that evening.

We would go to the play and then have the men drive us home. I could always conjure up a migraine headache if necessary.

When we arrived back at Connie's, Bob and Orazio were already there, and dinner was ready, being kept warm. Connie and my mom were angry with me. I made up some excuse about why we were late. Jerry and I bathed quickly, got dressed, and joined the family in the dining room. I discovered during dinner that Orazio spoke nearly no English. I spoke very little Italian although I could understand the language. Dom, Connie, and my mom, who did speak Italian, did most of the talking with Orazio while Jerry and I spoke with Bob, who sat across the table from us and the two children, Jay and Lisa, Connie's six-year-old daughter, who were both very talkative and amusing. When dinner was over, we left for the theater. Because Bob was the one with the car, he was the driver, but I noticed that Orazio quickly ushered Jerry to the front seat, leaving me to sit in the back, but I sat as far away from him as possible. When we got to the theater, waiting in line to enter, we unintentionally paired off: Bob with Jerry, and I with Orazio. I really would have preferred to be with Bob because we both were teachers, and I thought we had more in common.

I didn't know how much of the play Orazio understood, but he booed the villain, praised the hero, and wore the little orphan girl's bow (a replica prop everyone had been given) in his hair when she appeared. We all enjoyed ourselves, especially since the entire audience was interacting with the characters, booing, whistling and applauding, and sighing. When the play was over, Orazio suggested that we go to *Fazio's,* a nightclub that featured a live Big Band, to dance. He told us he happened to know the owner, who also was Italian; and since it was still early, about 10:30 p.m., he didn't want Bob to drive us home to Connie's. At his insistence, we all agreed. I thought, "What harm would there be? It's only for tonight."

Orazio struggled to communicate with us. In fact, he stuttered, even when he spoke in Italian. He tried to explain that he had always stuttered, even as a child. When we arrived at Fazio's, using some sort of hand gestures and speaking a bit of broken English, Orazio asked me to dance. As we were dancing, the owner spotted him and yelled, "*Oh, Orazio, dove siete stato? Non lo ho veduto in un molto tempo.*" Orazio answered, "*Sono stato occupato, ma lascilo lo presentano al mio fidanzata.*" The man was asking about Orazio's whereabouts, and here Orazio was telling him that I was his fiancée. I quickly replied, "No, no! I don't even know the man. He's a friend of my sister and brother-in-law." Orazio looked at his friend and said, "*Gli non presti alcun'attenzione. È il mio fidanzata.*" I just laughed and insisted it wasn't so. I really wasn't that attracted to him. As far as I was concerned, he was just another handsome womanizer, always too sure of himself.

I didn't know about the men, but Jerry and I usually ordered only one drink when we were out. However, we four must have had more than two drinks each that night because when we returned home, we entered the living room, where my mom and Connie were sitting, dancing the Conga, wearing sombreros, and laughing until we fell on the sofa. We had no idea where we had gotten the sombreros, but we certainly were giddy. The men left about one-thirty in the morning, and Jerry and I made plans to go to Mass that morning.

After attending a late Mass, we decided to have lunch and then visit the new art gallery. When we returned to Connie's later that afternoon, Orazio and Bob were there. I couldn't believe that Connie had invited them even though I had previously told her that I didn't want to date anyone. Jerry and Bob were in the den talking with Dom, and I was sitting on the living room floor playing a card game with Jay and Lisa. That afternoon Orazio was very quiet. He had come into the living room and was sitting on the sofa watching us play. I noticed he was wearing a gold medal on a chain and I asked about it. He said that his mother had given it to him long before he was transferred to the United States. He took the chain off and insisted I wear it. I had flashes of my silver ring that Memo took and the gold cuff links he had given me. Despite my objections, Orazio had already put the chain around my neck, holding the clasp so I wouldn't remove the chain although I tried. Rather than create a scene, I decided I would give it to Connie to return to him when I left.

I didn't know whether Connie and Dom had invited Orazio and Bob for dinner or if they just came. I was getting annoyed. Orazio was in the kitchen pretending to help my mother cook, and he kept addressing her as "Mamma." What was I to make of him? Was he just another player, especially when he said to me, *"Lo incitate a ritenere per la prima volta come un bambino nell'amor."* Whatever he was saying of being in love for the first time reminded me of Memo's letters. Since I was "fooled" more than once by men, I wasn't going to fall for Orazio's line, not this time.

After dinner, Bob left and Orazio remained. Connie decided that she would take Jerry and me sightseeing to landmarks and other points of interest in Milwaukee before driving Orazio to his apartment. I sat next to Connie, thinking that Orazio would sit in the back, but he didn't. He decided to sit in the front also. Because it was a tight squeeze, he had to put his arm around my shoulder. He decided to sing some Italian love songs although he couldn't carry a tune. When we stopped at a red light, the driver in the car next to ours shouted, *"Ah! Amore."* I just laughed.

The next morning Jerry and I had awakened early and were whispering, making plans for the day. Suddenly we heard the telephone in Connie's bedroom ring. Who could be calling this early? We heard, "I don't know where they're going. They're still sleeping." We decided we would not tell Connie of our plans. When she asked me at breakfast, I said, "We really don't know." The truth was that we planned to go shopping at the Mayfair Mall in a suburb in Milwaukee. Marshall Fields had just opened, and we wanted to look at the new fall fashions.

While we were shopping, we discovered a small, beautiful restaurant in the store and decided to eat lunch there. We had just been served, when we noticed Bob and Orazio walking to our table. We were shocked to see them. "How did you find us?"

"We found out from your sister that there isn't a Marshall Fields in Pittsburgh, and we figured that since girls like clothes, you both would be here shopping," Bob replied.

The answer sounded too much like one Orazio would have made. Then Bob, who did all the talking, said that there were day cruises on the *Milwaukee Clipper* that went from Milwaukee to Muskegon, Michigan. The ship left the following day, about eight o'clock in the morning, docked in Muskegon for an afternoon of sightseeing, and returned to Milwaukee about ten o'clock that night. I was more than a bit annoyed.

I said to the men, "No one asked us if we wanted to go."

Jerry whispered to me, "I don't really like being on the water, but I've never been on a cruise."

"Neither have I, but they made arrangements without asking us first."

"It sounds like fun. Let's go," she replied.

The Letters

I was certain that it was Orazio's plan not Bob's. The men claimed that they had already bought the tickets for the August 18 cruise, and the tickets were non-refundable. We didn't know if that were true, but we wanted to believe Bob. Since the men kept insisting they had already bought the tickets, we agreed to join them. I didn't know about Jerry, but there was another reason I suddenly agreed to accept their invitation.

The men arrived early Tuesday morning. As we walked to the ship from the parking lot, Orazio made sure that he was walking beside me, holding my arm. He claimed, "I helpa you" as though I needed help walking. Breakfast was buffet style, and where I was, he was. Muskegon was about 85 miles from Milwaukee, about a six-hour trip. There was a lot to do on board the ship, but after breakfast we just walked around the ship talking. Orazio was another Memo: charming, witty, and very attentive. During the cruise, he asked Bob to take a picture of the two of us standing against the railing on one of the decks with Lake Michigan behind us. Orazio put his arm around my shoulder and tilted his head on mine.

After reading the ship's program about all the activities on board, we paired off. Orazio wanted to take me to the ship's theater to see the full-length movie because he said it helped him learn English, but Jerry and Bob decided to go elsewhere. During the movie Orazio was holding my hand. Suddenly, he leaned over and kissed me. That's what Pedro had done the first time I went to a movie with him in Monterrey. This time I walked out of the movie. "Don Juan" was surprised, but he behaved for the rest of the cruise. We did meet up with Jerry and Bob sitting in lounge chairs on the deck and decided to explore other features of the ship together.

When we arrived in Muskegon, we did some sightseeing and shopping. I bought two small souvenirs for Jay and Lisa. I must admit we all had a day of fun, and despite Orazio's inability to speak English, we did understand what he was trying to say. He was amusing, and we spent much of the day laughing. Years later I learned that he had written a postcard on board ship and mailed it from Muskegon to his mother: "I have found the girl of my dreams."

The *Clipper*, which operated until 1970 and is now a National Historical Landmark, played a large part in Orazio's and my life. We had always planned to take a second cruise for one of our anniversaries, but we never did. I had always regretted not saving the 1959 brochure and postcard of the *Clipper*, but after reading Orazio's letters, written so long ago, I decided to write to the City of Muskegon, hoping a post card of the ship was still available. I had always wanted it to be framed along with the framed photo of the two of us on the deck of the *Clipper*.

Much to my surprise I received a letter from the President of the S.S. Milwaukee Clipper Preservation Corporation who responded to my letter and sent as gifts an original postcard like the ones sold on the ship in 1959. He also sent me two other postcards now sold in the ship's museum and a 1959 brochure, advertising the Daily Sailings of the *Clipper* and an explanation of all of the activities on board. As I looked at the brochure, I recalled the hours we spent playing a game of shuffleboard, lounging on one of the deck chairs, dancing in the ballroom, and touring Muskegon. That cruise was really a magical moment in our lives, but that day I was not interested. Orazio was too persistent, and he reminded me of Memo.

The following evening, Orazio came alone once more. Connie had guests: Danny, an attorney and retired naval officer, and his companion Mary Ann. Both were long time friends of Connie and Dom, and I had met them during other visits to Milwaukee. Danny invited all of us to dinner at the Great Lakes Naval Training Center in North Chicago for Thursday evening. The Center is the United States Navy's Headquarters Command for training recruits. Although Orazio knew Connie's friends, once more he was very quiet. It may have been his inability to speak English fluently. I had not seen Danny and Mary Ann for several years, and since they didn't know Jerry, she and I spent time talking with them. Orazio spoke with my mom as she asked him a few questions about his family, all who lived in Italy. Nevertheless, it was a pleasant evening.

Thursday evening at the Great Lakes Naval Training Center, Orazio wouldn't leave me alone. I was determined to talk with Jerry, to ask her if she would be willing to cut our vacation short. I didn't want to get involved with him. I remember both Orazio and I standing on a short bridge looking at the water. Orazio asked me if I at least liked his looks. He was quite handsome with wavy black hair and very seductive dark eyes. I just said, "I really haven't thought about it." I knew he worked for Universal Business Machines, but I wondered when he did work because he was at Connie's every afternoon. He started to call me, "*Amore.*" Other than that, I knew very little about him.

After a few minutes on the bridge, he told me he was in love with me. I replied, "Don't love me. I'll make your life miserable. I've had enough of love." He just ignored me, but he never left my side. I was frightened, annoyed, and angry with all of his attention; love terrified me. I couldn't confide in Jerry because she was unaware of how my relationship with Memo had ended, and she knew nothing of Pedro; my heart still had not totally healed. I couldn't take a chance. It had been less than a year that I had stopped dating. Did I want to trust another man?

Mary Ellen Cipolla Grasso

The following evening he was at Connie's again. I was pleasant, no longer angry. I realized that I was making him pay the price for my emotional problems and for the men who had loved me, claimed undying love, and then left me. In five years, four men of those I had dated had proposed to me. Two decided not to marry me. Two I loved, but there were many problems, and I felt that I was the wrong woman for both of them. It didn't make breaking up any easier. In fact, it may have been worse for me because I felt responsible for their unhappiness. Many years later, I met one of those men at my brother Buddy's funeral. John introduced me to his wife, and I chatted with them for a while. He had married the perfect woman for him. He was happy, and so was I. Even though I had lost contact with the other, Pedro, I never forgot about him, and I hoped he too had found happiness.

Connie's home was crowded with family and friends that evening, and I went out to the patio for some cooler air since the house was not air-conditioned. Orazio followed me, turned me around, and kissed me. I tried to pull away, but he just held me tighter and kissed me again.

"Good grief!" I thought. How do I get into these predicaments?" It was again Memo on the dance floor and Pedro on the hotel stairway. Had I initiated those responses from men? I seriously began again to consider a convent. Jerry and I left the next morning, a day earlier than we had planned. When we arrived at Jerry's home, her father said, "Who's this Italian who called wanting to know if you arrived home?" I answered, "If he calls again, just say we decided to do some sightseeing along the way." When I arrived home, my father had had a similar telephone call. I told him what to say if Orazio called again. I also explained that he was a friend of Connie and Dom's and there was no reason why he should be telephoning me.

Letters from Orazio

Shortly after I returned home, the letters and telephone calls began. The first letter was written on August 21, the day after Jerry and I left. The greeting was "*Amore mio.*" He wrote that he was expecting a telephone call from me, but I had not promised to call him, and he added in Italian, "Being in love with you is like a dream." He wrote that had he not met me, he probably would never have wanted to marry. Memo sometimes had a postscript about his typing. He wrote it wasn't the typewriter making the mistakes, but it was the typist. Orazio had a postscript saying he was so nervous writing to me that the writing looked as though he were using "the foot of a chicken." Like Memo, who wrote in Spanish, Orazio wrote only in Italian.

Orazio's second letter was dated August 25. He sent me a snapshot of a friend and him. They must have been skiing somewhere in Wisconsin. He wrote that he knew I wasn't certain of what he was writing, but instead of him not being certain of me, it was I who was unsure. He added that God had illuminated his mind to wait because he had to meet me, his love. He signed the letter, "*Per tutta la vita, Orazio.*" A day later he sent a second snapshot of him alone with this inscription: "*Non per guardarmi e pensare mi ma per pensare mi e guardarmi. Te amo per tutta la vita. Di cuore, Orazio.*" I wasn't sure what he meant: "Not to look at me and think about me, but to think about me and to look at me."

In his first letter he wrote that he had fallen in love with me and wanted to marry me. Nothing was going to change his mind. I swore that Memo and he must have had the same tutor to teach them how to write love letters, or maybe a Cyrano de Bergerac had written those letters. Their letters sounded exactly the same: same declarations of love, same experiences with women. Memo had claimed that he had never told any other girl that he loved her. Orazio wrote that he was tired of introducing each woman he dated as "This is my friend." He wanted to find the love of his life, get married, and introduce that woman as "my wife." As far as he was concerned, he was getting married. He even wrote to his mother that he was engaged. He may have been, but I wasn't. He was very persistent, wouldn't take "no" for an answer. He was in his thirties, had never married, and like Memo and Pedro came from a foreign country.

Two days later he wrote that he wanted nothing more than our happiness and was sure of it because he had a lot of faith in me. I didn't want to be responsible for Orazio's happiness. He wrote that "most people are never content, but when they find the person they have always dreamed of, they will never need to think about falling in love again because they will be as happy as I am now. My only thought is you. You are my only jewel of my life." I must have sent him a small gold key, which he referred to in his letters. As I reread his letters, I couldn't recall why I had sent the key to him nor remembered exactly what it symbolized.

He once wrote, "I wear it on a gold chain and will never remove it until I marry only you. I never tire of telling you I love you."

"What significance did that little key have for Orazio or for me?" I thought.

It wasn't until May 30, 2009, that my memory of the key was jogged when I visited on a whim Cassadaga, Florida, known as "The Psychic Center of the World." I remembered I had written to him that my heart was locked, and it was useless for him to believe we could ever be a couple. I had had enough of lying men. I must have been subconsciously proposing a challenge. Was he man enough, honest enough to unlock my heart that now lay dormant?

Orazio wrote every two or three days, and when he didn't write, he telephoned me when he visited Connie. Both Connie and my mother assured me that Orazio was "very much in love," and I should take him seriously. How could he be? He barely knew me. My mother telephoned me several times telling me what "a wonderful man he is." I learned he was thirty-five years old, not settled, nor seeking *amantes* and *passatempos*.

Why would I now believe my mother's or Connie's opinion of Orazio? After all, my parents liked Memo very much when he visited, believing he was sincere. I realize now that Greg Behrendt and Liz Tuccillo, co-authors of *He's Just Not That into You* are right. If a man really loves a woman, he wants to marry her; he gives no mixed messages or excuses; he's never too busy to call or write. He doesn't change his mind, and he's not cruel. Above all, he doesn't play games with her.

I was unaware that my dad was very concerned about Orazio's intentions. While I had never discussed my feelings with my dad after the incidents with Ray and Memo, my father knew how I really felt: the laughter was gone, replaced by a cloud of sadness. In a letter to Connie, my dad wrote that if Orazio was playing a game and decided to change his mind about wanting to marry me, he was first to talk with my dad, not me. I had not discussed Orazio with my dad nor made any decision about an engagement or even marriage. I thought my dad's letter was premature. Perhaps my mother, in a telephone call to my dad, had mentioned Orazio's desire to marry me. Connie told Orazio about my dad's concern, and in his next letter to me he wrote, "Only death could stop me from marrying you."

If I had thought that Memo wrote the most romantic, passionate letters, Orazio's were even more so. In the letter of August 29, he wrote, "You are the woman who will make me change my life and give me much happiness. *"Ti Amo, Adorata mia."* Many times he signed his letters, *"Tanti bacioni, Tuo Orazio."* Then in one letter he had this postscript: *"Poi ci ficciamo conti de questi baci."* Since I could read Italian, I laughed that he had written we would later settle the account of all the kisses he was sending me. I don't remember when or how it was that I fell in love with him or why it happened. This courtship came only through thirty-one letters written in just two months. We weren't dating, and we lived miles away from each other. In a letter I wrote to Orazio on October 12 (a letter Orazio had saved and I had found along with his) I tried to explain what had happened:

Today as I was driving to work, I thought to myself, 'How did this strange thing happen?' And I cannot answer. Were you really sent here a year ago for me? Was it destiny or just a coincidence? I don't know the answer, but I little care. I only care that you were sent, and that whatever magic there is that produces this thing called love, it finally touched me. When we were at the Great Lakes, I was fighting you inside of me. If you had not seen me after that, it would have been over because I had made up my mind that no man would interest me again. I'm glad you persisted. Even after I accepted the gold medal, I kept fighting you. Remember that Monday? I didn't want to like you because I knew that you held too much attraction for me. I accepted the Clipper date to prove to myself that you were a Casanova. I decided to play the game. But the game backfired on me. And the more I played, the deeper I was falling. Then I began to worry. I was sure by Wednesday that you were playing the big game of your life: That I was a joke to you, and that you would show your final hand before I left. And I also knew that I could be hurt because when you held my hand or kissed me I felt a sensation I had never felt before. But

The Letters

I had to know how you really felt even if it meant I would be hurt. I was miserable that week and the week I returned home – half wanting and half fighting. I just didn't want to be hurt again, and hearing of the "hundred" women who were in love with you, I didn't want to be number 101. But all of the time there was one person who knew, and He put His hand into the same game and set us both aright. I am not very religious, but I am sure that it was God who finally brought us together.

Was I just swept off my feet by an uncontrollable force, or was my meeting Orazio planned by divine intervention? Did my relationships with other men teach me the difference between infatuation and unconditional love? What I do know is that he was the right man for me. Orazio made his first trip to Lower Burrell the first weekend in September, just fourteen days after I had left Wisconsin. My mother had decided to return earlier than she had planned, and Orazio was anxious to see me again, but I wasn't sure his coming was a good idea. He always complained about the distance between us. He had written that he was "nervous because I am so far away." He also wrote, "You are right when you tell me to think carefully, but at this age I have to think I will never marry." But then he added, "Women I can find anywhere, but none like you. It is difficult to find love."

Orazio was in Lower Burrell only four days, never leaving my side. He even went to my parish priest without me and told him that we were getting married. Father Fusco said, "Her parents have said nothing to me. Do you have all the documents ready? Besides, the church bans must be announced three weeks before the wedding. When is this wedding?" Orazio had no idea, but he was sure that he would marry me. I don't know how it happened that just two weeks after he returned to Milwaukee we set a wedding date: November 21, 1959. He did say that he was afraid of losing me. I knew him better than any other man who had professed to love me and who had spent more time with me. Actually, Orazio was a combination of Memo and Pedro. That may have been my first attraction to him. Yet, he was different. He was not pretentious, not egotistical. He was genuine. He didn't ask me if I could live only on his salary or if I could live without all the conveniences I now have. He was still supporting his mother, paying mortgage for the home he had just built in Catania, Sicily, for his mother and him. Although he had older brothers, he was the sole support of his widowed mother, but he didn't make excuses about having to support her. He didn't ask me to move to Italy although I knew he loved his family, his friends, and his country.

I had no illusions about his having dated women in Milwaukee, but I did believe him when he said, "No more women." That was a promise Memo never made nor could keep. After that weekend, Orazio returned to his job at Universal Business Machines in Milwaukee and continued the frequent letter writing. He had written to his mother, asking her to get all of his documents in order and send them to him as soon as possible because he was getting married. He sent her a copy of the photo we had taken on the *Clipper* and asked for her Blessing. When she replied, she gave him her Blessing and wrote that I was "*una bella ragazza.*" She also told him that she was very happy because "he was of that certain age now," and she wanted to see him married with his own family. Orazio sent me the letter and asked me to write to her even if it were in English. His nephews, Gino or Lino, would translate it for her. His cousin Maria wrote to Orazio also. She was hurt that he hadn't written to her, and she was disappointed because "I don't even know her [my] name." I did write to Maria as well as several other members of his family.

Orazio even sent me the letter his oldest brother Donato had sent him, cautioning him not to make decisions too rapidly. Donato felt that Orazio was making a mistake rushing into marriage. Donato never approved of American women, but the only ones he knew were the ones he met when he was in dry dock. It was twenty years before he ever met me. Donato worked for an American oil corporation in charge of the technical aspects of a ship. He telephoned me from some port in the United States and said," Now be careful. If he makes a mistake, as men do, you must forgive him." I just told Donato, "There will be no mistakes, no double standards by either of us."

Pennsylvania

Orazio quit his job October 31, but not before speaking with the vice president of the Olivetti Corporation, who was visiting Universal Business Machines, requesting that Orazio be transferred permanently to the United States on a work visa, which he already held. In his last letter from Milwaukee, he apologized to me because he was taking me away from everything: my family, my friends, my career that I loved, and involvement with several service organizations. He also apologized for the fact that all he had was his last paycheck: $150.00. He planned to send $60.00 of that money to his mother for the months of October and November, leaving him only $90.00. I assured him that I still had my job, and we would manage. He marveled at my ability to save money. I remember his writing, "If I had saved my money and not spent it impulsively, I would be a rich man today."

When he was in Italy, he enjoyed skiing in the Alps, borrowing someone's Ferrari to speed along the highways, and having all of his suits and shirts tailored made, regardless of the cost. He never bought just one pair of shoes. It was always two or three pairs at a time. He promised his mother that he would never abandon her, and he never did.

During the month of October, my colleagues and friends kept saying, "Are you sure he's going to marry you? Remember what happened before. How can you trust him? You barely know him." But I did trust him. This was just not an infatuation. As Pepe wrote, "There are many types of love." In my case that had been true. Orazio's letters drew me close to his family, asking me to write to several members of his extended family as well as his immediate ones. He asked me to correspond with his mother. He wanted me not only to become "one of the family" but also to know them and they to know me. His mother, affectionately known as Mamma Elvira, began to send me pictures of the immediate family and her, and I began to feel a part of Orazio's family.

Orazio never lied to me. He told me about the Contessa in Italy with whom he had been having an affair. He even had me read the letters she wrote to him, sending the letters to him at his office in Milwaukee, and he showed me the pictures he had taken of her and her thirteen-year-old son while they were all skiing on the Alps. She was a beautiful blonde, but he never compared me with her. I still have those photographs in an album. When he first wrote that he was finished with other women, I wasn't sure, but he gave me no reason to disbelieve him. My relationship with Orazio was different. It was secure.

Our letters to one another were filled with sharing our daily activities and the ordinary moments of life. Once Orazio wrote, "Now that you have written my last name so many times on the envelopes when you write to me, are you comfortable with the name?" I hadn't thought about it, but actually I was. In several letters written before we were married, he signed them in English: "Your husband, Orazio."

The wedding plans began to take on the appearance of a theatrical production. Everyone wanted to help. Everyone offered advice. My aunts volunteered to make *biscotti* that would be passed to the guests during the reception, an Italian tradition. My sister-in-law Mary and her mother *Zia Maria* also baked *biscotti* and worked on decorations and favors. Jerry's father volunteered to address the invitations, using his talent for writing calligraphy.

Mary Ellen Cipolla Grasso

The Edna Hotel rushed their renovations through so that the reception could be held in the new dining room and guests could be accommodated in the newly decorated rooms. Friends of my parents planned and catered the rehearsal party held at my parents' home. My brother Buddy and my dad, who both were active in politics, insisted that many of the county and state politicians be invited, and the wedding list grew. I fought inviting so many people. The list was growing, nearing three hundred guests, but Bud said that he would pay a share of the reception expenses as long as those guests were invited. At that point, I let the "directors" and "producers" take over.

While my students were not invited, they did ask if they could attend the ceremony at the church even though they begged me not to marry. Some said, "If you marry, you'll never have time for us. You won't stay after school so we can talk with you. Who's going to direct the class plays?" I assured them that they were welcomed to attend the ceremony at church, and I would not abandon them. Those students whose parents were invited did go to the reception because all guests were permitted to bring their children. Even Father Fusco entered the preparations deciding that we must be married with a Solemn High Mass, celebrated for special occasions with three priests officiating. The ceremony would include my having two bouquets: one for me to carry and one to be presented to the Virgin Mary at a certain point during the marriage ceremony

The Wedding

Nearly all of the plans were completed when Orazio returned to Pennsylvania November 1, and we had only three weeks together before getting married. In all, we had been together fewer than six weeks, but it was as though I had known him for years. During the three weeks in November before the wedding, we went to movies, watched television, visited friends and family, and with help moved some of our clothes and household items into the apartment we had rented but had not occupied. We had no sexual relationship, and he admired me for wanting to wait. We were comfortable just being with family, doing nothing special. Sometimes he helped with the dishes by drying them, or we sat outside on the swing in the backyard watching the sunset.

A few of my intimate girl friends, all who were married, had an engagement party for us, and while Orazio could only speak very little English, one of the husbands, Walt, did the translating. What was remarkable was that Walt was the only one there that was not of Italian descent. I was given a gift of a large sewing box filled with all of the necessities. Later, Orazio asked me if American women could actually sew. The stereotypical image of American women came from the movies, but there were other American practices and idioms that confused him.

The concept of a wedding shower was difficult for him to understand because he translated literally. He understood the word *shower* to mean bathing, but a *wedding shower* made no sense. Since wedding showers were not part of the Italian culture, he had a strange image in his mind of what that was. He also couldn't figure out what *living on a shoestring* meant. I tried to explain that it meant a couple had so little money that what they did have resembled a thin shoestring. I knew there was a second meaning, but I didn't want to confuse him. Nevertheless, throughout the years there were other American practices and idioms that confused him.

Jerry, as well as the other bridesmaids, had a shower for me, and the cake, made by her mother, was a likeness of the *Milwaukee Clipper*. Orazio enjoyed hearing all the details and looking at the gifts, but he had trouble understanding why I had been given four showers. I explained that four different groups were giving them. He became very involved in the rituals of planning the wedding, unlike many Italian men.

The wedding rehearsal was held on November 20, and a buffet was held in my home for family, friends, and out-of-state guests. All evening, Orazio was anxious to speak with me, and he complained that he had a headache. He asked me to go with him to the drug store because there was a specific over-the-counter medication he wanted that we did not have at home. He was very nervous, and all I could think of was that he had changed his mind about getting married. Instead of going to the drug store, he parked on a country road not too far from my home. I just sat in the car quietly, waiting for his announcement. I could hardly breathe. He said, "I have a headache." I replied, "Orazio, is there something you want to say to me." He then admitted that he missed not having anyone from his family with him, and being with so many guests he did not personally know was unusual for him, and he became very sad. We talked for about thirty minutes, and I promised him that we would visit his family in two years. We discussed our future together, and I realized that the reality of the next day was his greatest fear. Would he be a good husband, a good father? Would I always love him as he loved me? Would he be able to say the marriage vows in English? He held me so tightly that I could barely catch my breath. He kept saying, "Don't ever leave me."

When we returned home, my parents were very concerned. I believe a few of my friends and relatives were also. I decided that it would be a perfect time to give him my wedding gift, a pair of gold cuff links with his initials engraved on them and a tie clip. I wanted him to wear them for the wedding. The men had decided to wear navy blue suits, not tuxedos. Orazio gave me a gold charm bracelet with a replica of the Milwaukee Clipper. That was the first of the many charms he gave me during our marriage. On our first anniversary he gave me a calendar charm of the month of November with a topaz marking the date. Every special occasion meant another charm: a small cottage for our first home, two tiny pairs of gold baby shoes with the names of our two children, Stephen and Susan, engraved on the soles, the Eiffel Tower for our visit to Paris, a gondola for Venice, a graduation cap for the doctorate I received, and many, many others. Every major city we visited meant another charm. For some reason, I have never had the last charm, #1 MOM, he gave me for Mother's Day, just eighteen days before he died unexpectedly, put on the bracelet.

Mamma Elvira wrote that it was Orazio who insisted that the Olivetti Corporation transfer him to the United States when Olivetti bought out Underwood and began sending their technicians and engineers from the plant in Ivrea, Italy, to the United States because all of the products would be only Olivetti designed and manufactured. She then added, "It was that he was supposed to meet you." However, because I had trouble reading the Italian handwriting, I never really understood her next sentence until now, until I reread her letter. On our first trip to Italy in 1961, she mentioned that when we were married she spent the entire day in the cathedral praying and asking God, "Why did you give me an American daughter-in-law?" At that time, I felt somewhat dismayed, thinking that she really disapproved of me or was disappointed that Orazio had not married an Italian.

Now rereading her letter, I realized that was not what she really meant. It was a heartbreaking statement. She wrote that I would only understand how she felt when I was a mother, knowing that my youngest son, whom I loved, was getting married in another country with no family to support him and share in his joy. She again emphasized that because he was "of a certain age," she wanted him to marry and have his own family, but he claimed that he had never found the right girl until he met me. She planned to go to the cathedral on our wedding day and sit there all day, pretending that she was at the wedding. The prayer to God was because if he had married a girl who lived in Italy, his family would have been able to participate. I cried when I read the letter again. I had never understood what she was trying to say to me. It is a beautiful letter, and one that I now treasure. No girl could have asked for a more loving mother-in-law.

We were married November 21, 1959, at 11:10 a.m. Because it was a Solemn High Mass, it was very long; at one time Orazio became faint, and a chair had to be brought to the altar for him. He did, however, recover quickly. All of the wedding vows were spoken in Italian, and he began to relax and smile. I am sure that the absence of his family saddened him although a few friends from Milwaukee were there to support him. Pictures of the wedding party were taken at the photographer's studio rather than the church, which made the ceremony even longer because we had to drive to the studio. We told the photographer that we wanted a lot of pictures taken that day because we wanted to make sure that Mamma Elvira was able to share all of the events. My parents received a 5" x 7" version of our wedding album, as did Mamma Elvira who also received all of the other random photographs taken that day. The reception, with an open bar, was scheduled between the hours of 3:00 to 6:30 p.m. with a hot and cold buffet being served at 4:00 p.m. However, a lunch had been served to the immediate family and out-of-state guest because most of us had not eaten breakfast with all of the excitement that morning.

The receiving line was long. Orazio thought it would never end; neither did I. I kept taking my shoes off, and the photographs show me at different heights. I knew most of the guests, but Orazio knew only a handful. Fortunately, many guests were bilingual, and he could speak with them. He really enjoyed, nevertheless, some of the rituals: the throwing of the bouquet and garter, cutting the first two slices of cake, saving the top layer of the cake in a box for our first anniversary, and feeding each other the first two slices. The photograph of that event shows him holding my left hand down because someone warned him that I was going to shove the slice of cake in his mouth, but I didn't have any intention of doing that.

Orazio and I left the reception about 6:00 p.m. Connie, who was my Matron of Honor, came with us to help me change quickly into traveling clothes because the photographer was also there to take the pictures of our leaving. We returned to say our goodbyes to family and friends, as was the custom of the day and the town. None of the guests seemed to care that we were leaving, as long as they could stay and party. I learned much later that my dad ordered supper for all of the guests that remained. The band played on as the reception continued. Before we left, several of my close friends presented us with a wedding basket that I had given to two of my friends when they married. It had a bottle of champagne, sandwiches, two slices of cake, some fruit, and a few cookies. We learned weeks later that the band played until 10:00 p.m.

We split our honeymoon between the Poconos and New York City. There were only eight honeymoon couples at the Pocono Resort, and I still remember the Thanksgiving Day dinner. It was quite a spread for only sixteen people, and we all wondered who would eat all that food. We connected with two other couples although many times all the couples were together. Orazio was the magnet, broken English and all. It was the first time I saw the effect he had on others. We really had a great time sled riding and having a snowball fight: the men against the women. I don't remember who won, but we had a lot of laughs. We even built a rather large snowman.

In New York, Orazio had an appointment with the Vice President of Olivetti, and the two discussed the possibility of his remaining in the United States with Olivetti. No commitments were made, but I wasn't worried. I still had my job at the high school. Orazio had potential, and I knew he would get a position eventually. The men at the Olivetti Headquarters were very encouraging. We did a lot of sightseeing even though it was very cold. Orazio happened to see a poster of the movie *Ben Hur* the last morning we were in New York, and he wanted us to go to the movies. I wanted him to see the show at the Rockefeller Center because we could always see the movie at some later date when we returned home. I'm glad he changed his mind because he really enjoyed the Rockefeller Dancers. He kept apologizing because he had been so insistent.

We returned home after eight days to our three-room furnished apartment above a garage. Connie had set the small kitchen table with a pink linen tablecloth and matching napkins. She had set out the china, the sterling silver tableware, the crystal glasses, and pink candles. She had even bought groceries for our breakfast the next morning. We had to eat early because I had to return to school. Orazio found a part time job for a few days. Someone in town needed the typewriters repaired for his business. Two weeks later, while I was at work, a representative of the Olivetti Corporation came to our apartment and offered Orazio one of three transfers: San Francisco, New York, or Chicago. When I returned home from school, I found him sitting in the living room quietly. He kept apologizing about the offer because he knew that I would be leaving my family and the job I loved, but I was delighted about his being able to remain with Olivetti.

We had a decision to make. San Francisco was too far from Italy. Orazio didn't want to live in New York City, so we settled on Chicago. It was ninety miles from Milwaukee where Orazio had several friends still working at Universal Business Machines, and Connie and Dom lived nearby. We had only been married about five weeks when he was transferred to Chicago. I was under contract, and I didn't feel it was fair to the principal or the students for me to leave early. The prinicpal would have to find a teacher who was certified to teach English and Spanish. Besides, we needed the money. I had promised Mamma Elvira that we would visit her in two years. Orazio left shortly after New Year's Day, a sad day for both of us. Just before we left for the airport, we looked around the apartment and tears came to our eyes. I told him that I would give up the apartment and go home to my parents until I could join him. I knew I would be too lonely without him. I seemed always to be saying goodbye to someone I loved.

Chicago

Orazio rented a room at the YMCA in Chicago, and once more the letter writing began. Those letters were filled with loneliness. He wrote almost everyday, long letters sharing his life and work with me. Telephoning me long distance was too expensive. He didn't have a car, so he couldn't visit Connie and Dom or his friends in Milwaukee, and the weekends were even lonelier for him. Sometimes on the weekend he got a ride to Milwaukee with someone who worked in Chicago but lived in Milwaukee. Because he couldn't read the menus, he relied on fast food restaurants, especially McDonald's and the International House of Pancakes because there were pictures on the menus. I don't remember crying the first time I read those letters, but I did cry rereading them now. What I do remember is that during our marriage he rarely ate again in any of the fast food restaurants.

Those two months must have been terrible for him. He was losing weight because he was eating only one substantial meal a day. He kept looking for an apartment, but he couldn't find an affordable one that was furnished in a location where he wanted us to live. His net pay was $75.00 a week, and he was concerned that we would have to live on only his salary. Yet, I wasn't worried because I did have some savings, and I would try to get a job substitute teaching even if it were for a few days a week. Still he was very lonely, living in a city where he had very few friends and no one to come home to at night.

The English language was still difficult for him. Olivetti made arrangements to send their Italian engineers and technicians to school to learn English, but Orazio had so much to learn that he would at times become discouraged, and I wasn't there to tutor him. In one letter I wrote to him I mentioned that I had attended a meeting at the Junior Women's Club because I was vice president of the organization and still had some projects for the year to complete, but afterward I would resign. The word *"club"* for him had a very different meaning. It was more like a private bar. He wrote that he was sorry I was giving up an activity I enjoyed with my friends, and he didn't want to be the one to keep me from having a good time. He added, "What will I do when you go to the club? I will be so lonely without you." I had to explain that it was an organization of women who did many things to help others, and I was resigning because I wanted to leave. After all, I would be moving to Chicago.

Although I kept busy at school, I had to resign my position as director of the class plays, but I promised the new director I would help him cast the spring production. My senior students, especially those in the Spanish classes, were very upset because I would not complete the year with them. They reminded me that they had not wanted me to marry because I would stop "loving them." I was glad that I had time to spend with them after school, just to talk and reassure them that they would be fine without me. I added that I couldn't move if my husband didn't find a suitable apartment. They answered, "We hope he doesn't find one until we graduate." Truly, I knew I would miss them all.

Orazio finally found a furnished apartment just four blocks from the Edgewater Beach Hotel. The apartment was located on Junior Terrace in a brownstone that had been converted into apartments. It was two blocks west of a park and the lake. There was no elevator, and the apartment was on the fourth floor, but there was a Laundromat in the basement. Orazio seemed to be excited about his find, especially since Connie had seen the apartment and thought he had made a very good choice. The bus stop was on the corner of the building, so his getting to work was easier than when he lived at the YMCA.

Now his letters were filled with details about the apartment. He asked the superintendent to make sure the apartment was painted because it had not been done before he moved in. The superintendent painted but didn't clean the apartment. Every evening Orazio spent time cleaning with the products Connie had helped him buy. He wrote explicit details about cleaning the bathroom, the kitchen, the stove and refrigerator, the windows. He sent me measurements for all of the windows, but I sent him curtains for only the living room ones. When he wrote that there were six windows in the bedroom, I assumed the bedroom was or had been a sunroom. He was so proud of his hanging the curtains in the living room because he wanted everything to be "perfect "for me. His love was unconditional. We had taken a giant leap of faith when we married, but Orazio was the right man for me, and I was the woman he was meant to marry.

He no longer ate in restaurants but tried cooking at home. I remember one letter he wrote when he decided he would make steak for dinner. Connie had given him a few pots and pans to use. He had gone to the supermarket and bought what he thought was a steak, since the package was labeled, "Ground round steak." He didn't understand the word "*ground,*" but he cooked the meat in a frying pan. He wrote that the steak "broke all apart," but he cooked it anyway. He then cooked some spaghetti, added an egg and the meat, and declared, "It was good." He was so proud of spending his evenings in his home, cleaning and trying to cook for himself. He mentioned that he was sleeping on the sofa in the living room instead of the bed because he was waiting for me to come before sleeping on the new sheets I had given him. Finally his back began to hurt, and he decided to use the bed.

He had no idea that I had a hope chest filled with linens that my parents or I had bought through the years. Ah, those hope chests! Every girl that I knew had one. In fact, at high school graduations in my town and the neighboring ones, the girls received a miniature Lane Hope Chest from the John Fedan Furniture Company. It was very good advertising because many girls either received a Lane Hope Chest as a graduation or engagement gift or bought one when they began to work. I still have two miniature chests filled with costume jewelry from the 1950's.

I finally resigned on March 1, and Orazio took several days off from work to fly to Pennsylvania for the move. We rented a U-Haul and moved just a few of our household items because Orazio told me there was only one closet in the apartment and no cabinets in the kitchen, just one shelf. During the trip to Chicago he kept saying, "You made a man of me, and I like saying 'my wife.'" I liked writing *Mary Ellen Grasso*. How could I not love this man? I remember driving to the apartment and parking. He was so anxious to show me the apartment that he didn't even want to take a suitcase out of the car. Four flights meant eight stairways with landings in between each one.

The apartment was clean, but all I could think of was unloading the U-Haul. Good grief! How many trips would we have to make? Fortunately, one of the other tenants helped Orazio with the television set we had received as a wedding gift from my parents and some of the larger boxes. For the first time I hated all the clothes I had ever bought. Where would I put them? I didn't complain though; I just soldiered on. Orazio was so excited that he bounded up the stairs.

I was exhausted when we finished unloading the U-Haul, even too tired to eat, but Orazio insisted we go out to one of the nearby restaurants so that first we could also return the trailer to the U-Haul agency. We would not have been able to park the trailer overnight near our apartment. I got my second wind, but after dinner and climbing those steps one more time, I just fell asleep on the sofa while Orazio connected the television set. He finally awakened me about midnight, and when I walked into the bedroom, I realized I was right. It had been a small sunroom. The bed was pushed against the windows, and there was only one way to get in and out of the bed: crawling over Orazio. Because he would be up earlier than I, he took the side that was open to the living room. I had the side against the windows. Well, I thought, at least there's no chance of my falling out of bed.

But then I realized that there were no curtains or blinds, and I have a tragic flaw: I can't sleep with any light in the room, not even a sliver. Unfortunately, the streetlights lit up the room, and I knew that when the sun rose, I would be wide-awake and cranky. While I took a bath, Orazio tried to cover some of the windows with whatever newspapers he could find in the boxes, but there weren't enough. However, once I was in bed, I just threw the covers over my head and fell asleep instantly. Romance that night was out of the question.

I spent the next two weeks unpacking boxes and trying to store clothing and household items. The bedroom had a small alcove on one side that held a pole to hang suit jackets and trousers. Below the suits was a chest with three drawers. That was for Orazio. I telephoned the superintendent to ask if he had another chest of five or six drawers for me. He did. In fact two custodians delivered two chests of drawers. One was placed in the kitchen for linens and tools. The other was placed in a very small alcove between the kitchen and bathroom for some of my clothes.

Still, there was no place to store dishes, glasses, and tableware. I managed to coax a steel white cabinet out of the superintendent to be used as a pantry and to store dishes, glasses, and tableware. I placed my cookbooks, the telephone, the mail, and stationery on the only shelf available on one of the kitchen walls. The sink was set on steel legs so I kept the pots and pans under the sink as well as detergents, bleach, and other cleaning items. Much later I made a white cotton skirt with elastic for the sink to hide those items.

There was a fireplace in the living room that couldn't be used because it had no chimney, but I cut out a few portraits from an Italian calendar Orazio had given me, framed some reproduced artwork by famous Italian artists, and placed the frames on the mantle. Everything else we had brought went into that one walk-in closet: Orazio's and my clothes (our overcoats, suits, dresses and shirts, shoes and boots), small electrical appliances such as the cake mixer and toaster, the vacuum cleaner, brooms, mops, a bucket, and whatever else was around. We needed drapes for the bedroom, but we really couldn't afford them. The rent was $105.00 a month, and we were sending a monthly check to Mamma Elvira for the mortgage on Orazio's home back in Catania.

The following weekend when we went to visit Connie and Dom, she and I went shopping at Gimbel's Department Store, and I found some yellow, blue, and green-stripped sheets on a clearance table. I still had the measurements for the bedroom windows, so I bought enough sheets to use as drapes. The rods were still above the windows, and all I had to do was to make the hems for the rods. I didn't have a sewing machine, but Connie did, and I spent the weekend making drapes. I also bought inexpensive window blinds. After Orazio had installed the blinds and the drapes, the bedroom was transformed into a very cheerful room. When we moved from that apartment a year later, I converted the drapes to sheets for twin beds, for they still had a lot of use. Today two of those sheets are used as slip covers I made for the dining room table leaves.

We now felt comfortable in our home, and I didn't believe anything else would be a problem until Orazio called me from work one day to ask me to pick him up about 5:30 in the afternoon from the Olivetti office on Michigan Avenue. I assumed that I would know how to get there. I didn't bother to ask Orazio for directions.

I thought, "Hadn't we driven to the apartment when we first arrived? I know the route."

What I didn't know was the because of the heavy traffic at that time of the afternoon, the lanes were configured differently. There were more lanes traveling north than south, and I was traveling south. Just as I entered the overpass and began driving in the far right lane, I noticed all the cards facing me. I panicked. Why were those cars in my lane? Seconds later I was surrounded by four policemen on motorcycles. Within seconds all traffic stopped as one of the officers tried to reroute the drivers in my line to another one. Traffic was stalled. Suddenly another officer came to my car, asked me to open the window and began shouting, "Lady where do you think you're going? What do you think you're doing? Are you an idiot? Don't you see the direction of the cars?" I just looked at him and started to blubber, "What am I doing wrong? I just want to go to Michigan Avenue to get my husband. It's just to my right." I sobbed and sobbed. I couldn't catch my breath, and the officer couldn't understand a word I was saying. I finally got calmed down, and I again explained about my situation. To my surprise, two of the officers decided to escort me off the ramp and down to the street behind Michigan Avenue where Orazio was waiting for me.

One of the officers said, "Are you her husband?"

The Letters

I thought Orazio was going to faint at the sight of the policemen, "What did she do?" he asked

"Well," answered the officer, "she almost got herself killed. I suggest you drive, take her home, and have her lie down. She's a very nervous woman."

Then the officer turned to me and said kindly, "You'll be all right. You're going to have to learn how to drive here in Chicago." I finally did, but there was always something new about the city and Orazio to learn.

Then one Saturday night as he was sleeping, I heard him shout, "I'm not a bastard. I'm not a bastard." I was puzzled. Was it a nightmare? I didn't want to awaken him, but the next morning I questioned him, "What were you shouting about last night? About not being a bastard?"

"I never knew my father. Only my brothers did. My dad went to Argentina when I was two years old, and we never saw him again."

He knew that during World War I, Orazio's father Nicola Grasso, a captain in the Italian army, was stationed in Catania. Nicola was the only biological son of a *contadino*, a farmer. He did have, however, two adopted brothers who inherited the tomato farm and became very successful selling tomatoes to a cannery. Nicola and Elvira Grimaldi met in Catania, fell in love, and married before the war had ended. Sadly, they were star-crossed lovers. Elvira was an educated beautiful young girl, a *Signorina*, who came from a well-to-do family.

When the war ended, Nicola took his young wife and his first-born son to Nochera Inferiore, near Naples, to live. Nicola's parents were glad to have him home, believing that his wife would be another pair of hands to work on the farm and that eventually his son would also become a farmer. Elvira was unaccustomed to working, especially on a farm. She was very unhappy and wanted to return to Catania, a large industrial city. Nicola and Elvira moved back to Catania where Nicola worked in his brother-in-law's factory, making stringed musical instruments. He went from being an officer in a uniform, giving orders, to being an employee in a factory. He was unhappy living in the city. For nine years the couple traveled back and forth, from the country to the city. Nicola's mother wanted her eldest grandson, who was about six or seven years of age, to work in the fields. Elvira wanted him to become educated, even some day going to the university. She now had three sons, and all she could think about was that they all would become farmers. The couple began to argue, and during one of the more heated arguments, Nicola took the gun that was in a drawer and shot his wife just missing her side.

Leaving Nochera Inferiore with her three boys, Donato, Giovanni, and Orazio, she returned to her parents' home in Catania. Nicola immediately followed her, professing his love for her and urging her to move to Argentina, considered the New World in the Americas, away from both families. Like many other immigrants who crossed the ocean, the men went first, finding a job first and later a home to rent. Several times he sent money for his family to follow him, but Elvira's family, fearing for her safety, persuaded her to remain in Catania. Who would protect her in a strange country? For a short time the couple corresponded by mail, she making excuses and he asking for forgiveness. Then the letters from Nicola ceased. The couple simply lost track of each other. I never would have known of these details if Zia Giovanna, Mamma Elvira's youngest sister, had not told them to me a few years later. Neither Orazio nor his brothers were ever told about the details.

The Letters

Orazio and I spent the day just talking. He was distressed because he never knew his father or anything about him except that he had abandoned them and lived in Buenos Aires. He wanted to go to Buenos Aires to find his father, but I discouraged him. I thought about Rueben, my pen pal who lived there. We had been exchanging letters for at least ten years, sharing information about our families and our lives, never meeting, just corresponding by mail. I had confidence in Ruben and was certain he could help us. I wrote to him giving whatever details Orazio knew: Nicola's birth date and the approximate date he had left Italy. Much to our surprise, Reuben sent us not only the events of Nicola's life in Argentina but also his death certificate. Through research, Rueben discovered there was a large supermarket in the city called Nicola Grasso and Son. He visited the market and spoke with the son. Unfortunately, Reuben mentioned that a man in the United States was seeking his father, adding that, perhaps, Orazio was also his son. The Argentinian had no idea, but he gave Reuben the address of his mother. Reuben did visit her and told her that Orazio was searching for his father. I now believe that fearing a law-suit and the possibility of losing the supermarket, she denied knowing anything about that Nicola Grasso, claiming that her husband was born in Argentina. She claimed that she was legally married in a Catholic church. She knew of no record of a divorce, civil or otherwise. But that wasn't unusual. There were Italian immigrants at that time who married a second wife without having been divorced.

However, the death certificate verified Orazio's father's birth date and the origin of his birth: Italy. The certificate also recorded the date and time of death, the cause of death, the doctor's signature, and Nicola's last address. Reuben went to the home and spoke with the landlord, who along with his daughter had witnessed Nicola's death from a massive stroke at age 55. According to the information Reuben received, Nicola was separated from his wife and was just renting a room. When Reuben sent all the documents and details to us, he refused any payment for his trouble or the cost of the certificate. He asked only that his son would like a cowboy suit. I asked him to send me an outline of his son's foot and the size of clothing he wore. We sent him the complete outfit, including the hat, a leather belt and holster, and a toy gun with paper caps.

On our next visit to Catania, we gave Mamma Elvira a copy of the death certificate, but gave her no other details. All other documents we gave to Giovanni, Orazio's brother, for safekeeping and to share them with Donato the next time he came home from sea. Mamma Elvira held the certificate and cried as Orazio translated it for her. "I wish I had known he was ill. I would have brought him back home and taken care of him. I always loved him." I told her that Reuben had gone to the cemetery where he was buried and found a beautiful tombstone at the head of his grave. She seemed to be consoled by that information. It was during that visit that I had learned all of the other details when I spent an afternoon with Zia Giovanna. That same summer Zia Marietta gave me a 5x7 studio portrait of Nicola in his uniform, one of the few portraits she knew still existed. For years I never wanted to display it, but a year before Orazio died, I had it restored and framed. I placed it on an antique oak end table next to one of Mamma Elvira when she was about the same age as he. I was no longer angry. He is Orazio's father and my children's grandfather. Many times Orazio would pick up the photo and look at it. Then one day I came home from work and found a note next to a bud vase with a rose in it that he must have picked from the yard: "Thank you for the picture. I love you, Orazio."

But our problems never ceased, especially with the apartment and the laundry room. I'll never forget one laundry day when I placed a batch of Orazio's white dress shirts, briefs, and undershirts into an empty washer. I put detergent in the washer and sat down to read. When the wash cycle had ended, I went over to the machine to remove the white shirts. All the clothes were a bright pink. Someone must have dyed an article of clothing, but didn't bother to run a cycle of bleach before leaving the laundry room. This time crying would never help. It took me three wash cycles, using bleach each time, to restore all of the clothes to their original color: white. That was eighty-five cents extra I hadn't planned to spend: seventy-five cents for the washer and ten cents for the dryer.

The apartment was another problem. It was always too cold since the heat was turned off at nine o'clock at night and not turned on until eight o'clock in the morning, long after I had made breakfast for Orazio, and he had already gone to work. The winter weather in Chicago was brutal, but the weather we could live with; it was the bugs that bothered us. The apartment had a major problem: large roaches everyone else called "water bugs." They marched in formation every night all around the kitchen floor baseboard. Sometimes they crawled on the furniture. No matter how hard we tried to eliminate them, they multiplied. Twice exterminators came, but they couldn't control those roaches. I was told that the apartment below me was very untidy, and that garbage was on the floor. One of the exterminators was surprised to see our apartment. He said it was one of the cleanest in the building. He also was astonished to see it so well decorated and especially liked the pictures on the mantle. The roach problem was never solved, but the tenants below us were evicted. Orazio and I had decided that when our lease was up, we would try to find another apartment to rent. Neither one of us was used to the various insects that invaded our apartment, the strong odors of cooking coming from the hallways, and the plastic bags of trash left on the floor near the chute by children who were supposed to dispose of them properly but seldom did. A few other tenants and I, afraid of an additional infestation, would take the time to throw the bags down the chute. I didn't complain though to Orazio. I knew that he worried more about our financial situation and not being able to have much money for entertainment.

Although Orazio and I had very little money, there were a lot of free attractions in Chicago. There were the Museum of Science and Industry, the National History Museum, the art galleries, Lincoln Park, the beaches, and the flower gardens. Chicago had a wealth of diversified events for everyone. We could go to the Schubert Theater for a $1.00 each (second balcony) to see the off-Broadway shows and have dinner for 99 cents at a small restaurant on State Street: a T-bone steak, a baked potato, a salad, a roll, a cookie, and a beverage. The bus was 25 cents each way, and for less than $5.00 we had a wonderful Saturday evening date. We never minded saving dimes and quarters for the Laundromat located in the basement, but shopping for groceries was a bit difficult. I made sure that I had planned a menu for each week before writing a shopping list. I bought only the essentials, and I did a lot of comparative shopping by reading the newspaper advertisements and cutting out coupons.

I could never buy a large bottle of bleach or a large box of detergent. Those sizes were too expensive. Orazio was paid weekly so I really couldn't stock up on groceries. Besides the refrigerator was just 14 cubic feet with a very small freezer compartment that held one ice cube tray and enough room for two small packages of meat, so I had to shop every other day. Besides, I couldn't carry heavy bags of groceries four blocks and then up eight flights of stairs. Furthermore, just money for the rental of our apartment and the mortgage in Italy took nearly a half-month's pay. I was grateful to my uncles, who were butchers, who taught me how to use the cheaper cuts of meats. I had been cooking since I was eight years of age, and I learned how to make many tasty dishes with leftovers.

During April, I began to look for a teaching position for the fall term. My brother-in-law had made a connection with an administrator of the Chicago schools, and my sister gave me the names of three suburban high schools, about thirty-five miles from Chicago. I sent resumes first to the suburban schools and was surprised to learn that there was a full-time substitute position for nine weeks open at Mt. Prospect High School. The teacher was taking a maternity leave in just a few days, and the department head was anxious to hire someone who could start immediately. I was scheduled for an interview and hired that same day to begin on the following Monday.

I was so excited that I developed a migraine headache on my first day of work. I took a Fiorinal before leaving home, hoping I would be fine. Except that usually when I took that prescription I needed to go to bed, but I didn't want to call in sick, not the first day. Instead of getting better I got worse. I took a second pill, but it had no effect. The teacher in the classroom next to mine, Janice Harmon, also suffered from migraines, and she offered me one of her Fiorinal pills. By my fifth class, I could barely walk. My speech was garbled, and I leaned on the slate board trying to write. One of the students left the room to report me to the principal who then escorted me to the infirmary, and I heard him say to the school nurse, "Good grief! We hired a drug addict from Chicago." I tried to explain, but I was making no sense. Finally, Janice came into the infirmary and mentioned that I had taken Fiorinal, which is a narcotic. Janice asked me if she could check my purse, and I nodded. She found a small empty pill bottle, and the principal called the doctor, who confirmed that I was a patient who suffered with migraines and he had prescribed the medication. He told the principal to have me drink a lot of black coffee. Now the cafeteria manager was involved.

Someone telephoned Orazio, and a co-worker drove him to the high school. The school nurse tried, instead, to get me to drink some orange juice, but that turned out to be a disaster. Now the custodians had to be summoned. Who else would know? It was the overdose at Duke University all over again. All I wanted to do was sleep. It was seven o'clock at night before I could walk to my car with help so that Orazio could drive me home. I was sure that I would never get hired to a full-time position because all three schools were all part of District 214, and I was afraid the news would travel. But I was fortunate. During the time I was at Mt. Prospect, I was hired by Arlington Heights High School for the following year to teach English and to serve as technical director for the class plays. Arlington, also part of District 214, offered me a dream position, making $7,000, $2,000 more a year than I had been earning at Arnold High School. Orazio couldn't have been happier for me. He knew how much I loved teaching.

In addition to teaching four English classes as a substitute at Mt. Prospect, I also taught one public speaking class and coached the debate team for the nine weeks I was there. I had a major in speech as well as in journalism, Spanish, and English. The interscholastic debates for the year were over, and I was scheduled to emphasize the giving of several types of speeches suitable for public speaking. I was very serious about giving the class directions for presenting their persuasive speeches as their next project. I was coaching them saying, "Don't throw your hands into the air. Make sure that you face your audience. The students in the back of the room need to hear you speak, so don't look at the floor, and don't look at me. Above all else, boys, don't put your hands in your pockets and play with anything." That statement had just rolled out of my mouth when I heard snickers. Thank heavens that the dismissal bang rang!

I had forgotten all about the incident until the next afternoon when all of the students had left the school. I was walking through the nearly vacant hallway, and I heard, "Mrs. Grasso!" I looked up the stairway, and there were the principal, the vice principal, and the dean of students standing on the landing with their hands in their pockets. The principal said sternly, "Are you giving new instructions to our students?" Like a fool, I tried to explain that I meant coins or keys. I felt the heat rising from my neck to my face. The men were laughing, and one of them said, "News travels fast in this school." For the next few days I avoided eating in the cafeteria. The students were scheduled to begin giving their speeches the following week. I must admit that the speeches were excellent, and the students were perfect ladies and gentlemen. No coins or keys were rattled. I finally began again to enjoy teaching. It was only the daily commuting that was not enjoyable.

Driving seventy miles a day on the Kennedy Expressway was hectic, but trying to get home early so that I could park in front of our brownstone instead of parking several blocks away was another problem, especially when it rained and the wind turned my umbrella inside out and sometimes shoved me into a wall of a building. At least it was spring, and there was no snow.

Trying to find a parking spot should have been the least of my worries. Once more a simple toothache became a major medical incident. I had forgotten about the dental problem at Duke University when I went to the dentist in Chicago for what should have been a simple procedure: replacing a filling that was missing. I was in quite a bit of pain before I left the office, and the dentist gave me an envelope with pills to alleviate the pain. He did write the name of the medication on the envelope, but I wasn't familiar with the name. I was instructed to take two pills every four hours, which I did.

By morning Orazio was unable to awaken me. He was frantic, "Wake up! Wake up!" He telephoned the dentist because he had no idea what to do or whom to call. The dentist felt that Orazio sounded desperate, and he decided to call a rescue service. According to Orazio, minutes later a rescue vehicle arrived with two men dressed in blue uniforms and carrying medical bags. They took my vital signs, gave me an injection after looking at the pills, and placed an oxygen mask on my face. They did manage to awaken me and get me on my feet. They insisted that I first walk around the apartment. I wanted to lie down. Then they had me walking up and down the stairs with them. My legs felt like rubber, and they had to hold me up. They made me walk a block or two outside even though I complained I was cold. They kept urging me, "Stay awake! Talk to us!" I just wanted to lie down, but they wouldn't let me.

Sometime later, the men had me in the kitchen preparing brunch for all of us, but they stood next to me helping. They wouldn't let me sit down. They kept asking me questions that I had trouble answering. They stayed with me until late afternoon, frequently checking my vital signs and giving me a second injection. I have no idea why I wasn't taken to a hospital, but Orazio later told me that they were in constant contact with someone else by telephone during the hours they were with me. They didn't leave me until I was stable and wide-awake, advising me to avoid any pain medication because I am extremely sensitive to it. They had Orazio sign some papers for the City of Chicago although he did not read the papers. He just wanted to be assured that I was all right. For days, Orazio and I worried about paying for the medical service. There was no medical insurance that we knew of in 1960.

After that episode, I ceased complaining about the long drive to Arlington.

I really shouldn't have minded the drive on the expressway because having two incomes was a blessing, but because Orazio believed a bill for medical expenses was on the way, he now believed our trip to Italy would have to be cancelled, and I realized my dream of our owning a home was over. Because we never received a bill from a hospital or the city, we were certain that we could definitely go to Italy next summer, in 1961. Nevertheless, we still kept to a strict budget. Airplane tickets to Sicily were expensive, and we did want to take gifts to the family.

We were still learning a lot about each other, and Orazio once told me that people who are born near an active volcano sometimes take on characteristics of the volcano: a quick explosion and then calmness. I kept waiting for that first argument, the first explosion, but it didn't happen by him.

It was our first anniversary, and I was very excited about having a celebration just for the two of us. I baked a cake and decorated it with the cornucopia from our wedding cake. We had saved the top layer, but it was in my parent's freezer in Pennsylvania. I made one of his special entrees for dinner and set the table as it was for our first breakfast after our honeymoon. Usually he was home by six o'clock in the evening. I had gotten dressed as though we would be going out on a date, and I sat and waited. I waited and waited and waited. No Orazio. I thought that maybe he had stopped to buy a bouquet of flowers. About 8:30, I put away all the food in the refrigerator. I had made several calls to his office, but no one replied. I couldn't imagine what had happened. I left the cake on the table and got ready for bed. If he had been in an accident, I would have been called. At 10:30 I heard the lock in the door turn. In walked Orazio, smiling and brimming with news. He had been playing billiards with some of the men from work. They had first gone to dinner. I was speechless.

He walked into the kitchen to hang his coat in the hall closet and spied the cake on the table. I was quiet as he read, "Happy Anniversary." He turned and looked at me.

"At least you could have called me. How did you forget today?" I said. I was angry!

"Today? What day is it?" he asked.

I answered, "Did you forget already? You saw the cake. You read the inscription." My volcano erupted. I wasn't born near one, and I rarely got angry, but I was hurt.

I expected him to be as romantic as I was that day. He just looked at me. Suddenly, I calmed down. He'd gone into the bedroom for the gift he had bought: the calendar charm.

"I didn't forget. I just forgot the date," he apologized. He explained that he had never gone out with the men to play billiards although they had asked him many times. I was crying; he was holding me tightly and apologizing. He never raised his voice.

Through the years of our marriage, Orazio had many memory lapses, but I never again took them seriously. He was just being Orazio. A day earlier, a day later, it made little difference to me. He made celebrations for ordinary days when there was nothing special to celebrate, and those days are now all the sweeter, all the ones I now remember. He did remember, however, the major holidays.

The Letters

We spent our first Christmas at Connie and Dom's home, but we had decorated our apartment with a silver tree we had received as a bonus when we purchased an end table for the living room. We weren't going to have a tree since we couldn't afford one, and we wouldn't be home for the holiday. Orazio had mentioned several times that he had always wanted a Lionel train with tracks he had once seen in a movie, but he never got one. They were too expensive and unavailable in Catania. I happened to read of an offer made by Quaker Oats cereal. The offer was printed on the container: Send twenty coupons, I believe, and $19.95 for the train and tracks. The engine blew smoke, and I knew Orazio would be happy with it. I remember eating a lot of oatmeal and saving the money. The train would be his Christmas gift from me.

In those days, Christmas was celebrated differently in Catania. *Befana*, the witch, left gifts for the children on January 6. There was no Santa Claus and no tree. Many homes did have the Nativity Scene displayed. Gifts for the adults were not exchanged. Christmas Eve was the day that was celebrated with family, and Orazio told me that wherever he was on the day before Christmas Eve, he made sure that he returned home for that holiday. I had managed to save an additional $35.00 to buy gifts for my parents, Connie and Dom, and their children. I was so excited about shopping in the department stores on State Street. The stores were always decorated with animated figures and beautiful scenes built around a theme.

I managed to find a pair of wool gloves for my father for just $3.00 and a nylon slip for my mom. The sales clerk put them in gift boxes for me. I bought mittens and knit caps for Jay and Lisa, but I couldn't find a suitable gift for Connie and Dom. I still had a little money left, but I decided to take the bus and go home. As I was walking to the bus stop I was so happy that it seemed as though the packages I was carrying had gotten lighter. However, what began as a happy day for me, turned out to be a sad one instead. I always had a bus token in my coat pocket so I wouldn't have to search in my purse for one. I was carrying my packages but had my purse on my shoulder. I got into the bus, sat down, and tried to swing my purse onto my lap. Where was my purse? All I had were the shoulder straps dangling alone. A thief had cut my purse away. I started to cry loudly, "Why me? Why me? That's all the money I had." I couldn't stop crying. My wallet was gone, my keys, my leather gloves that Mamma Elvira had sent me. I didn't even have a handkerchief to wipe my nose. Some of the people on the bus tried to console me, but I would have none of their sympathy. How was I going to save enough money for gifts again?

When I returned home, Orazio had purchased a revolving light for the silver tree now set up in the living room. There were no ornaments on the tree, but the light wheel with several colors made the branches twinkle as if there were. I just blubbered, "Someone stole my purse by cutting the straps. Everything that was in it is now gone. I don't have any more money. I can't finish shopping." Orazio just hugged me and said, "Everything will be fine. Look at how pretty our tree looks." I stopped crying, looked at the tree, and kissed him. For me, he had brought light into the darkness of my day.

He was the one who worked extra hours so he could replace the money that had been stolen. He helped me replace my driver's license, my Gulf credit card, and the keys. His Christmas gift to me was a leather wallet. I always knew from his letters that he was compassionate. We kept and used the tree in the living room for many years though we always had a fresh green tree in the family room when we bought our first home.

The Letters

A few weeks after the holidays in 1961, I had my second exposure to the chemistry Orazio had with strangers he met, especially one he had become acquainted with on the bus he rode to and from work. I was surprised when he brought home a "freedom fighter" from Hungary as our guest for dinner. At first, the young man, whose name I no longer remember but I will call Taz, was very cordial. He spoke English well, and during dinner we spoke about our families. After dinner we sat in the living room having espresso coffee. The conversation suddenly switched to the Hungarian revolt in 1956. He had been among those Hungarians who revolted against their Communist rulers. He began to criticize Americans, and I became offended. He believed that he was entitled to an apartment, a job, and financial assistance because as he said, "We fought for America." He explained he was angry because, "America didn't come to help us." According to Taz, "Hungary had appealed to the United States, who did not back their Hungarian friend. Then Great Britain, France, and Israel invaded Egypt to recover the Suez Canal that had been nationalized by Egypt, and the United States joined Russia to condemn the action and even helped the United Nations arrange a ceasefire. Using tanks, Russia then smashed our revolt in Hungary." As he stood up, he kept pointing his finger at me and shouting, "America owes us! You owe us!" He was getting very angry.

At that point, Orazio stood up and said, "This is interesting, but we need to go to bed. It's now late, and my wife gets up early. We will continue this the next time you come." We said, "Good night," and he left. I just looked bewildered at Orazio, "Surely you won't invite him again." Orazio replied, "I've known him for a few months, and the first time I saw him he looked sad. I just started to talk with him. He said that he was from Hungary and didn't have a job. He was living temporarily with another Hungarian. I felt sorry for him. He was on the same bus this afternoon, and I decided to invite him for dinner. He looked hungry." I never heard about him again, but sometime later Orazio told me that he had met him once more, but Taz was leaving the Chicago area. I'm glad he did because there would have been no second invitation.

Once more we had settled into a routine. Then we received a letter sent by the agency that held the rental on our apartment. Did we plan to renew our lease when it came due?

Orazio suggested that we find another apartment closer to Arlington Heights. He didn't want me to continuing driving on the Kennedy Expressway, especially during the winter. He decided that he could take the train to Chicago from the station near the high school. We had only one car and could not afford to buy a second one. I could leave him at the station at 7:00 in the morning, and he would be at work by 8:30. He would return at 6:30 in the evening, and I would be waiting to take him home. We did look at a few apartments, but I wanted to buy a house instead of renting. Most of the two bedroom apartments we looked at were unfurnished and had rental fees of about $160 a month or more, much more than we could afford. Also, we would need to buy furniture.

I really wanted to buy a house instead of renting. He wanted to go to Italy. Then one day while driving around, still looking for an apartment, we chanced upon a very small town: Wheeling, Illinois. It was considered a bedroom subdivision. There were only a drugstore, a Jewel Supermarket, an Ace Hardware, a Gulf gasoline station, a Laundromat, and a frozen custard store, as well as a small shopping area, maybe a block long, that included the post office. There was one subdivision of very small homes, all of them alike, and an elementary school, named after the poet Carl Sandburg. We noticed a billboard with an advertisement for twenty-five new homes. I said, "Why don't we just look at the models."

He agreed, but he said, "We're not buying this year, maybe when we return from Italy."

The models were lovely. The homes, with an attached one-car garage, were on a quarter acre lot and included nearly all major kitchen appliances, even a garbage disposal. A refrigerator was not included, but a washer and a dryer, enclosed in a closet in the family room, were. Three bedrooms, two bathrooms, a combination living and dining room, and a very large family room were more than we had ever hoped for. We walked through all of the models and noticed that all of them had ample closet space. The driveways were of cement, not asphalt. We had found what we wanted, but Orazio was unconvinced. I just had to find a way to persuade him. He did agree to talk with a sales representative who gave us some basic figures for the $18,000 home. The mortgage payment was within our budget and less than renting an apartment, but we would need furniture. Still I wanted the house.

But we had another problem. We had only a Gulf credit card, and it was only for gasoline. We were told that we needed to show that we had good credit and had a history of paying our bills. We had only paid cash for everything we bought so we had no reliable credit history. The builder suggested we apply for a department store credit card. Because I knew I would eventually need a sewing machine, whether we bought the house or not, I suggested to Orazio that we purchase one at Carson, Pirie, Scott & Co. on the monthly installment plan. He agreed, but he still wasn't totally convinced about purchasing the house. The trip to Italy was on his mind.

Driving home from Wheeling, I promised Orazio that we could have both on several conditions. We would take brown-bag lunches to work instead of his eating out and I eating at the cafeteria. For the next year we would go nowhere that cost money:

Mary Ellen Cipolla Grasso

the movies, the off-Broadway shows. Because only twenty-five homes were to be built, I was anxious to sign a contract, and the next day we did. But we were short $500 for the twenty percent down payment. The builder did put a month's hold on the lot we wanted with just a small down payment. I wrote to my father asking for a loan. He gave it to us, but with a request that he didn't want us to repay him in small payments. He wrote, "When you get $500 together, then send me a check." We made sure that every payday we set aside money to repay the loan. We finally sent him the check, and he returned it, torn in small pieces, along with a note: "Now that you have saved $500, let this be the start of your savings plan." We never forgot his advice, and we did follow it. I used to call money that we had saved as "rusty money." We wouldn't use it.

Italy

The day we closed on the house and were given the keys to our home, I sat in the sales office, held on tightly to the keys, and cried. Having our own home meant a lot to both of us. We needed furniture and began shopping. We bought queen-sized mattresses, which we placed on the floor, and from Gimbel's Department Store we purchased a walnut wood double dresser, a chest of drawers, an end table, and two twin beds for just $150. Dom said he could easily join the headboards together to make a queen-sized one. The bedroom set was a floor model as was the tangerine sofa and the Danish chair we bought a few weeks later in Arlington Heights for the family room. We were surprised when we learned that many of the shopkeepers gave a twenty percent discount to local teachers.

One of my classes at Arnold High School had given us a card table with four chairs as a wedding gift, and that became our kitchen table set. I had never known of an AMC refrigerator, but I happened to see one in a department store window on State Street. It was one of the first refrigerators with a bottom freezer. Because it had been on display, I was able to buy it for half price. With my new sewing machine, I made café curtains for the kitchen window as well as all of the drapes. Now that our house was "furnished," we could begin to plan for our trip to Italy. We were happy and in love.

We were both very excited and started to pack a month before the trip. We planned to stay two weeks with the family and then take a train to tour the major cities in Italy. It was my first trip, and

Mary Ellen Cipolla Grasso

Orazio wanted to show me his country. We started to buy gifts for the family, but because I wasn't sure what would be appropriate for everyone, I had Orazio make the selections. I remember so well getting off the plane in Catania and walking on the tarmac towards at least one hundred of Orazio's extended family. All I could see was a very tall women standing in the front holding a large bouquet of red roses. It was Mamma Elvira, who was five feet eleven inches tall, holding a wide gold bracelet. She was crying as she embraced me. I was crying so hard that I couldn't hear Orazio trying to introduce me to everyone. He kept shouting, "This is my wife. This is my wife, Marilena." I was given bouquets of beautiful flowers and smothered with hugs and kisses. I couldn't remember who was an uncle and who was a cousin.

Orazio was finally home in the country he loved, surrounded by his family and friends. Some of the men went with him to the baggage carrier to get our luggage. It was as though a celebrity had arrived. I was just beginning to get a migraine headache, and with so much emotion I knew the headache would only get worse. I followed Orazio into someone's car, not knowing what was next. We were told that we would be going to Orazio's home where a few of the women had prepared a homecoming feast for about twenty-five relatives. Most of Orazio's favorite dishes had been prepared as well as a large kettle of soup and a pasta dish. I knew that I wouldn't be able to eat much, if anything. Mamma Elvira sat next to Orazio, urging him to eat: "*Mangia, mangia.*" I did manage to eat a bowl of soup, but I became nauseated. I whispered to Orazio that I had a migraine and couldn't eat anything else. I needed to lie down. He told me to lie on the sofa. As I did, I heard someone say, "Why didn't you tell us what she likes to eat?" He tried to explain, but they were unconvinced. Finally, I fell asleep.

When I awoke, some of the relatives were sitting on the balcony, and those with young children had gone home. The kitchen and

183

dining room had been cleaned, and the women were talking quietly in the family room. I still had the headache. I needed the medication, which was packed. Orazio came in to tell me that we would be staying at our sister-in-law Fina's home because it was larger, and Mamma Elvira wanted to be with us. By the next morning I was fine, and I had no trouble eating the delicious food that was prepared for all of the other meals. However, I noticed that there was a small case of marmalade and jellies because someone advised Fina that Americans liked jelly on their bread for breakfast. Unfortunately, that is one thing I don't really like because I find jellies to be too sweet. However, I did try to use some. But a small case?

It wasn't too long that morning before the telephone began to ring. The usual question was asked: *"Como e Marilena?"* Several aunts followed their telephone calls with visits to check up on me, the American. Some even thought I might be pregnant. After all it was two years since we were married. They would then sit out on the balcony wanting to get more acquainted with the American their nephew chose to marry. I always enjoyed visiting with family because I forever learned more about Orazio's antics when he was young. Mamma Elvira was always the one to tell me about her *birichino*, the naughty boy that I loved.

It seemed as though when he was about eleven years old he began to skip school now and then. In the morning he would make sure he had his books and other supplies for school, kissed his mother goodbye, and went off to class. Each afternoon he returned when school was dismissed with traces of ink on his fingers, indicating that he had been at school and telling her tales about what happened at school. After a month or so, his teacher gave him a letter to give to his mother, requesting a conference about his frequent absences. He knew he would be punished, maybe forever. What could he do? He decided to speak to one of the women who cleaned the common areas of the building where he lived. He gave her a few *liras* to stand in for his mother. The woman was poor and agreed to go to the conference for the extra money.

Several weeks later, by chance, Mamma Elvira, who always dressed well and wore a fashionable hat, happened to be at the same market as the teacher. When they were both waiting at the cheese counter for service, they struck up a casual conversation without first introducing themselves. When Mamma Elvira heard that the teacher taught in the same school where Orazio attended, she said, "My son, Orazio, goes to the same school. Perhaps you know him."

The teacher was stunned. "Is your son Orazio Grasso? I just met his mother recently. She is a poor cleaning women who speaks the Sicilian dialect, not Italian. She promised me that he would not miss school again, but he is still not attending everyday." Mamma Elvira had heard enough. "I can assure you that Orazio will be in school everyday." And he was. Mamma Elvira knew how to keep her three sons in line.

His sister-in-law Fina, Donato's wife, and cousins Gianni and Tita occupied the fifth floor of a large apartment building. Zia Angela (Tita's widowed mother) lived with them, and since she was a seamstress, she wanted to make me two outfits and a terry cloth beach robe, which she did. I just had to select the material, buttons, and zippers and take them to her. Since it was summer, the movie theater across the street opened the roof and walls for cooler air. At first I didn't know why either Mamma Elvira or Zia Angela would take turns checking the marquee in the morning to see what was playing. I thought that they were planning to go to the movie theater, but when it became dark, they took their chairs, sat on the balcony, and watched the movie. Some nights I joined them. We had an excellent view and the sound was perfect. I had now become officially one of the Grasso family.

We were given many wedding gifts from the relatives: sets of embroidered table linens with twelve napkins and beautiful ceramic sculptures. Orazio received a gold ring from his mother, and I received a watch, two bracelets, and a necklace. Zia Marietta and Zio Paolo gave me an oval-shaped onyx ring surrounded by small diamonds, and Fina gave me a lapel pin. It was customary to give the bride gold jewelry as an investment. Should the couple ever need money, the gold could be sold.

We didn't always eat home because so many of the relatives and friends invited us to eat either at their home or at a restaurant, but the most unusual invitation was one by Orazio's friend Lorenzo. He had invited not only us but also two of our cousins, Gennaro and Cristina. The invitation was for dinner at his home. When we arrived at his home, we were invited into the living room where we met his wife Isabella, his two children, and his mother-in-law Rosina. We were asked to sit for a while. About a half-hour later Lorenzo said, "It's too hot to eat at home, so we decided to take you out for dinner." Rosina and the youngest child remained at home. Gennaro drove us around the beach area a while because Lorenzo wanted to find the "perfect" place for me. He selected a restaurant on the beach. There was a great ceremony about ordering. Two large bottles of wine were placed on the table. Steamed clams and sea urchins were ordered as well as olives, cheese, bread, and linguine with a clam sauce. When dinner was over, the waiter presented the bill to Lorenzo who passed it on to Orazio and Gennaro. I was shocked to see that those two paid the bill. I said nothing.

On our way home, Lorenzo suggested we stop at another beach restaurant for cold watermelon. Once more, Orazio and Gennaro paid the bill. When we arrived at Lorenzo's home, he asked me to send each of his two sons cowboy outfits with leather boots and hats. I told him I couldn't. In truth I was angry. Driving home I was reprimanded by both men. "You shouldn't have said that. We knew he didn't have money, but it was the gesture. You should have said, 'Of course' and then not sent them with the excuse that you didn't know their sizes." I had a lot to learn about Italian culture.

One of the most memorable moments of the first trip to Italy was the night Mamma Elvira took Orazio and me to a nightclub. Without our knowledge, she had made reservations for the three of us requesting a table near the band. I had not seen her more beautiful nor happier than she was that night. Her slate-gray-blue eyes sparkled as she urged us to dance, "Go! Go! I want to see you two dancing together." She adored her son. One only needed to glance at her face to know that.

Walking to the dance floor, we looked around the club and noticed a long banquet table on the mezzanine set with a number of covered silver steam platters. We were intrigued. We danced two sets before the band took a break, and we returned to our table. I asked the waiter, who was now at our table opening up a bottle of champagne Mamma Elvira had ordered, if the banquet table was for a wedding party. He said, "No. It's for the Baroness sitting two tables away from you. She is here nearly every evening." Orazio added, "Watch. She will select an escort among those handsome, well-dressed men sitting in the back of the room." After a few moments, one man at a time came to her table and then sat for a few minutes. Each of them kissed her hand; some lit a cigarette for her. Each sat and chatted a while with her and then left the table. After a short period of time, she called the waiter who talked to one of the men: her selection for the evening. Orazio and I were again dancing, but I couldn't keep my eyes off the ritual and the couple.

As they walked to the dance floor, I noticed that she was not young, perhaps in her late fifties. She and her escort were dancing near us, and I could see that she was heavily made-up. She was wearing a black dress with three tiers of tassels that moved when she danced. Her escort held her closely. He was very attentive and appeared to be quite engaging, his eyes only for her. Orazio and I again returned to our table to sit with Mamma Elvira who whispered, "He's a gigolo." A bit later the waiter led the couple to the banquet table. I assumed that others in the club would be joining them, but they were alone. Who was going to eat all of that food? I wondered what the club did with all the leftover food. What happened to all of the other gigolos? They were no longer sitting in the back of the room.

Meanwhile Mamma Elvira had ordered dinner and a bottle of wine. She preferred wine with her dinner. She had ordered an entree she knew Orazio and I would like: grilled fresh fish. She thought Orazio was too thin at 145 pounds, and she kept urging him to eat more. The meal was delicious. She had even ordered a pastry for us, but it was the entire evening that was so memorable, especially when she said in Italian, "Was it like this when you got married?" Orazio held her hand and replied, "Mamma, it was just like this, but this is much better because you are here with us." That evening was her attempt to recreate a wedding reception that she couldn't attend.

Our days there were filled with sightseeing trips: Siracusa (Syracuse), Taormina, and Etna. The first time we took a trip to Mount Etna, a barrier did not surround the mouth of the volcano, and I was too afraid to get close. I knew I wouldn't get near even if there were a barrier, as there was years later. No encouragements would change my mind. I looked at the lava on the ground, fascinated by it. I still have a large reproduction of a photograph of one of the major eruptions. It shows hot lava coming down the mountain and surrounding a building. I also have a plate commemorating the loss of a restaurant, La Siciliana di La Rosa, during one of the eruptions. On the center of the plate is a hand-drawn picture of the erupting volcano, and on the back is an inscription: *Restorante del Buon Recordo, 1983*. I don't know what I expected lava to look like, but later I bought a ring and a necklace made from the cooled lava. They are lovely, reminding me of onyx, and I always receive many compliments when I wear them today. I still recall one summer when the family spent a Sunday at Zia Marietta and Zio Paolo's villa in Mount Etna. There were small eruptions coming from the volcano. I was frightened, but my sister-in-law Fina calmly said, "Oh, the old man is smoking his pipe. Don't worry."

Medieval Taormina on the east coast of Sicily, half way between Messina and Catania on the Ionian Sea, was a wonderland for me. It is still a popular tourist attraction, and when we were there in 1961, it was called the Riviera of Italy. While Syracuse is south of Catania, Taormina is north of it and Etna. Since no cars were permitted to enter the town or park in it, I found the town to be a pedestrian's paradise. The town is on a very high cliff, and I can still see in my mind's eye Isola Bella Bay, a spectacular view of a natural reserve below the town. The public square was filled with tourists, and the small boutiques that lined the streets were filled with souvenirs that I found to be much cheaper than those in Catania. Orazio, who loved to shop, made the rounds with me. He could always barter with the shopkeepers, a talent I didn't have. Mamma Elvira and a few of the other members of the family who came with us sat on benches in the square while Orazio and I, along with some cousins, roamed around the town.

The Letters

Taormina is isolated because of its location, but the beauty of the town attracts thousands of Europeans. One of the attractions for me was the Greek theater. I remember sitting on the steps with Orazio watching the construction of a set for a Greek play that was to be presented later that summer. The crew had just completed constructing a circular stage for the chorus of the play to use. I was told that theater is the second largest theater of its kind in Sicily. I would have liked to have been able to return later that year to see the production, but I knew that was impossible. Later we visited the grottos and saw some of the most magnificent miniature religious displays I had ever seen. I had taken dozens of photographs that year, but unfortunately I have very few. I had mailed about twenty rolls of film to a developing plant, failing to write my name on each roll. They were lost in transit, and I was able to recover fewer than half of the photographs. We spent the remainder of the afternoon visiting historical monuments and churches such as the *Duomo*, the cathedral that dates from the Thirteen Century.

While Taormina has the second largest Greek theater in Sicily, it is Syracuse that has the largest. The difference between the two theaters is that the steps of the theater in Syracuse were cut from stone and had not deteriorated as those in Taormina. Visiting that theater, Orazio and I noticed a number of stone "boxes" decorated with sculptures and inscriptions surrounding the theater. Our nephew Gino explained that they were sarcophagi, once used as the burial coffins for only the best actors. One happened to be opened, giving us a chance to look inside. They were simply stone boxes. They appeared small to us, but the only explanation we received by a workman cleaning the sarcophagus was that the actors were really of short stature.

Driving around the city, we saw more than enough beautiful birds. I found Syracuse to be a charming, clean city and the beach very inviting, but I wanted to go to the Orsi Regional Museum, considered one of the best museums in Sicily, and Orazio came reluctantly. He had been there before. Gino was our guide. There were Greek and Roman treasures to see there, all with detailed explanations to read. I was fortunate that Gino added additional information. I wanted to read everything, to see everything, but time was limited. That day we were fortunate to watch a group of archaeologists and their interns uncovering a new find. We stopped to watch them for a while. For a minute, I wished I could I could join them. Memories of past years came to mind.

We did as much sightseeing as we could during that first trip to Sicily since we planned to stay in Catania only two weeks. The morning we were to leave, Mamma Elvira got ready to come with us to the airport to see us off. She was sitting in the family room wearing her hat and holding her purse waiting for us, but at the last minute she couldn't leave. She just sat and cried. Gennaro and Cristina were going to drive us to the airport, but we all just cried with her. Italians are very emotional. Orazio and I promised that we would return, but we didn't tell her that we would still be in Italy sightseeing for two weeks. Rather than leave from Rome to return to Chicago, Orazio had changed our departure from Rome to Milan. He wanted me to see the mainland of Italy, not just Sicily. He had lived and worked many years in Ivrea, which was in north Italy. It seemed as if all we did that morning was cry, at home and at the airport where so many relatives had come to say goodbye. Orazio, no doubt, was the favored one, but I had been treated like a princess.

I understood how difficult it must have been for Orazio to leave Italy once again. I remembered his letters to me when he had apologized for taking me away from my home, my family, and friends, but Chicago was only an eight-hour trip by car. Italy was miles and hours away, and those trips were very expensive. We still needed to furnish our home, plant grass in the front and backyards, and landscape the yards. All that would take money. Between the two of us, we were making only $12,000 a year.

We had no idea when we would return to Italy again. However, this trip was like a second honeymoon, and Orazio was anxious to show me as much as possible. Since he had visited those cities and had seen their landmarks many times before, he sometimes would not go with me to see the historical sites of a specific city or town. I would take the guidebook he had purchased for me, go alone into a cathedral or museum while he sat outside, fed the pigeons, and talked with strangers. I have photographs of him sitting on the steps of a building barefoot surrounded by pigeons. However, he did go to the Vatican with me. I still remember that Michelangelo's sculpture *Pieta* was on the floor of the Sistine Chapel, and I marveled at the beauty of it. I walked around it, wanting to touch it because it looked real. I did lightly touch an arm. We spent a day at the Vatican because I believed I might never get to see it again, and I wanted to see everything. But I did return a few years later. That time *Pieta* was encased in glass for security reasons, and no one could get close to it. It wasn't even at eye level. We didn't have enough time to visit all of Rome, but I made sure that I dropped some coins in the Fountain of Trevi. I made a wish that we would return. We did go to the Coliseum where Orazio hired one of the guides who not only described everything clearly but also gave us a reenactment of some of the scenes he was describing.

In Florence we attended a fenced outdoor concert one evening. As usually Orazio assumed he was the vocalist as he sang the lyrics to some of the songs. If an orchestra or band was playing, Orazio was singing. Sitting next to us were several young men from Holland. One of them was getting married in a few weeks and told us this was the last trip he would take as a bachelor with his friends. While we were there, he had an artist draw an excellent portrait of me. He gave it to Orazio and said, "It is for you. Remember that she will always be this young in your eyes." Orazio had it framed, and it still hangs on one of the walls in my home. We had planned to leave the following day, but Orazio had not confirmed our plane reservations. When he telephoned that morning to verify the flight information, he was told that his seats had been resold and the plane was filled. He was supposed to confirm our trip twenty-four hours before the flight left. We had no other recourse except to go to an Alitalia travel agency as soon as possible.

But, when we arrived in Florence, I noticed that a small diamond from the onyx ring that Zio Paolo and Zia Marietta had given me as a wedding gift was missing. Small diamond baguettes surrounded the oval shaped stone. I was very distraught, but Orazio said he knew a jeweler who had a small shop on Ponte Vecchio. Ponte Vecchio in Florence was the only bridge that was not destroyed during World War II when the Germans retreated from Italy. That year the plaza and the bridge were covered with young men and women, hippies, who lounged or slept on the bridge and in the nearby plaza. Those sleeping on the floor of the bridge made it difficult for us to walk around them. Trash littered the floor of the bridge, and I slipped on a half-eaten piece of fruit. It was our first exposure to that culture but not our last. We found the jeweler, and he agreed to replace the baguette. He told us that the ring would be ready in an hour. That gave us time that day to see Michelangelo's *David* and try to find Dante's home. We decided to walk even though the heat was unbearable, and I wasn't wearing a hat or using an umbrella.

We walked and walked. I kept checking the guidebook, but it was of no help. We asked a lot of people, but no one seemed to know where Dante's house was. Finally we came across a building that had a small brass plate attached on one side that read, "The poet

193

Dante lived here." No wonder no one seemed to be able to give us directions. I had taken a snapshot of the plaque, but that too was a photo I lost among others.

The next day we planned to find the house that Robert Browning and his wife, Elizabeth Barrett, rented. I wanted to take photographs and to be able to tell my high school students about it. But there was no museum and no house, not then. At least we couldn't find it. What we did find were narrow streets filled with traffic and drivers on mopeds that zigzagged around other vehicles. We gave up the search and went to dinner. Confirming our flight to Venice that day was on neither of our minds. There were still sites Orazio wanted me to visit, and I still had not see the sculpture of David.

Because we both felt uncomfortable with the conditions of the city, we were anxious to leave Florence and decided to cut our trip by one day. It was not the Florence Orazio remembered or the one I read about in my travel guidebook. The day we planned to leave, we did go to the Alitalia Travel Agency where the agent said he would try to help us, perhaps not by plane but maybe by train. We had our luggage with us because we had to check out of the hotel. The agent was busy with a client, so we just sat quietly waiting until he could talk with us. Suddenly a very irate American couple walked in. They had plane tickets with KLM, the Dutch airline. The man began screaming loudly. He was uncontrollable. The agent couldn't even talk with him. He was arrogant. He wanted his tickets changed to the next Alitalia flight because he had missed his KLM one. When he was told that no seats were available, he shouted, "Throw the Italians off! Throw two of your Italians off! We're the ones spending the money here in their country! Throw off the last two who made reservations!" I was ashamed that I was an American. He grabbed the agent by his shirt and tried to pull him closer.

Orazio walked out to find a policeman, but someone who was just passing by the agency who heard the swearing and threatening of the agent had already called one. All I could think of was a book I had recently read and had discussed with my honors English class. The book, *The Ugly America*, written by William J. Lederes and Eugene Burdick in 1958 was a best seller. While the book exposed American corruption in Southeast Asia, the title became a new word. While it refers especially to Americans for their behavior when they travel abroad, it also refers to any traveler abroad who acts both arrogantly and superior. I now can only recall that two police officers took the couple out of the agency. Although the agent was noticeably nervous, he handled our case in a very professional manner and thanked us for our patience. He not only got us tickets on the afternoon train to Venice but also refunded the difference between the cost of the train tickets and those of the plane.

Once we arrived at our hotel in Venice, we could finally relax in this city. Well, for me, almost. Walking in St. Mark's Square, I had to contend with the pigeons who seemed to love everyone else but me. The moment one came near me it landed on my head or arm to do its untidy business. Another one nibbled on my toes that stuck out from my sandals, and another sat on my shoulder and pecked my ear. I tried feeding the pigeons, but all they did was eat the treats Orazio handed to me and continued to torment me. That was not enough to stop me from visiting St. Mark's Basilica even though my hair smelled and my blouse was stained. We did go back to the hotel so I could bathe, wash my hair, and change my clothes before going to dinner. After dinner, we walked around the city. I expected to see garbage floating in the canal, but the canal was very clean. I was looking forward to riding in one of the canals, but that night I just wanted to have a good night's sleep. Venice seemed so calm and peaceful after our days in Florence.

The Letters

While I was getting ready for bed, Orazio opened the French doors for us so we could enjoy some cool air, but along with the cooler air, we were serenaded by some music coming from the street. I could hear every sound: the noise from the canal as the paddles from the gondoliers struck the water, the voices of people sitting at the tables on the sidewalk below our hotel, and the footsteps of those walking along the boardwalk. Orazio was oblivious to the sounds. He had visited Venice many times and was accustomed to the noises.

The following morning after breakfast, Orazio hired a guide recommended by the hotel. Many university students were employed as guides in many of the cities and towns and on tour buses to earn money. We had an excellent guide. I wanted to take a ride on the gondola, but Dario, our guide, suggested that we wait until it was his cousin's turn to take passengers. The gondoliers worked in rotation and tourists took whoever was available. We just kept walking around until Dario's cousin was at the gate. Dario motioned for us to follow him as he asked his cousin if he could take the three us to the Island of Murano for a price slightly lower than the one listed. He agreed. Orazio had been to the Murano factory, but he wanted me to see it because glass blowing was becoming a dying art. The skill of the glass blowers was passed from father to son, but even in 1961 there were sons who were not interested in glass blowing. During the demonstration, the glass blower made a small pale yellow unicorn and then handed it to me. I treasured it, and I did mourn the loss of it when I moved in 1998. I had had it for 37 years, but it broke during the move. I still have the candy dish I bought that day at the Murano factory. We were only in Venice two days, but we vowed that we would return.

Our last stop was Turino (Turin) where Orazio's cousins, Franco and his wife, Tita, lived. Orazio had not seen them in many years, but when they met it was as though it had been only yesterday that they had seen each other. We were there only a day, but I was happy to meet them both. They had lost their home and all of their possessions during World War II. Now they lived in a small cottage provided by the factory where Franco was the factory's only watchman. We spent an afternoon with them, and while Orazio and Franco talked about days long past and the effects of the war on many members of the family, Tita stood up, hurried to her bedroom, and came out with a small white package she wanted to show me. I unwrapped the package to see only an embroidered white handkerchief with some rubble in it from their home bombed during the war.

Crying, she said to me, "This is all I have left. We will never be able to own another home. We have never recovered."

I had no words for her. I hugged her as tears streamed down my face. What could I say to her – this woman who for two days couldn't find her toddlers, using a spoon and her bare hands to dig through the rubble that once was her home, only to find a single white handkerchief.

Not too many years later one of her sons came to visit us. We were delighted to share time with him. We learned that his younger brother was a gifted pianist, living and working in Paris. Unfortunately, a few years later, both young men died within a short time of each other.

After our visit to Turin, we left for Milan. We were there only a day, hardly enough time to sightsee, but we were ready to return to our home in America. Orazio even missed a mug of American coffee. I had become so much a part of Orazio's family and his beloved country that I was sad when we left. I now understood how difficult it must have been for him and his family when he decided to marry me, give up his life in Italy, and live in the United

The Letters

States, and I realized how much he loved me. I was certain that we would return, for I had become a Grasso.

Wheeling, Illinois

Could I ever have thought that thirty-one letters, written just two years earlier, would have changed my life? I was sure that family, friends, and colleagues would never have thought our marriage would have lasted even a year. Here were two people who didn't speak the same language, who had a very, very short courtship, who came from different lifestyles and cultures, and who didn't have a sexual relationship before marriage. Orazio was unique. Above all else he loved his family, but he also was loyal to his friends. In his eyes everyone was a friend. The president and one of the vice presidents of the college where I later taught were his friends as were my secretaries, the neighbors on the block, his colleagues, even those who were hired to maintain our home. Orazio was kind and generous. He would give his last ten dollars to any member of the family or to one of his friends who needed it.

We had finally settled into our home and began to enjoy a social life with Orazio's colleagues, but once more our life was about to change when our first child, Stephen, was born in March of 1963. Orazio was overcome with joy. For the first few weeks, he felt awkward holding Stephen, afraid he was hurting him if he held him close to his chest. But the love for his son overcame his fear of parenthood. Saturday mornings he insisted I sleep while he got up early to take care of Stephen. I never thought that he would change diapers, feed him, or bath him, but he did. Now he was anxious for Mamma Elvira to meet her grandson, and we began to plan a second trip to Catania, but we wanted to wait until Stephen was two years old. However, after the first three months of Stephen's birth, there was a rift in our relationship.

The Letters

When we first moved to Wheeling, we discovered that most of the couples in that subdivision were much younger than we. The men went to work, but the women remained at home with their children. One of our neighbors, Laura was just eighteen, and her husband, Harry, was nineteen or twenty. They had a child that was just a year old and the couple had many problems. Many times Orazio made sandwiches for Harry because his wife rarely cooked, and Harry complained to Orazio that he was always hungry. He worked two jobs, sometimes three, trying to pay all of the bills. Once after eating some hearty homemade beef soup at our home, he asked me to give his wife the recipe. I did, but when she realized that she had to cut up the vegetables, she simply said, "That's too much work for me." Several times she asked me to pay for her dry cleaning, but she never paid me back. I was one of the few women in that subdivision that had a career.

I remember the first party we were invited to attend before we had Stephen. At first, the evening was very pleasant. We snacked, played cards, and then charades. Later the men threw their keys on the floor. Orazio didn't. He wanted to know why. Then one of the men told him they were going to dive into the pile to get someone else's keys. They would then go home with the wife of the owner of the keys. Orazio refused, and I had no intention of staying. We left, and we never accepted another invitation. Nevertheless, a few of the couples still came to our home some evenings just to visit.

However, several weeks later, four of the women came to visit me one Saturday morning. They seemed to be quite serious. Each of them had a business card of a therapist or a psychologist. They told me that I was keeping Orazio from attending the parties and having a good time. They believed I needed help. I didn't; they did. I discovered that they entertained the Omar Bread man after his morning deliveries when they invited me to have breakfast with them. They were the first of the "desperate housewives." Most of them were ten years younger than I and had at least two or three children. Some were having affairs, and I knew about them because they had confided in me.

Unfortunately some of their behavior ended in tragedy when one of the men who lived about three houses away from ours, and often visited us with his wife, hanged himself, leaving the garage door open so that his wife, who had left after a violent argument, would find him when she returned.

Orazio and I were asleep and heard neither the siren of the ambulance nor the commotion made by many other people who were in the street when they saw the flashing lights from the cars of two police officers who had followed her home because she was driving erratically. Our bedroom was to the back of our home, and all we heard was a loud noise coming from our family room. I got up to check the noise and found only that a large painting in our family room had fallen to the floor. I didn't see the police cars from the window of our front door, nor did I hear the screams. I heard about the incident the next morning from one of the secretaries when I arrived at work and asked me about it. Nevertheless, there were always marital problems with some of the younger couples.

Sometimes Joanne, whose home was to the right of ours, would have her children wait for me when they returned from school until I got home from work. Many times I would find the children sitting on the stoop. At first I didn't know why they were there, but the oldest said, "Mama told us to stay with you until she gets home." I later learned through Janet that she and another woman were having affairs in the afternoons with two young men that worked at a motel. Meanwhile, Harry and Laura divorced following an enraged argument. Harry broke the sink in the bathroom, destroyed the chandelier in the entry hall, and trashed the kitchen. I had no idea what married life was like for the other couples. I didn't seem to have anything in common with the younger women, and I was not always comfortable speaking with them. I only knew that both the men and women were unhappy.

If I went grocery shopping alone on Saturday mornings, while Orazio did some yard work, several of the women would go to my home as soon as I left, wanting something they claimed they needed: a Brillo pad, a couple of eggs, a cup of sugar, a few slices of bread, or a pound of spaghetti. But they seldom left. They would still be there sitting in the kitchen with Orazio when I returned, drinking coffee, and eating toast or graham crackers. A few times they stayed for lunch, inviting their husbands to join them. Shortly after those episodes, Orazio decided that we should leave the house on Saturday mornings to go grocery shopping together. It was only then that no one needed anything. Yet, there were other requests. Sometimes the women would ask me to drive them in the evening to the frozen custard stand for a cone, but they really just wanted to "hang out" with other young men and women there. I drove them only once, and when I learned what they really wanted, I never took them again. Another time they begged me to go grocery shopping with them so that we could "bond together." This time Laura wanted me to pay for her groceries because she didn't have enough money. I simply refused, and I was never asked again.

Joanne's Saturday morning visits and social invitations to Orazio and me were more than just wanting to borrow an item or invite us to some event. She was becoming infatuated with Orazio. All the signs were there. She was having serious marital problems and was considering a divorce. I was ill in bed one day, shortly before our son was born. She came to visit and to tell me that she was in love with Orazio, wanted to marry him, and asked me to give him a divorce that he had not asked me for. I said, "Look, Joanne, I know my husband well. He may wine and dine you, might even romance you, but he won't leave me and not just because I am pregnant." I remembered Orazio's brother's letters about Orazio making a mistake. It all came to a head one afternoon a few months later while I was wheeling Stephen down the block in his carriage. I noticed that Harriet, another neighbor, had her arm bandaged. I had babysat her son several times, and I had tutored her husband because he was in danger of losing his new promotion. His new position required that he write proposals and results of experiments, but one of his superiors told him that the papers had many dangling modifiers, thus obscuring the meaning. I stopped to ask her if she was all right.

She said, "Who told you?"

I answered, "No one told me anything. I just saw the bandage. Your arm is bandaged. It's in a sling."

By the time I had walked around the block, Joanne had spoken with Orazio, accusing me of having a "big mouth" after Harriet had telephoned her. I couldn't understand why Orazio was angry with me. Obviously he had known whatever had happened to Harriet, but he had never told me. I tried to explain, but he defended Joanne. I was very hurt. Was he having an affair with Joanne? But when? Neither he nor Joanne had a car at that time. He no longer went out to lunch because the owner of the new company he worked for had lunch delivered for the men who worked there. Orazio was always either at home after work because I picked him up from the train station or at work. He also wasn't a very good liar. A week later, I told him that since it was summer, I was going to visit my parents with our son for a while. I added, "You need to decide what it is you want." He was very quiet. He drove us to the airport, came into the plane to make sure we were settled, and snapped a picture with my camera of Stephen and me sitting in the plane. He kissed us both and left.

During the two months I was away, he telephoned frequently and wrote many letters, almost every other day. He missed us, he was lonely, he accidentally bleached a load of his clothes and ruined them all, he bought tuna for cats instead of for people, and he never loved anyone but me. The first week of August he drove to Pennsylvania to take us home. I had never told my parents why I had left him for so long that summer. He cried when he saw us and said, "Don't ever leave me again. You and Stephen are my life. I can't live without you two." Joanne did get a divorce and later married someone else who lived in the neighborhood. As a matter of fact, there were a number of divorces that occurred during those years that we lived in Wheeling. We were very happy that we became close friends with two other couples nearer our age, Dorothy and Nate, and Polly and Chuck, who were happily married with strong family values, and life for us once more became tranquil. It was now time that Stephen met his *Nonna Elvira*.

 London

We settled on a date for our second trip to Italy, but we decided that first we would spend five days in London and five days in Paris before going to Catania. It had been four years since we had been there, and I wanted Stephen to meet his Italian family, especially his *Nonna*. We arrived in London, but our luggage didn't. We learned that it was sent to China and then back to the O'Hare Airport in Chicago, but no one knew where it was at that time. A representative from TWA took us out shopping for a few clothes but not enough for ten days. Most of the time Orazio was at the airport checking the baggage department, and Stephen and I went sightseeing to a nearby historical museum or to see other landmarks. We decided to make the best of a bad situation. At times Orazio joined us, and we did more sightseeing. Several days later we were evicted from the hotel because we "looked suspicious." Personnel at the hotel assumed we would just leave one day without paying since we had only one small carry-on bag and no other luggage. Once more the representative from TWA had to intervene on our behalf. He assured the hotel manager that we really had lost the luggage, and even their office tried to locate it, but they couldn't find it. Hotel personnel had no idea how difficult the visit was for us.

Not having changes of clothing was a real problem. The day we went to the Palace to see the changing of the guards it rained and rained, and we were soaked. We had to send our clothes that we were wearing to the laundry. Since I had only one dress, I had to stay in the hotel room and wear a robe until the laundry was returned. We had been given a budget of only two hundred dollars for clothes for the three of us; that amount wasn't enough money for me to buy another dress other than the black shirtdress I was wearing when I left the Chicago airport. Instead, I decided to buy a robe, and I was glad I had. We left London after five days, hoping the luggage would be in Paris. It wasn't, but at least it didn't rain. Once more we just decided to make the best of an unexpected situation.

Paris

At the Paris airport we hired a driver of a small black limousine to take us to our hotel. On the way there he happened to see his eight-year-old son Luc with his backpack standing on a street corner. He asked us if he could pick him up and take him home because he was coming from school. Orazio said, "No problema." Luc had been entertaining Stephen in the back seat, and his father, Jean, mentioned that he was also a guide. We decided to hire him for the next day so we could visit the Bastille and see other attractions. The next morning Jean divulged that his son was not attending school but was on a summer vacation. His wife worked, and there was no one to take care of Luc, and Jean had to find ways to take care of him. Would we mind he came with us? We had no objections.

At the end of that day, I told Orazio that he should pay Jean before we got out of the limousine, but Jean said, "We'll settle later. I'm sure that you would like to see more of Paris and the surrounding areas. Besides my brother-in-law is a chef at an excellent restaurant near a small park. I can take you there for an early dinner, and after your son eats, Luc can play in the park with him. Children get restless easily." For the next four days Jean drove us all over Paris, stopping to visit museums, historical landmarks, and the countryside. We did go to the restaurant that Jean had told us about. His brother-in-law Philippe specialized in sauces for broiled steak. We invited Jean and Luc to eat with us, but Philippe suggested that he pack a small basket for Luc and Stephen, and they could eat at one of the vacant tables outside. We were hesitant, but Jean assured us that we could see the boys from our table near the window, and Luc was very responsible. Because it was early, the restaurant had very few customers, and the four of us were able to get acquainted. The steak sauce was delicious, and we enjoyed our dinner and the time with the men. Both Frenchmen spoke English fluently. We kept our eyes on Luc and Stephen because the park was within our sight. At the end of each day Orazio wanted to pay Jean, but he kept saying, "We'll settle later."

When we went to lunch, we always invited Jean and Luc to eat with us. I remember that I had ordered a side of spaghetti with octopus, but I wasn't expecting it to be topped with the ink of the octopus. I set it aside, saying, "I don't think I'll eat that." Luc had brought a sandwich and some fruit that day, but he told his father that it was a shame that the spaghetti would just be wasted. Since I wasn't going to eat it, I asked Luc if he wanted it. He first looked at his father, who nodded, and Luc devoured the spaghetti. Luc thought it was delicious. He also ate his sandwich and shared the fruit with Stephen. I was worried about Orazio's paying Jean, but for Jean, it was always "later." When Orazio and I went to the top of the Eiffel Tower, Luc and Jean stayed in the park taking care of Stephen. Luc had brought a couple of his toys with him that day to entertain Stephen. I never stood close to the front of the tower but stood at the back. Once more I was terrified of the height. When we got into the limousine to return to the hotel, Jean said he would drive us to the airport the next morning. Would we mind if we shared the limousine with another client who was leaving at the same time as we? We had no objections.

At the airport, the other couple left first. They paid their portion of the trip and left. When we arrived at the Alitalia entrance, Jean and Orazio took our luggage inside. I glanced at the men as I was helping Stephen out of the limousine, and I saw Orazio was having a heated discussion with Jean. All I could think about was the bill. I figured it was astronomical. We would have to pay it. Finally, Orazio came over and said, "He won't take any money."

I answered, "What do you mean he won't take any money? We hired him."

Orazio tried to explain, "Jean said that we were the only clients to pay for their lunches each day, and we had no objection to his son's being in the limousine with us."

Now and then Orazio would give Luc some American coins he still had, and once he gave him a dollar "for your expert baby sitting service." Jean told Orazio, "I just considered these few days were our vacation. I enjoyed myself. So did Luc." Finally, at our instance, Jean accepted a very small amount of money for his son.

Leaving Paris, we knew that we would have a long flight ahead of us. We had to change airlines to fly first to Rome and then to Catania. As luck would have it, the president of Alitalia was on board with us on the flight to Rome. He was very engaging, talking with the passengers as he went up and down the aisles. As he did he accidentally tripped Orazio, who fell down as he was going to the restroom. He helped Orazio up, spoke with him, making sure he wasn't hurt, and then gave him his business card saying, "If you have any trouble on your trip to Rome or Catania, use my card. I will be happy to help you." Later during the flight, he spoke with Orazio again, who mentioned our lost luggage. He gave Orazio the name of someone to contact at the airport's Lost Baggage Department who could help us and asked Orazio to use the card he gave him.

We had the same experience our guide with Antonio in Rome as we did with Jean the first time I visited the city in 1961. Antonio took us everywhere tourists visit: the Fountain of Trevi, the Roman Forum, the Coliseum, the Villa Borghese, the Apian Way, and many other historical sites during the days we were in Rome, including a well-known nightclub near The Seven Hills of Rome. When he drove us to the airport, he refused payment. He, too, said, "I never take a vacation. This one, driving with you two, was mine." That same year a university student in Venice, who served as our guide and had been recommended to us by one of the hotel administrators, refused his fee. Fabrizio told us that he never had American tourists who not only paid for his lunch and dinner but also walked with him instead of in front or in back of him. Orazio spoke several languages as well as most of the Italian dialects, and Fabrizio enjoyed speaking his dialect with Orazio for a few minutes. There was no pretence with Orazio. He was very personable, genuinely interested in people, and never arrogant. The guides enjoyed being with him and didn't really treat us as clients, especially Antonio who sang Italian songs with Orazio as we were driving along the Apian Way. At least Antonio could sing.

Long after we returned to America, Orazio and I often recalled the night we went with Antonio to the Seven Hills of Rome to a nightclub that was frequented by beautiful call girls. Antonio had mentioned that those girls lived in a hotel nearby and earned a lot of money. Orazio began talking with two men seated at a table next to ours. Being Orazio, he joined the two tables so he could converse easily. One of the men was an elderly handicapped gentleman. The other man was his nephew, Dario, who said he was 28 and was usually the one who accompanied his uncle to nightclubs to watch the entertainment. Because of the uncle's handicap, he seldom went out, and he did look forward to watching the floorshows. While we were getting acquainted, we all noticed a young woman circulating the club, stopping at tables to speak to some of the young men. The entertainment had ended, and only the orchestra was playing as a few couples were still dancing. Many of the customers, no doubt who were tourists, had left.

Mary Ellen Cipolla Grasso

Clerks at most of the hotels and limousine or taxi drivers usually recommended to tourists the Seven Hills of Rome as a night stop known for excellent cuisine, dancing, and entertainment.

It was obvious that she hadn't connected with anyone before coming to our table. She ignored Antonio and Orazio, but set her sights on Dario, flirting with him, caressing his arm and shoulder, and suggesting that they dance. When he didn't respond, she began her routine with the uncle, who was starting to fall asleep. I wasn't sure how old he was, but I judged him to be in his seventies. For me, the attention she gave him became embarrassing as she sat on his lap, whispering in his ear while trying to awaken him.

She even begged and said aloud, "Look, I have to make money tonight. The man standing near the bar expects me to do so."

Finally, Orazio, who could no longer keep quiet, said, "*Signorina*, don't you see that the gentlemen are not going to bed with you. One is not interested, and other can't perform. Just leave. Tonight is not your night. Understand?"

I was not the only one surprised by Orazio's brazen remarks, but so were Antonio and Dario. And the girl? She scurried away.

Catania, Sicily

When we arrived in Rome, Orazio did contact the Head of the Luggage Department who was able to find our luggage. Unfortunately, two of the pieces, made of canvas, had been slashed. Upon investigation, we found that Orazio's two new suits were gone. All of the gifts we had brought for the women, such as nylon stocking, nylon slips, and nightgowns, were also missing as well as some of Stephen's and my clothes. All of the disposable diapers, not available in Italy, were gone. I had brought them in case he needed one at bedtime. Fortunately, he never did. Personnel at Alitalia, meanwhile, taped the luggage for our flight to Catania and gave us a check to replace the luggage. I was just happy that we had a three-hour layover to get that help from Alitalia before going to Catania and grateful to the president for giving us his card, which we did use. Several months later, after we had returned to Wheeling, Alitalia sent us a second check for the loss of the items, which we had filed in our report at Rome.

Our return trip to Catania was just as exciting as the first one. Once more, family and friends filled the entrance to the tarmac, waving and calling our names. This time I wasn't the attraction; it was the blond, blue-eyed two-year-old grandson, holding on to his beloved, but ragged, teddy bear. It had been picked clean of fur, and Mamma Elvira said that she would buy him a new one that very day. I tried to explain that he had new ones at home, but Teddy was his favorite. On our flight to Catania, Orazio had to "rescue" Teddy from a trash can where he had been thrown because Stephen had forgotten him on the plane from Rome and the cleaning crew just threw it away. Stephen was crying hysterically, refusing to walk a step further, when he realized Teddy was missing.

Once more a feast had been prepared for us. Mamma Elvira wanted Stephen to sit on her lap so she could feed him, but he had been eating with a spoon and fork since he was one year's old. I was always rushing in the morning, and I would give him his breakfast, but he had to learn to eat by himself. He was very proud of his skill to do so and kept saying, "No, Nonna. I eat by myself." She was very disappointed saying, "You brought me a little man, not a baby." That was another of the cultural differences I noticed. Stephen became quite ill with an intestinal virus, and Mamma took over, telephoning her doctor who made a house call. He prescribed a diet of carrots and rice and gave me a prescription for injections, which I would have to give. I didn't know how to do that so Gianni volunteered. After a few days Stephen was no better and tired of the diet. He screamed each time he was given an injection, which stung. A friend of Orazio's urged me as an American citizen to go to the Signorella American Naval Air Station in Sicily for help. There one of the doctors gave me a small bottle of Paregoric, an antidiarrheal drug used at that time without a prescription. In three days Stephen was well. Mamma Elvira adored her grandson, and in her eyes he could do no wrong. One morning he was eating a slice of bread with jelly and putting his sticky hands on the newly painted walls in the hall. Several times I cleaned the wall and asked him to stop, but he just went on. I swatted him once on his behind, and Mamma took a wooden spoon out of a drawer threatening me, "How dare you touch that sweet child. He can do whatever he wants here." In many Italian families, even today, children are pampered, especially the boys. As men they adore their mothers who continued pampering them.

The Letters

As time went on, I noticed the many cultural differences between the Italian nationals and the Italian-Americans, especially with Orazio's family and friends. I remember Orazio once saying, "Let me be the man at work and on the street, but the boy at home." I saw this demonstrated many times. Once the men came home, the wives were in control. The men called them, *"Gioia and Amore mio,"* and the women pampered them. During the summers the men in Orazio's family would have cabanas set up on the beach for their family, as did many other men. The cabanas were portable, and they surrounded the beach of the Ionia Sea in Catania. The various bright colors of the cabanas gave the beach a festive look. Used as a dressing room and a room for the children to nap, the cabanas were also a place for storing the charcoal grills, beach chairs, the children's toys, beach towels, and changes of clothing.

I recall how quickly the women and children got ready in the morning. The beds were made, the house tidied, and the beach bags and baskets packed for the day. When we arrived, I noticed that all of the children roamed the beach, playing on the water's edge. I was the nervous mother, constantly keeping my eyes on Stephen as well as my young nieces and nephews. Everyone else seemed to be relaxing and enjoying herself. Mamma Elvira and her friend took off their dresses and sun bathed in their slips. Orazio was snorkeling with a few of the teenagers, and I was running back and forth from the cabana to the beach and back again. My sisters-in-law, Fina and Pippa, and my cousin Tita wanted me to relax, assuring me that the teenage cousins would take care of the children. How could that be? Some of them were swimming or snorkeling.

When it was time for lunch, a few of the boys were told, "Go see what you can find in the sea." Others were sent across the road to buy bread, cheese, and olives as one of the women started the grill. I remember the sea urchins and the fish that were prepared

Mary Ellen Cipolla Grasso

for us. Lunch was all very casual: a hunk of bread, a handful of
olives, a slice of cheese, and some fish. I ate a sea urchin, but it
wasn't my favorite food. Usually the baskets from home had fruit.
After lunch, it was time to nap. The children were put to sleep on
the cots in the cabana, and the adults just sat in the lounge chairs
under an umbrella, napping or talking. The young men chased the
girls under the watchful eyes of their mothers and grandmothers.
I happened to notice the son of Mamma Elvira's friend, a young
man of about twenty years of age. I thought that he should be
working, not playing with some girl or another every day. I asked
the woman about her son and asked why he wasn't working. She
was shocked, "Oh, no! He studies very hard at the university, and
he needs this time to relax. He's just a young boy. His father and
I support him." Her eyes glowed with pride as she talked about
him.

Usually, the men came to the beach after work. Orazio would
spend many days with his cousins, his nephews and their friends
snorkeling, his passion, or playing cards. I recall so vividly the
return of the men from work whose first questions to their wives
were, "How was your day? How were the children?" Then the
drama started. The women would say, "Oh, it has been so difficult chasing after the children. We're exhausted. You have no idea
what it is like." I couldn't believe what I was hearing. The women
had spent the day laughing, swimming, gossiping, and relaxing. I
was chasing children. But then, I was even more surprised when
the men comforted them. "I know, love, it's very difficult. You
must watch them every minute. They can be mischievous. I have
an idea. Let's eat here. I don't want you to return home to prepare supper, especially when you are so exhausted." Off went the
teenagers across the road to purchase pizza, freshly baked bread,
roasted chicken, steamed clams, or whatever was available. There
were always cheese and olives left over from lunch as well as the
fruit. The men walked up and down the beach with their wives,

talked with friends who also were there, played with the children, relaxed on a lounge chair, and everyone had a very good time.

After a few days of this scenario, I asked my cousin Gianni about these rituals. He told me, "I know. It's a game we men play. Besides it's too hot to return home. Look how happy everyone is." He was right. Those Italians knew how to relax and enjoy themselves. That summer was enjoyable. At one point Mamma Elvira said to me, "Look at our women here. They have such a good life. They don't have to work. Why don't you move here to Catania?" I explained that I really enjoyed teaching. For me it wasn't work. The truth was that Orazio had made the transition to the United States easily and never asked me to move to Italy.

Home Again

My life in Illinois had become very exciting. I never knew who would be coming to dinner or who would be staying for the weekend: one extra person or four or maybe more. Orazio's letters never revealed that side of him. He wrote only of his love for me. I grew accustomed to having Orazio bring guests home unannounced. I recall that five years after we were married he telephoned me one Friday afternoon to tell me that two new technicians, Georgio and Alberto, from Italy were in the office. They had been sent to Chicago for one year as Orazio had once been sent to Milwaukee. Orazio asked me if Georgio and Alberto could have dinner with us and then spend the weekend at our home. I remembered Orazio's letters and how lonely he was when he first moved to Chicago and how much he missed having a home cooked meal.

Of course they were welcomed. I could always stretch a meal as my mother did when my dad or my siblings and I also invited unplanned guests for dinner. By that time Orazio had bought a used Volkswagen from one of our neighbors who moved to Maryland, so I no longer had to drive that extra trip to the train station because his car was parked there. The men came every Friday evening and left every Monday morning. Because Orazio and I wanted them to enjoy themselves and to visit the historic landmarks of Chicago and the surrounding areas, we spent the weekends just sightseeing or going to museums. Since Saturday was my cleaning day, everyone helped clean the house so that we could leave early. Neither of the men was married, but doing chores presented no problem.

Some weekends they preferred to stay at home, sit on the patio, and just reminisce. They were younger than Orazio and had not experienced World War II first hand. Orazio never mentioned anything to me about his war experiences, but it was during those times at home with the men that I learned he had joined the resistance movement, helping to smuggle British and American paratroopers into safe houses such as convents. He had, however, served in the military, according to the documents he presented before we were married and was honorably discharged. But then I remembered the photograph Mamma Elvira had given me of Donato, Giovanni, Orazio, and her. Orazio must have been about six years old. He is wearing a uniform of an organization that all boys belonged to when Benito Mussolini ruled Italy. The organization, called *Figli della Lupa*, was part of an educational reform movement much like the Hitler Youth Movement. Children were required to study composition and penmanship. Fascist cartoons and quotes by Mussolini were also part of the curriculum. Before Mussolini, there had been Boy Scouts in Italy, but the Fascists suppressed them. Orazio did remember the youth movement, *Sons of the Wolf*, preached nationalism and intolerance towards other nations. He even remembered being instructed to throw rocks at the synagogues and protestant churches. The name, *Figli della Lupa*, was based on the twins Romulous and Remus raised by a female wolf. According to the myth, the twins were the sons of Mars, God of War, and Princess Rhea Silva. The twins were abandoned on the River Tiber and found by a shepherd. Romulus, who killed Remus after an argument, became the first king of Rome, where the shepherd had found them on the bank of the River Tiber. Older boys in the organization wore a full uniform, but the younger ones, eight to ten years old, wore only the jacket and cap. That is the uniform Orazio is wearing in the photograph.

I did know that during our trips to Italy no one spoke about the war except when Mamma Elvira told me about eating grass. She said she would clean it well, sauté garlic with the grass, and then mix it with spaghetti. I also did learn from Zio Paulo that the family evacuated to Mt. Etna during the periods of the heavy bombings in Sicily once the American and British broke through. Their experiences were certainly far different from mine. No wonder Orazio never spoke to me about his, not even mentioning that one of his brothers spent three years in a German prisoner of war camp.

During those discussions with Alberto and Georgio, Orazio recalled our visiting Laura in Rome, a cousin of a family member. She and her father had joined the resistance movement in secret, not even letting her mother know. Every night she and her dad would leave their home, but never at the same time. Laura told her mother that she was working at various hospitals, rolling bandages for the wounded. However, neighbors convinced her mother that she was a whore, making money, out with a number of German soldiers who now occupied Italy. She and her father never returned home at the same time to avoid detection. On one of those nights, her mother was waiting for her with a large stick and beat her nearly to death, leaving her with injuries that remained for the rest of her life.

When her father visited her in the hospital, he apologized for not defending her. He knew his wife would try then to defend their daughter's reputation, but he couldn't trust his wife with the knowledge that he and their daughter was part of the resistance movement. The Germans would have killed his family as well as any other members of the movement. When I met Laura, she limped, and there were still scars from the beating. That day she and Orazio exchanged many unbelievable stories of the resistance movement during that period. Orazio never did tell me why he had joined the movement after he was medically discharged from the service, having been injured when a bomb detonated under water near the Coast Guard ship he was on. I did learn, however, that he took risks by buying olive oil for the family from the black market when the oil was nearly impossible to obtain.

Other weekends, Georgio and Alberto also spent a lot of time playing with Stephen or helping Orazio, especially during the Christmas holiday. They had never trimmed a Christmas tree, but they enjoyed helping Orazio select one, cutting it to fit the stand, and then putting ornaments on the tree. All three set the electric train under the tree and then played with it for a while. Georgio and Alberto both wanted to put the angel on the top of the tree. Shopping at the mall during Christmas was a highlight for them. Italy did not have a Santa available to talk with children; he was yet not part of the culture in Italy. We must have walked around the mall several times, making sure that we missed nothing: not the baby ducks in the pond, not the talking Christmas tree, not any of the other animated displays. Before they left Chicago, they bought a few American appliances, including a toaster and blender. We missed them when they left. Georgio and Alberto made that year special for all of us, especially Orazio.

We were now settled although sometimes Mother Nature played her hand in our life upsetting it. Usually I awakened at five o'clock in the morning to get ready for work and to take Stephen to his sitter's home. That particular morning, the sky was clear. I walked out the front door to get the half-gallon of milk that had been placed in the box on our stoop by the milkman. In the distance I saw a giant funnel rearing its head in my direction. I turned on the radio to hear the news and asked Orazio to open the trap door that led to the crawl space under the house. I looked out on the patio and decided to take the canvas lounge chairs into the house so they wouldn't blow away. I tried to open the patio glass doors, but I couldn't. I saw the swing set in the backyard that had been cemented into the ground fly out, cement posts and all, and fly away up in the air as though it were made of aluminum foil. Behind it was a doghouse from someone else's yard and a large storage shed flying up and away.

By the time Orazio opened the trap door to the crawl space, the tornado had left our subdivision, and all seemed quiet and calm again. But as I drove to work, I noticed that the homes on each end of the block had serious damage. Their roofs were destroyed. Other than our backyard, we were fortunate that we had very little damage except for a few cracked windows. When I got to school, I learned that classes were cancelled because the apartment building where most of the faculty lived had no roof, and the heavy rains had flooded their apartments. Many students volunteered to go there to try to protect the faculty apartments. Looters had already arrived.

If it wasn't a tornado, the snowstorms were brutal. Electricity was unavailable for a week or two at a time. There was no warm water because my home was an all-electric one. Restaurants were closed, so there was no way to eat a hot meal. Taking a shower or bathing was near torture: ice cold water. There never seemed to be enough blankets to keep us warm at night, and I can recall that once when we had no electricity, Stephen slept in our bed wearing his snowsuit. I was thankful that his sitter's home had electricity, and Marie would make sure he had a bath and three hot meals. Even though we left our faucets opened slightly to avoid a pipe bursting, I was shocked one afternoon to find three rooms flooded because the hot water heater in a closet in the family room had burst, and water was flowing out the door from our home into the garage. Only the fire department was available to pump out the very cold water, but every step we took there was a squishing sound from the floor as beads of water came through. Since there was no electricity, no fans could be used to dry the living room carpet, and Orazio had to remove it the following day so the wood floor underneath could dry.

Despite the fact that it took at least a month to have the floor coverings replaced, we had no plans to move from Wheeling. We had become intimate friends with two Italian couples who also lived in the Chicago area, and we spent many afternoons with them during the weekends at our home. Our lives now had a certain rhythm to them as we enjoyed the comforts of everyday living, and our love for one another grew day-by-day.

Our life was never dull, however. I remember Carmine. He too had been sent from Italy to work with the same company as Orazio. They became fast friends, but only once did he visit us at home. He married an Italian-American who worked in the bridal department of one of the stores on State Street. I met her only once, on her wedding day, and I thought they were ill-matched. She was American and followed the lifestyle of the country, but he did not. They divorced before their first anniversary. A few years later he met and married Miss Italy who was in the pageant for Miss Universe. They too divorced about six years later, but Carmine was heart broken. Orazio decided to invite him home every weekend after that because Carmine was very depressed. One evening, I suddenly woke up to hear the sliding glass doors in the family room open. I put on a robe and dashed outside. There Carmine was in his pajamas, running around the yard with a very large screwdriver he had gotten from our garage. He kept saying, "I'm going to kill myself. I'm going to kill myself."

I was running after him, pleading with him. Finally, I went to wake up Orazio.

I shook him, "Orazio, Orazio, come outside. Carmine is going to stab himself with our screwdriver. He wants to kill himself."

Orazio sat up in bed, looked at me, and said, "Come to bed. It's Italian drama. He's not going to kill himself. He wants attention." He lay back in bed and instantly fell asleep.

A few minutes later I heard the back door close. Carmine was back in his bedroom, and the screwdriver was on the end table in the family room. Carmine never returned to our home, but Orazio learned that he had finally accepted the divorce after moving from the area.

Unfortunately, the first of Orazio's many health problems occurred in 1964. He awakened one night with severe chest pains. I wanted to call 911, but he insisted it was just indigestion. By the next day he was no better, so we drove to see his doctor in Chicago who decided to hospitalize him. Orazio was having an acute gallbladder attack, and surgery was necessary. It was scheduled for the Monday after Easter. Orazio insisted that he wanted to spend Easter at home and wanted to be released. I spoke with his doctor and told him that, knowing Orazio he would not return after the holiday. Easter Sunday Stephen and I went to the hospital to visit him. We met him in the recreation room. He was in a wheelchair holding an Easter basket that parents could purchase from the hospital gift shop for their children. We had a very nice visit and Stephen enjoyed riding on his dad's lap or pushing his wheelchair. Stephen and I spent most of the afternoon with him, and Orazio finally accepted the fact that he would have surgery the next day, the first of many he would have to endure.

But who would have thought that an incident in 1965 would have been one of my most traumatic. It happened several weeks before Christmas. I had promised Stephen that I would take him to the Randhurst Shopping Center, the first largest enclosed regional mall. We would look at all the decorations, visit Santa, buy him new shoes and do a little Christmas shopping. He was anxious to

talk with Santa and be the one to select a gift for his dad. He had
never done so before, but at nearly three years of age, he insisted
he was old enough to do so. Randhurst was beautifully decorated,
including a pond with baby ducks swimming in it. I bought a few
gifts for the family, his shoes, and he selected a tie for Orazio's
gift. I was also carrying his small lunch box with a sandwich, a
thermos of juice, and a cookie. We sat down on a nearby bench
as he ate his snack. When he was finished, he wanted to go to the
Talking Christmas Tree he had seen earlier. As we began walking,
he spotted a candy store and asked if he could have a few chocolates. He wanted to carry the small bag of several chocolates that
we had purchased. As we continued walking through the mall, I
was holding his hand, but the packages kept slipping. I didn't have
a large shopping bag, so I stopped at the Talking Tree to arrange
the packages as he talked to whoever was operating the tree. I
reached down to hold his hand, but he had gone in a split second.

I called his name, but there was no answer. I started to walk
around the mall. No Stephen appeared. I checked every place
children were. Perhaps he was among them. He wasn't. I walked
in and out of stores. Someone gave me a large shopping bag for
my packages, but I had no idea who it was. I had Security send an
announcement over the loudspeaker: "Blond boy with blue eyes,
about thee years old, wearing a sailor suit, is missing. If anyone
sees him, call the Security Office or take him there." Apparently
no one saw him. I spoke with several of the Salvation Army bell
ringers. No one had seen him. I was frantic. Security had called
the Mt. Prospect police department, and an officer was sent to
talk with me. It was getting late. I kept walking the mall, going
in and out of stores. Was he with Santa? Did he go to the Duck
Pond? Was he where gifts were being wrapped? Was he in a rest
room?

Finally, the police officer caught up with me. He sat with me trying to calm me. By that time I was sobbing, "He's gone! He's gone!" Scenes flashed through my mind. I thought only of the worst scenario. I told the officer, "I can't go home without him. What will I tell my husband?" It was nearly ten o'clock at night, and stores were beginning to close.

The officer said, "You will need to come to the police station with me. Obviously he isn't here. He might have been taken."

I couldn't breathe. The lights were dimming as stores closed. I couldn't move. My heart was palpitating. Suddenly we heard footsteps coming down the quiet hall. A few shopkeepers were leaving. In the distance I saw a child running down the hall, carrying a small bag, and dragging a jacket.

I heard a small voice saying, "Mommy, where have you been? I have been looking for you."

Walking behind him was a store clerk who said, "Is this your son, the one in the announcement? I didn't think he was lost. He wasn't crying. I assumed someone from his family was shopping in our store. He was just looking at the decorations and wasn't wearing a sailor suit."

Of course not, I thought to myself. He was dragging the jacket. I scooped Stephen up in my arms, hugged him so tightly that he said, "You're squishing me." When I arrived home, Orazio had already telephoned Marie, Stephen's sitter, earlier in the evening who told him that I was probably still shopping. He wasn't worried until we arrived home, and Stephen said, "Mommy got lost." I was expecting Orazio to explode with anger when I told him what had happened, but he didn't. All he said was, "I wish I had been with you."

I never forgot that incident and years later when I was shopping at the Hollywood Mall in Florida, I found a boy about three or four years old roaming the mall and crying. It was the Friday after Thanksgiving, a traditional shopping day. The mall was crowded with children. No one seemed to notice the boy, but I was uncomfortable leaving him alone. I asked him his name. He said, "Kevin."

"Are you alone?

"No, I can't find my mom."

"Well, Kevin, do you see that man over there in a uniform with a badge? I'm, going to ask him where his office is so someone can find your mom."

I spoke to the officer, introduced Kevin to him, and told him that I would take Kevin to the Security Office where the usual announcement was sent over the loudspeaker. About an hour later, I returned to the Security Office, but no one had claimed him. Kevin was no longer crying and was busy coloring a book with crayons. I knew Kevin was safe, and I could continue my shopping.

We spent the Christmas holiday in Milwaukee with Connie and Dom enjoying their traditional Christmas Eve party and the excitement of Christmas morning when Jay, Lisa, and Stephen found that Santa had arrived.

Then suddenly after we returned home, there was another unexpected turn in our lives. Following a heavy snowstorm, Orazio began shoveling the snow on the driveway and circular walkway as the banks of snow on either side got higher and higher. It seemed to be impossible to keep the driveway and the walkway cleared. I had wanted him to purchase a snow blower the year before, but he insisted that the exercise was good for him. After the second week he began to complain about a severe back pain, making it difficult for him to walk and nearly impossible to pick up the heavy equipment at work for repairs. Finally he made an appointment with his the doctor who recommended an orthopedic surgeon. The diagnosis was a spinal disc hernia with a spinal deformity. At first he was placed in a removable body cast, which meant a leave of absence from his work. However the body cast and the pain medication were of little help. He seemed to be unable to do anything for himself, and I became his fulltime caretaker. It was then his doctor advised surgery. As fate would have it, I was pregnant. When we first learned of the pregnancy, we were delighted. But I soon became stressed. "Why now?" I thought. How were we going to manage economically: the mortgage, medical bills (without health insurance not available in those days), utilities, food, and other incidentals. We had wanted to have another child, but not now. Teachers were paid on a ten-month's basis unlike today when they may choose to have their salary divided into twelve months. I knew that I would have to take a leave of absence for the fall term, maybe for the entire school term. That would be a year without that income.

I was right. Orazio needed a double spine fusion, which was scheduled for April. The hospital was in Chicago, about an hour's drive away. Who would take responsibility for Stephen after preschool? Who would pick him up? I took a leave of absence for two days, and fortunately his teacher agreed to keep him at school until I returned on other days, which would be about 6:30 p.m. It was only for a few days. I couldn't rely on neighbors or friends because unlike today most families had only one car. For the next two weeks, I would visit Orazio only on Saturdays and Sundays, taking Stephen with me. Still the question of finances kept me awake at night, but I never worried Orazio. My parents telephoned frequently inviting us to visit them for six weeks or more. My dad suggested we close the house when the school term was over so Orazio could recuperate at their home and my mom would help care for Stephen. We agreed. My dad had asked me casually about remembering to pay the mortgage and when I told him that we had the money to cover the summer utilities and the mortgage and that I had cancelled the telephone,he just sighed, "Good for you." I realized then that he had insisted we visit them so that we could reduce our expenses. All we would have to pay was the mortgage as well as two utility bills: water and electricity. He had hoped I would do that, but he would never tell me to do so.

Those six weeks were filled with visiting typical tourist attractions. Stephen especially enjoyed the Idlewild Story Book Forest in Ligonier, Pennsylvania, with storybook characters such as Little Boy Blue and Miss Muffet and other life-sized models of fairy tales. He walked in and out of the Gingerbread House and the house of the Old Lady Who Lived in a Shoe. We went to Conneaut Lake Park where the largest natural lake is and where Orazio and Stephen were fascinated by the hundreds of fish jumping out of the water. Grandpa made sure that Stephen enjoyed himself on the rides in the Kiddieland Amusement Park, an attraction for families with young children. Stephen especially enjoyed gardening with Grandpa because he said, "Men have to work." Orazio found his sense of humor during those weeks, and I was no longer distressed.

Paty

When we returned home, we were back to our normal routine, what-ever that was for us. Since I was on leave, Stephen wanted to stay home with me, but I insisted he go to preschool at least for three half days. I needed time to decorate the nursery and just rest. How-ever, I never expected anyone from my past to enter my life again. I received a letter from one of Memo's nieces, Maria Rosa's daughter Paty (the Spanish spelling). I had received a picture of her in 1959. On the back she wrote, "Para Tia Marielena." This time she asked if we would sponsor her as an international student for one year so that she could learn English. I had received a booklet of post cards from Paty's Aunt Yolanda E. de Cabello after Memo and I no longer wrote. Yolanda signed hers, "Your friend." I had exchanged Christmas cards with Paty's family and her grandparents and I also exchanged Christmas greetings. I had never forgotten them, and I truly still held affection for them.

At the time Paty wrote me in 1966, I was pregnant with Susan and had taken a leave of absence for the coming school year. I knew it would be difficult to drive Paty to school every morning from Wheeling, but Orazio had agreed to our sponsoring her and suggested that he drive her to the high school on his way to the train station. He knew nothing about Memo or the fact that Paty was his niece. I had cho-sen never to tell him. Just before the fall session, Paty's father, Jorge Sevilla, brought her to our home. She lived with us only two months. Orazio, never having any experience with teenagers, was having a bit of a problem adjusting to a fifteen-year-old girl who sometimes left her snack tray under the bed instead of taking it to the kitchen. His experience was limited to only three-year-old Stephen. Furthermore,

I felt guilty because Paty could not partake of all of the high school experiences. International students need to live with a family that has teenagers attending the same high school.

During those two months, Paty made friends with a girl from Arlington Heights, Christy, who had met her in one of their classes. Paty needed to immerse herself in the language as well as the culture of America and its high schools. She had become familiar with Christy's family, and they invited her to live with them. Paty spoke with one of the school's counselors, a friend of mine, who came to my home one afternoon to tell me that Paty wanted to live with Christy but was afraid to tell me. I agreed that it would be a good move. She could walk to school, join a club activity or two, attend the basketball and football games, and just hang out with other American teenagers. However, we did see her often, and when we went to Milwaukee on weekends to visit Connie and her family, she would come with us.

I never asked her father about Memo, his brother-in-law, during the few days Jorge was with us, nor did I ever ask Paty about her uncle. Neither she nor her father had ever spoken of him while they were at our home. After all, it had been nine years since I last saw Memo. I do regret not giving Memo's gold cuff links to Jorge or Paty to return them to him. Memo had given them to me during that first summer because he wanted me to have something of his. His grandmother had given them to him on his fifteenth birthday, and I did wear them many times. Shirts and blouses that needed cuff links were one of the fashions during that period. I recalled the first summer we went swimming at Vista Hermosa. He wanted my sterling silver ring that I had worn for two years. It was my favorite piece of jewelry. I had never taken it off. I was reluctant to give it to him, but he wanted something of mine to keep close to him, so I did. I still have his cuff links somewhere in my home, but I don't know what he did with my ring.

Susan

Those events were in the past, and I now looked forward to the birth of our second child. In those days there was no way to determine the gender of the baby, and I was sure it was going to be another boy, but we were blessed with a daughter. Orazio thought Susan was "the most beautiful baby in the nursery." Instead of the blond, blue-eyed, calm baby I was expecting, she was full of energy with sparse black hair and very dark eyes. At nine months she walked. At ten and a half months she used her crib as a trampoline as she bounced herself on the crib mattress, catching herself on the railing with those tiny hands and flipping out of the crib. We could hear the sound of the summersault as she hit the floor and went scampering to her brother's room to awaken him. At a year old, she destroyed the Jack-in-the Box she had received from Santa Claus by jumping up and down on him, until he could not longer jump out of the box when the crank was turned. She had inherited her father's coarse thick black curly hair, his dark eyes that squinted when he smiled, his personality and sense of humor, his adventurous spirit, and his ability to socialize easily. She was the mischievous one, the *monella*. We never complained, however, about this feisty child we almost lost when she was two and a half months old.

Once more Chicago and the surrounding suburbs were hit with a harsh snowstorm during the winter of 1967. I recall that snow from the drifts covered the sliding glass door of the patio entrance. Our driveway must have been about two feet thick with snow, and the roads were equally as bad, for they had disappeared under the drifts. All schools in the area were closed, as were many of the offices in Chicago. I was relieved to be home on maternity leave. First Stephen became ill. I had managed to take him to the pediatrician before the storm really hit our area and able to get a prescription from the nearby Rexall drugstore. Two days later Susan became ill, and I noticed that she had trouble breathing. The roads had not been cleared, and I could only speak with the pediatrician, who said that he would telephone a prescription to the pharmacist. Since Orazio couldn't drive because of the roads, he decided to walk, more like trudge, the eight blocks to the drugstore with Nate, a neighbor. When they arrived there, they found only a high school student who worked part time, in the store. He was trapped, for he had no way of getting home, and he certainly couldn't help Orazio. It took Orazio and Nate nearly two hours to make that useless trip because they couldn't tell the sidewalks from the streets and at times turned the wrong corner. When Orazio returned home without any medication, I again called the doctor who instructed me to give Susan a third of a teaspoon of Stephen's medication. For five days Orazio and I took turns holding Susan upright at night, patting her back, diapering her face down, and also taking care of Stephen. By Saturday we were exhausted, especially Orazio, who for several days kept clearing the driveway and walkway with the power motor he finally had bought. As soon as he thought the driveway and walkway were cleared, another heavy snowstorm covered them. In one case in the area, a father had to deliver his child because the helicopter that was sent with paramedics could not land. It was bitter cold, but at least our electricity was functioning. There were other times that we had no electricity, and the water pipes were frozen.

Finally, when some of the roads in Wheeling had been cleared and passable, we took Susan to the emergency room of Holy Family Hospital in Arlington Heights while one of our friends, Polly, volunteered to stay with Stephen, who was now recovering: no fever, no cough, no other symptoms. Susan was x-rayed and found to have double viral pneumonia. The radiologist scolded us, "Why haven't you taken her here sooner?" All I could say through tears was, "We tried." She was immediately put under an oxygen tent. Needles with wires were put in that frail body. She was too sick even to cry. At that time there were sixty-six children in the hospital, most very ill. Because there was a shortage of oxygen tents, as soon as one child began to improve, the tent was removed and placed with another child. The hospital was staffed by one of the Catholic orders of nuns who had not left for many days, and they, too, were exhausted. Their white habits were dirty, but those nuns were efficient and very professional. A few mothers remained with them to help not only their children but also the other children whose parents could not make the trip, and we were all saddened by the death of the toddler whose room was next to Susan's.

Taxis were not available because some of the roads had not been cleared in Wheeling, and those that were had only one-way signs because snow was banked on either side of the road and covered one lane. I couldn't drive to the hospital, but I kept in touch with the doctor frequently, or he telephoned me. The news was grim. He told me to prepare for the worst. She wasn't going to make it. She wasn't eating, and she had gone down to her birth weight: seven pounds. Formula had to be flown in by helicopter for all of the babies, and the helicopters were usually late. I was so fortunate to have Orazio who was always encouraging me, giving me hope. Because the main roads were cleared in Chicago and Arlington Heights, where Holy Family was located, he stopped every evening when he departed from the train after work to check on Susan. Since the cars at that time had snow tires and chains on the tires, he was able to drive to the hospital and then drive home.

One of those evenings he found her lying in her own vomit. She was pale, not moving. He rang for help, but no one came.

He decided to take matters into his own hands and went to get clean linens from the linen room, but no crib sheets were available. He took one of whatever sheets were available as well as a gown, much too large for her, but it was clean. He took her out of the oxygen tent and crib. Holding her on his lap, wires and all as best he could, he removed her soiled diaper and gown, washed her, and put the clean diaper and nightgown on her. He then put her on the recliner next to the crib, removed the dirty sheets, and folded the large sheet to fit the crib. One of the nurses finally answered his earlier call and told him just to throw the diaper in the pail and the dirty linens in a corner on the floor. She checked the needles and wires and then left. Orazio rocked Susan until she fell asleep and then put her back into the crib, making sure that the tent was secure. When he arrived home, there were not enough words to tell him how much I loved him.

I finally was able two days later to hire a taxi to take me to the hospital. The hospital had a chapel, and before going into her room, I walked into the chapel, sat on a pew, and cried. I prayed, "God, if you are going to take her, please give me the strength to accept this loss. I don't think I can do it." I walked into her room to see this frail child with wires everywhere. I was afraid this was the last time I would see her. I called her name, but she didn't open her eyes. She was barely eating, according to the chart hanging on the foot of the crib. Mother Superior came in to talk with me and to tell me that the formulas had not as yet arrived. She, too, gave me little hope, trying to console me. I was determined to stay there until her soy formula arrived. My fear was that no nurse had the time to hold her while she was feeding. There were just too many children that needed attention. I telephone Orazio and told him that I was not going to leave the hospital until I could feed her. The helicopter did arrive finally at 7:30 p.m., and formulas were quickly delivered to the rooms. I took Susan out of the crib to feed her, but she had forgotten how to nurse. I did manage, however, to get her to drink two ounces although it took over an hour. I had to keep squeezing her checks so that she would open her mouth. Before I put her back in her crib and under the oxygen tent, I held her a bit longer and sang a lullaby, thinking it might be the last time but praying it wouldn't be. She fell asleep. I laid her in the crib and left with a heavy heart. Stephen was asleep when I got home, and Orazio had made dinner for us. He was the optimist, encouraging me, but we both had trouble sleeping. Early the next morning the doctor telephoned us. We were waiting for the worst. He said, "I can't account for it, but she's going to make it. She passed the crisis, but she is still very sick. Then he added, "I must prepare you both. Don't be upset, but she may be mentally handicapped because of the high fevers, over 104 F. Just have patience." But we were ready to deal with any other problem. We were happy that we had not lost her.

Despite the fact that it took her a month to recover completely, while Orazio and I complained about the weather, we still had no desire to leave Wheeling although we did try to sell the house in order to purchase a larger home, but we had no buyers. Instead, we had added an addition to the house: a large bedroom, a work room for Orazio, office space for me, and a 6' X 17' walk-in closet that had space for the sewing machine. Since we had no attic or basement, the closet held our winter clothing, the luggage, Christmas decorations, and any other item that needed to be stored.

We did go, however, to Florida during spring break to enjoy the warn weather while visiting my parents, who had moved permanently from Pennsylvania to Florida. At first, they had purchased a condominium to spend only the winters in Florida, but after traveling back and forth for a few years, they decided to sell the condominium and purchase a larger home. Stephen especially enjoyed the attention he received from my dad; since the months Susan was ill, he got very little. We kept saying, "Be quiet, your sister is sick," or "Don't go into her room." My mother spent a lot of time playing with Susan, giving her measuring spoons to rattle, small lids to bang, and we began to notice many changes. For the first time in months, she was laughing, banging lids, interacting with her brother, and trying to talk. It was though she had awakened from a long sleep. Orazio and I had taken the doctor at his word, and instead of stimulating Susan, we had treated her as though she was intellectually limited, but she was a different child when we returned home.

Orazio left for home, but I remained with my parents for another two weeks. During those weeks at my parents' home, I had an unexpected visitor. I answered the doorbell one day to find Goldie Ronk, my former fiancé's mother, standing on the porch. I had not seen her in years, and I was surprised that she would be visiting. I learned that she and her husband had remained friends with my parents long after Ray and I were no longer a couple. Ray and his family lived in Sunrise, Florida, not far from Oakland Park where my parents lived. Goldie had come to visit my mother. She sat across the table from me as my mother prepared lunch. I was feeding Susan her pureed meat and vegetables. Goldie mentioned that Ray had suffered a massive heart attack but was now well. He and his wife had two children, and she showed me only a picture of her grandson.

Suddenly she said, "You should have been my daughter-in-law."

I simply answered, "Ray had other ideas. He thought otherwise."

"You were too strong for him," Goldie answered.

We had lunch and continued talking. I mentioned that I was living in Chicago and teaching. That was the last time she ever visited my parents. My mother liked her and couldn't understand why Goldie had broken off the relationship.

I returned to my position at Arlington Heights in September, hiring a nanny for Stephen and Susan. Marie, Stephen's former baby sitter, had moved to Michigan with her family, and it was difficult to find a sitter who had transportation. I placed a classified ad in the newspaper and interviewed several women. I hired one, Abbey, whose husband was in Vietnam and who had a two-year old child of her own. She could take the job only if her child could be with her. Abbey also assured me that she would be able to handle all three children. She had suitable references, and I seemed to have no choice. I had to work to help with the economical situation. There was no medical insurance at that time. Besides, I always worried about Orazio's health. In addition to the two major surgeries he had during the early years of out marriage, he had had five minor surgeries during the past few years. One of those was supposed to be a simple procedure that any doctor could perform in his office: the removal of a small pre-cancerous tumor behind his ear. Dr. Lawson thought it would be a good type of surgery for residents in Wesley Memorial Hospital in Chicago to view, and Dr. Lawson asked Orazio if he were willing to sign a permission form, explaining to both of us that Orazio would need only to remove his shirt. He would have no anesthesia. The surgery would take less than a half hour, and there would be a short question and answer period. He would then be free to go home.

I sat in chair in the hall near the operating room, reading a magazine. Sometime later, I noticed a nurse hurrying out of the room and scurrying down the hall. There seemed to be a lot of activity as I saw other doctors enter the room. Another nurse gave me Orazio's clothes and shoes, and said, "There's a small problem. Orazio needs to be anesthetized and must be in a surgical gown.

Dr. Lawson will talk to you later, but Orazio's fine." I just looked at her, "Orazio's fine? How could he be fine?"

"Well, he has everyone laughing."

I was puzzled. This was supposed to be simple: cut, remove, stitch. I started to pace the hallway. Finally I sat down. About two and a half hours later, Dr. Lawson explained that instead of a small tumor near the surface, it was one that had long roots extending down Orazio's neck, and the roots were intertwined.

"Well, what was funny? I was told that 'everyone was laughing."

"You know Orazio. If he has an audience, he has to entertain them. He even had me laughing."

Orazio was home on sick leave for several days and told me that Abbey seemed to be a competent nanny. All seemed well for about a month with Abbey. Then I received a telephone call from a neighbor who told me that Stephen was outside several mornings with only his pants on. He was barefoot and shirtless. The fall weather in Illinois is usually cold at that time. She told me that she took him home and spoke with the sitter, who didn't know he was gone. Then I began to notice that Susan was always in bed with her shoes on when I returned home, also wearing a wet diaper. I asked Abbey about that, but she told me that she was just getting ready to change Susan's diaper, and she had put her in the crib while she was getting a small basin of water to wash her. Yet, the diaper pail was always filled with soiled diapers. I had a diaper service that was a gift from my parents, but I always seemed to be running out of the allotted number of diapers.

I noticed that the kitchen floor was usually very dirty, and dishes were left in the sink although I had a dishwasher. I questioned

Abbey, but she always blamed Stephen. She said that he wouldn't sit and eat at the table. Later I received a photograph of her child playing in the sandbox with Susan's stroller. No wonder it always had traces of sand in it. Finally, I decided that I would make an unexpected visit mid-morning on a Friday, pretending that I had left graded papers at home. I had an hour break between classes and got permission to leave. When I arrived home, I saw Stephen eating from a jar of marshmallow cream and Susan standing in her crib with her shoes on. Abbey was diapering her son with one of Susan's diapers. It was easy to identify them because all were marked with "Grasso." I was infuriated. Taken by surprise she began to cry, apologizing and giving me all sorts of excuses. I knew she would not go home until I paid her for the week. I just said, "I'll be back at four o'clock this afternoon so that I can pay you. We'll talk then." When I returned, I did pay her for the week as well as fired her.

All I could think of was, "How can I replace Marie? The woman Stephen called Aunt Marie." When Stephen was just an infant, she would place him in his carrier on the counter as she prepared dinner and explain every step to him, not that he understood, but he was fascinated by what she was doing and he watched her intently. Some afternoons when I picked him up, Marie would have tea ready, and I would sit and chat with her for a short time. It was then that I noticed how interested he was in what Marie was doing. I had no idea that Marie was spending so much time with him. When he was just an infant, I used to hold him on my lap while I was reading my news magazines. While he looked at the pictures, I would point to words in the pictures, such as truck, soap, elephant, telephone, and desk. It was the only way I could read and keep him occupied. Then I remembered that day when he was about ten months of age sitting in his high chair watching me prepare dinner. I didn't explain what I was doing, but I heard an impatient, "Tell me, Mommy." I knew that he had a large vocabulary for his age, but I wasn't aware that he used short sentences. "When was it," I thought to myself, "that he went from words to sentences?" I had just a few days to find someone like Marie for Susan and a pre-school for Stephen, not just a day care. Fortunately I saw an ad on the bulletin board in the supermarket where I shopped and found a competent sitter for Susan, Beverley, a former nurse who had three boys, two who attended elementary school. Beverley lived near the high school and enjoyed having a little girl to care for. She even made clothes for Susan and her doll. I then found an excellent new pre-school for Stephen at a church near our home.

The months passed by quickly. It was now late May, and Paty was getting ready to leave in June to return to Mexico. Connie came to say goodbye and give Paty a gift she had bought. Paty came with Christy to see Connie. We had given Paty a camera and film for Christmas, and she wanted to take pictures of everyone she knew. I was sorry to see her leave because I had not spent as much time with her as I would have liked.

I corresponded with her now and then until 1969 when she sent me a record she and her three brothers, Oswaldo, Kiko (Ricardo), and Jorge, known as *Los Hermanos Sevilla*, had recorded for a record company, and then I never heard from her again. My life was a road filled with twists and turns, and the next road was one that was totally unexpected and one that changed our lives.

An Unexpected Move

In June of 1968 I had to resign my teaching position at the high school because Stephen would be entering kindergarten, which unfortunately was held for only a half day. I never considered taking a leave of absence for a year because there were no private kindergartens in that area that had after school care. Neither were we able to hire a sitter who was willing to take Stephen from his elementary school to our home for just four hours in the afternoon. I did have an excellent sitter for Susan, but Beverly lived in Arlington Heights, just a few blocks away from the high school and didn't have a car to pick up Stephen from the Wheeling kindergarten. It was for those reasons that I felt I had to resign. Orazio and I never considered leaving the Wheeling school district. But, that all changed July of that year when we decided to fly to Ft. Lauderdale, Florida, to visit my parents who now lived there permanently. Orazio stayed for only two weeks before returning home. I planned to stay two weeks more and then fly home with the children.

My colleagues had asked me to visit Nova High School, a public school in Broward County because the school had been featured in *Life* magazine and was considered to be on the cutting edge of new educational techniques. My father drove me to the area although he was not really acquainted with Davie, the neighborhood where the school was located in a larger area called University Park. Not only was the high school located there, but also Nova University and the Junior College of Broward County. Davie was a small rural town with a Western motif. University Park was just acres of sand and buildings. I believed I was entering Nova High

The Letters

School when I saw a building that had a prominent sign: "Administration." There was no other identification. I walked into the building and stopped at the receptionist's desk where I was given a paper to fill out. I was quite impressed. I thought that Nova was taking a survey to see what effect the article in the magazine had on readers nationwide. I completed the first page of questions about where I lived, my occupation, the school and colleges I had attended, my interests and activities, and other personal questions. I thought, "This is some inclusive survey." I turned the paper over and continued.

When I came to the question, "How many words do you type a minute?" I asked the secretary, "Why does the school care about my typing skills?"

She replied, "Aren't your here for the secretarial job?"

"Isn't this Nova High School?" I answered. "I just came to visit."

"You're at the Junior College of Broward County."

We both just laughed so loudly over our misunderstandings that the Dean of Academic Affairs came out of his office to tell us classes were still in session. We tried to explain, but he asked me, instead, to follow him to his office, and before the afternoon was over, he had me speak with the Division Director of Communications and the Department Head of English. While we three were talking, he telephoned the Vice President of Academic Affairs, telling him he had an applicant for the vacant English position and asked him if he would interview me the following day. I wasn't aware that the vice president had agreed and set a time for the appointment. The dean explained to me that an English position was available because the instructor had resigned suddenly to join her husband in California. He was supposed to be there for six months before being deployed to Vietnam. I told the dean I wasn't interested, but he urged me to keep the interview with the vice president the following day. I explained that I wasn't an applicant, but I agreed that I would meet with the vice president out of courtesy.

I attended the interview the next morning wearing a sundress and sandals, the only suitable "dress" I had for such an occasion. I was just on a vacation in Florida with two young children. During the interview, I explained that since I wasn't looking for a job, I did not have the required resume with me. Nevertheless, August must have been a lucky month for Orazio and me because I was offered a position after meeting with the vice president, contingent on my resume and references. I was also given an application to complete and then return it the following day with a photograph attached. I didn't have a photograph, but I did take one at a mall, four pictures for a dollar. Orientation for new faculty was August 14, just ten days later. I wasn't certain I wanted the position, but when I telephoned Orazio that evening telling him of the possible offer, he urged me to accept the position if it were offered. He told me that had always wanted to go to a warmer climate. Even my parents urged me to accept the position, telling me that while there were no public kindergartens in Ft. Lauderdale, there were private ones with after school care, including one near their home; and since I would only be teaching three days a week, Monday, Wednesday, and Friday, my mother would take care of Susan the three days I worked. Orazio took care of the children Monday after work because I taught a night class from 7:00 to 10:00 P.M. and chose to remain at the college all day on Mondays rather than leave after my twelve o'clock class. Doing so gave me a chance to grade papers and develop curriculum.

Once more I was convinced it was divine intervention. Orazio and I had tried to sell our home three years earlier because we needed a larger one, but we couldn't. Instead we added the addition to it. This time everything happened so quickly. I was offered the position once BCC's administration and Board of Trustees received all references. I left the children with my parents and returned to Wheeling for the Labor Day weekend to sign papers for the realtor and to make sure the house and all appliances were spotless because the house would go on the market the day after Labor Day. With my father's advice, I had bought a used Ford station wagon that had air conditioning and low mileage for $750. By the time I returned to Wheeling, I had already started teaching at the college, and a car was necessary. Since there were no classes on Labor Day, and I didn't teach on Tuesdays, I decided to return to Ft. Lauderdale Tuesday morning, giving me more time to make plans with Orazio. We thought it would take a few months to sell the house. We were wrong. The first couple to view the home Tuesday afternoon bought it immediately at our asking price. Three weeks later Orazio moved to Ft. Lauderdale, and we went to live in a furnished duplex I had rented. Our furniture was placed in storage, and on the second day that Orazio was in Ft. Lauderdale, someone from Kraynak Office Machines telephoned him, offering him a position. His previous employer had contacted the company about his moving to that area and gave the company our phone number. Orazio started work the next day and remained with Kraynak for twenty-one years, retiring in 1989.

The Move to Florida

Moving to Florida was the best move we ever made. I loved my position, teaching English composition and the traditional and contemporary literature courses. I served first as an instructor and then a professor for twelve years. I served later as the department head for eighteen additional years, retiring in 1998. My title kept changing. At one time I was Department Head of English, then it was English, Journalism, Speech, and later ESL (English as a Second Language) was added. As the student enrollment and departments grew, I kept shedding one department. I finally was just Department Head of English, and the college became Broward Community College. It is now Broward College, a four-year college. Orazio liked working at Kraynak and very quickly made friends among his superiors and colleagues.

For the first year in Ft. Lauderdale, we lived in two different furnished apartments. Once more I was commuting about thirty miles a day, and Orazio felt that we should purchase a home near the college because I had to begin classes at eight o'clock in the morning, and he didn't have to work until nine. My father, who was a realtor, suggested Plantation, fifteen miles west of Ft. Lauderdale. I must have looked at fifty houses in Plantation. None of them appealed to me. When I first mentioned to Orazio, while he was still in Wheeling and I was looking for a house, that the cost of the house I liked was in the Plantation Park subdivision and cost $34,000, he thought I had lost my mind. I do believe that smoke was coming out of the telephone, or the volcano had erupted.

He yelled, "That much? I said look for a house no more that $20,000!"

I just quietly answered, "Well, there's another one at $28,000. It also has four bedrooms. We'll look at all of the models when you come here."

Known as "The Dream City," Plantation became the site of our dream home. We bought the more expensive one because Orazio wanted a swimming pool and a circular drive in a large home suitable for entertaining. I wanted a self-cleaning oven, an air-conditioned laundry room, an office suitable for a library, and a third bathroom, all which were included in the more expensive and larger model. If we had added those items to the less expensive model, it would have cost much more. I didn't need to convince Orazio about his choice. Our move to Plantation Park was the best choice we ever made.

Right: The beautiful and be-loved Mamma Elvira the first time I met her.

Left: A vacation with Grandma Cipolla and Susan was transformed into a bubbly child, full of laughter.

Left: Steve and Grace in Holly-wood, Florida, in 1964, their first year as snowbirds.

Right: Susan, with Dorothy the "naughty doll" that went everywhere with her, and Stephen in Wheeling, Illinois.

Right: Orazio's oldest brother, Donato, who had many misconceptions of American women.

Left: The Italian technicians from the Olivetti company, Georgio and Alberto, with Stephen. They spent a year with us every weekend in 1963 and 1964. Two years later we visted them in Milan.

Right: Grandma Cipolla loved reading books to her grandchildren

Left: According to Stephen, all men must work, and he was helping Orazino dismantle an adding machine for parts.

Right:. Our "monella" who destroyed her Jack-in-the-Box on Christmas Day by jumping up and down on it.

Left: We spent many summers with our sister-in-law Fina and her two children, Gino and Lino in Catania, Sicily.

Left: Orazio with his brother Giovanni on our last trip to Italy in 1997.

Bottom: Our nephew Lino receiving a trophy for water polo.

Right: Susan's first trip to Italy having her portrait panted in Venice.

Left: Mamma Elvira with Giovanni, Orazio and Donato. The boys are wearing the mandatory uniform for the youth movement, *Figli della Lupa,* during World War II.

Top: Elvira and Pippo Grimaldi with Orazio on their balcony in Catania on our last trip to Italy.

Bottom: International student Paty Sevilla, Memo's niece, with her brothers, Oswaldo, Kiko, and Jorge in 1968. Known as the Hermanos Sevilla, they had cut their first record and sent a copy to me.

Top: Angela Grillo and Orazio who discovered that his child-hood friend from Catania and her husband, Carmelo, were also living in Plantation, Florida

Bottom: Orazio with the Dr. Pepper Challenge Trophy for his soccer team in 1978. The trophy was donated to the Plantation Historical Museum and Society after his death.

Left: Daniela LaRocca with her dad, Aldo, waiting for entrance into the church in Taromina, Sicily, for her wedding.

Right: Nicola Grasso, the father Orazio never knew.

255

Top: Tita, Fina, and Lino at home in Catania.

Bottom: Aurelio, Pippo, Nunzia, Elvira, and Giovanni visiting Disney World the year Susan and Joe were married.

Orazio and Lino had to wear red "sarongs" in order to enter a church in Sicily. The church did not permit shorts for men or women in 1980.

Plantation

Our life was never lacking interest, never ordinary, and always filled with excitement. But I never expected a large group of seamen from a Norwegian ship in dry dock to be invited to our home. I came home from work one afternoon to see the kitchen sink filled with freshly caught fish packed in ice cubes. I walked out to the patio to find some men swimming in the pool, some playing billiards, and some grilling steaks. Orazio cheerfully introduced me to the men, adding that the children were playing with neighborhood friends at their homes. A few of the men were happy to tell me of the gift they had brought: the fish piled in the sink. They began to give me instructions about scaling them, gutting them, filleting, and wrapping them before storing them in the freezer for "many delicious meals."

I just laughed. "Gentlemen, I'm not a Norwegian wife. I don't clean fish." Without a second's thought they said, "Oh, don't worry. We'll do it for you." They took the fish outside, placed them in a galvanized tub we had, and began to scale and gut the fish. In no time the fish were cleaned, filleted, wrapped, and stored in our large freezer along with the wild boar and quail friends had given to us. Then the men took the remains and planted them under our mango tree as fertilizer. Nothing was wasted. They even cleaned the tub, the knives, and the kitchen sink. I really enjoyed talking with them as they worked or played billiards. Orazio explained that every time the ship was in dry dock in Ft. Lauderdale, he was scheduled to repair all of their office machines. At times it took him more than one day. He added that the crew always invited him for coffee and for meals. His invitation for a grilled steak dinner was his way of thanking them. Orazio and I had an exciting afternoon and evening, and we and our children got to meet some interesting men and learn about their families and life in Norway.

But there were other interesting, unexpected times. Orazio was taking an evening class at the community college: English as a Second Language. One evening the class was dismissed early. I also had a class from 7:00 to 10:00 p.m., but I didn't arrive home until 10:15. There in the kitchen was the ESL class of about ten men that Orazio had invited. Someone had made Turkish coffee, and the men were sitting around the table drinking coffee and eating sweet rolls they had brought. Everyone was trying to speak English, but it sounded like the Tower of Babel. I greeted them, sat down, spoke with them for a half hour or so, and then left to go to bed. I fell asleep, but the party continued. Orazio's letters had never revealed that side of him, but I was easy going and accustomed to having Orazio bring guests home, many times not announced.

Once it was a Brazilian tourist he had met in Miami. They had struck up a conversation while both were visiting an attraction. We had the daughter of an Italian friend of ours living with us for a year to study English at the college, and Orazio had taken her to Miami for the day when he met the tourist. He invited the man, whose name I no longer remember, to spend the evening with us. We spent several hours with him enjoying great conversation, the espresso coffee Orazio brewed, and the cinnamon-sugar toast I made. When our guest returned to Brazil, he sent us a beautiful pictorial book about his country with a note thanking us for our hospitality. He, too, had a stereotypical image of Americans before coming to our home.

The Letters

Another time it was Luigi, an Italian Orazio had met in Chicago sixteen years before. They both had double spine fusions and were in the same hospital room with six other men who constantly pulled pranks on the nurses. One night they called a pizzeria and had pizza delivered to their hospital room. Then one of them buzzed the nurse's station for an emergency. The emergency? Join them for a pizza party, but the men were not supposed to eat pizza, so they invited the nurses who would look the other way. Luigi was vacationing in Miami and came to visit Orazio. It was a surprise visit. Orazio and I had just bought a basket of fresh escargot, and I was preparing half of them with sauce that evening for dinner. I would need to prepare the entire basketful for an extra guest, but I didn't have enough homemade sauce for the extra escargot. I did have a jar of prepared sauce, but I knew Luigi always said that he never ate canned or prepared sauces. I asked Orazio to take him out for about a half hour so I could add the jar of sauce with my homemade one. I modified it a bit and quickly got rid of the jar and label. At dinner Luigi declared, "See, Orazio, you are lucky. Your wife never uses canned goods. I know. I can always tell. This is the best homemade sauce I have ever tasted."

Aside from friends and strangers, we especially enjoyed entertaining members of our Italian families who came for a month or more, all wanting to visit Disney World. Lino, Maria, and their two children, Donato and Diletta, came for a month's vacation. The first night they arrived, Orazio was so excited that he burned the meat he was grilling, and I overcooked the vegetables. I heard him tell Maria, "Don't say anything. She's American." The second night I prepared a stuffed chicken dinner while Orazio, Maria, and Lino took the children to the beach. When they returned, I set the stuffed chicken on a large serving plate surrounded with roasted potatoes and carrots, but Lino was not aware that poultry in the United States is dressed before being sold because only live poultry were sold in Italy. They were in cages and the housewife would select the one she preferred. Lino assumed that I had not cleaned the cavity. He whispered to his children, "Don't say anything." When I opened the cavity and scooped out the stuffing, Lino asked if he could taste it. I explained what it was as he took a spoonful. "It's delicious. I thought you didn't gut the chicken."

He then told us that when his father, Donato, took them to the airport, his final words were, "Don't expect food like your mother makes. Americans just open cans and eat. You will probably lose weight, but just don't make trouble with your uncle." However, Maria and Lino didn't lose weight during that trip; they gained a few pounds. Chocolate chip pancakes were always a breakfast favorite.

Lino even ate Diletta's teething biscuits. I had bought several boxes for her, and I noticed that there were seldom any biscuits. I couldn't imagine what had happened. Did our German shepherd, Lady, get them from the pantry? She was known to burn her nose when she tried to take the lid off a frying pan of sautéing beef chunks when I walked out of the kitchen for a short time, and she once ate an entire Angel Food cake I had made and placed on the counter. I asked if anyone had seen Lady take the biscuits. I heard Lino say, "*Zia*, I ate them with my coffee. I thought they were biscotti."

"Lino," I said, "you read English. Besides, didn't you see a baby's picture on the box?"

"I didn't pay any attention. They were good dipped in the American coffee with milk."

What could I say? I just laughed. He had also discovered the American mug of coffee with milk.

The Letters

Years later, fifteen-year-old Diletta came for a year to study English at the community college on a special visa for international students. She was extremely intelligent and learned English quickly. Orazio did not allow her to date any of the American students because she was too young, but that never became a problem. She not only became immersed in the ESL classes and student activities but also enjoyed trips we took to Key West, Orlando, Disney World, and Miami.

We introduced all the members of the family who visited us to the American culture. Gianni, Tita, and Fina were surprised with all the sales in the stores, and Gianni was the first to take the flyers from the Sunday newspaper to read all of the advertisements, and "**SALE**" always caught his attention. On one of our afternoon shopping trips, he bought a dust buster for his home after using mine when they came to visit. He was delighted because it was on sale. He also bought a camera one day, and when he saw an advertisement that it was on sale the following day, Orazio took him to Kmart where he had purchased it with the camera and receipt and was quite surprised when he was given a refund for the difference between the two prices. Fina and Tita also could not believe that it was possible to return an item for a refund once it had been purchased, and the customer walked out of the store. We took a cruise to the Bahamas, and Gianni fancied two lanterns that he had to buy that he had seen in one of the shops. We had no idea why he wanted them, but he said he was going to make two hanging lights out of them by turning them upside down and rewiring them. I did get to see the beautiful lights he had fashioned from the lanterns hanging in his home when Orazio and I returned to Italy two years later.

They always teased Orazio and me about our drinking a large mug of American coffee. Finally one morning Fina said, "All right, let's taste that flavored water you two drink." A surprise look came on their faces as they began drinking it, and Tita declared, "It tastes like coffee." The supermarket they found to be amazing, but that was true for any of the family who came for the first time. They would stand in the cereal aisle just counting the different brands and types, and Gianni, Tita, and Fina were no different. Their favorite food was baked Virginia ham, pancakes, and waffles with maple syrup, and our thick cut porterhouse or T-bone steaks that we grilled.

Orazio's brother Giovanni and his wife Pippa came for Stephen's wedding, and his daughter Elvira and her husband Pippo, along with their two sons, Giovanni and Aurelio, came for Susan's. Rather than cook typical Italian dishes, I introduced all of them to other dishes, such as chili con carne, stuffed cabbage rolls, roasted turkey, and cream or fruit pies as desserts.

They also learned a lot about the American culture. I happened to be repairing the hem of a sheet on the sewing machine, and Elvira was astonished. She said, "I thought Americans would just throw it away and get a new one." She also was surprised to see my large sewing basket with all the various spools of colored thread, needles, buttons, a pincushion, tape measures, and other trinkets used for sewing or repairing items. Much of their knowledge of an American household came from our movies.

For Orazio and me everyday was a holiday, but there were days of sadness. One year we planned to return to Italy so that then three-year-old Susan could finally meet her *Nonna*. Susan was our *birochina*, a carbon copy of her father. The tickets were purchased, and I had begun to shop for the trip. We had invited Mamma Elvira many times to visit us, but she never did. Unfortunately, before we could leave, Mamma Elvira became ill. I urged Orazio to leave first because school was still in session. Alone he could spend more time with his mother. We had no idea how ill she was.

The Letters

Unfortunately, while he was waiting at the London airport for his flight to Rome, she died of a heart attack. When our nephew Gino called me in the middle of the night to tell me of her death, I begged him to try to hold the burial for another day even if the doctor had to post date the death certificate. The custom in Sicily then was that the deceased were not embalmed. Anyone who died in the morning was buried at sunset. I knew if Orazio arrived to find that not only had his beloved mother died but also had been entered in the mausoleum, it would be more than he could bear.

He was so distraught when he called me after the funeral that I wasn't sure he would ever come home. Meanwhile, I had cancelled the flight tickets for the children and me. I felt guilty about not being with him, not being able to console him, comfort him. I spoke with his brother Giovanni and my sister-in-law Pippa. They told me he was very depressed, still grieving, not certain he was ready to leave, not sure he wanted to. He wrote several letters, but writing nothing about coming home. Stephen wrote him a letter, telling him he missed him. Susan drew a picture. I telephoned him, but when I did, he just cried. Finally, he returned six weeks later. He was still wearing the black arm band around his coat jacket and a black tie when I picked him up from the Miami airport, but I was never embraced as hard as I was that day. All he could say was "Don't ever leave me." Would he ever be the same? He wasn't, at least not for a while. Many afternoons when he came home from work, he just went to bed. He grieved not only for the loss of his mother but also for the loss of his bond to Catania. Mamma Elvira was the one who kept everyone together. I loved her, and I still miss her. She always referred to me as her daughter, not her daughter-in-law, and her sons' wives could do no wrong. Anytime Giovanni or Donato would complain to her about something their wives did or didn't do, she would say, "Go home! Your wife is an angel. I raised you. If there is any trouble, it's your fault."

I recalled an incident she had told me about Giovanni. When Orazio left Italy, Giovanni moved into Orazio's home to care for his mother. After a number of years, he decided to renovate the kitchen. He removed the wood cabinets and marble counter tops and installed blue American Youngstown Steel kitchen cabinets, American style counter tops as well as new appliances. He then gave an order: "The oven is not to be used." For several months Mamma Elvira and Pippa avoided using the oven. Then one evening, Mamma Elvire decided to make pizza. Giovanni worked for the railroad and that day he worked the late shift: 3:00 P.M. to 11:00 P.M. Mamma Elvira, Pippa, and the three children, Nicola, Elvira, and Giovanna, enjoyed the pizza. Mamma had saved a large portion for Giovanni.

When Giovanni returned home, he smelled the odor of fresh bread. "Who used the oven?" he bellowed. "Didn't I say not to use it?"

Mamma faced him, shook her finger at him and said, "I did." He continued shouting. Mamma just said, "Go to bed," and he did without saying another word. She was so angry that she sat down and ate his portion.

The next day, he apologized and said, "Mamma, I'll take the pizza to work for my dinner."

She just looked at him and said, "I ate it last night." Not another word was said, and the oven was back in use.

I regretted the fact that she never got to see her granddaughter who resembles her. I loved Mamma's sense of humor, her smile, her strength, and her love of family. It took many months for Orazio to heal and for us to continue with our normal activities.

One was a trip to Mexico that Orazio always wanted to take, and we finally took that trip in 1982 with two of our friends, Gil and Joyce, who also were our neighbors. Our plan was to visit Mexico City and Cancun. From the moment we landed at the Mexico City Airport, I noticed the difference from the years when I lived there. The polluted air hung heavy above us as we rode in a taxi to our hotel. We looked out the window and remarked about the number of homeless people sitting or lying on the sidewalk. Sometimes it was an entire family huddled together. The taxi driver told us that many of those families had come from the rural areas looking for work, a better life, but often they did not have the skills for jobs that were available. This was not the Mexico I remembered and loved.

"Perhaps," I thought to myself, "once we begin to tour the city, it will be as I remembered it." But it wasn't. Traffic was a nightmare, and the once blue skies were now veiled by smog. The taxi was old and in need of repair, but the driver was pleasant and pointed out some landmarks for us. The boats at Xochimilco were no longer covered with flowers. Instead, the flowers were painted on the boats. The Zocalo was far more crowded than I recalled although it still attracted me. Even the beautiful Chapultepec Park had changed. There were homeless families there too. There were also other changes, some for the better. A beautiful basilica to the Virgin of Guadalupe had been built, but where once the cloak with the image of the Virgin hung at eye level, it now hung high above the altar and to the back of the church, behind the altar. I watched some of the visitors and members of the clergy crawl on their knees from outside the basilica all the way to the altar. It was a moving experience for all of us. As I stood looking at the image of the Virgin, tears began to stream down my face. Once more I saw the ill, the handicapped in wheelchairs or on crutches, and the parents holding their very sick children, hoping for a miracle.

Despite the disappointment I felt, visiting Mexico City once more brought back the days of my youth and unforgettable memories. Nevertheless, we four did have wonderful new experiences to remember, especially the evening we went out to dinner at a small restaurant. It was late, and there were few patrons there. A young man came to our table and said he would be serving us because he spoke some English and he wanted to describe the entrees for us. Orazio and I had already made our selections and were just talking between ourselves. I had ordered my favorite, "*capretto*," meat from a young goat, roasted on a large rotisserie. Gil and Joyce were still trying to make a selection. As they continued looking at their menus, they questioned the server who would describe each entrée. Now and then Joyce or Gil would say, "That sounds good. What about this other one?" Finally, they made their choices. At least they thought they had. Unfortunately, the server didn't know as much English as he thought he did because when the dinners were served, Joyce and Gil were served six entrees, not just two. The waiter kept writing down as their selections, the ones they were deciding about. He heard, "That sounds good." The table was filled with plates, and Gil kept saying, "Orazio help me eat some of this food." Actually only a few forkfuls were eaten from each of the extra four entrees. Yet, it's a wonder we ate at all we were laughing so hard.

Our server came to the table with the bill and asked us if anything was wrong. I tried to explain in Spanish. Orazio explained in Italian. Gil tried to explain in English, but it was useless. All Gil heard was "You ordered. You ordered." We just looked at each other and laughed. What else could we do?

One of the highlights was going to see the *Forklorica Dancers* at the theater. Orazio had press credentials from Italy, and we were able to get orchestra seats. I recalled all those afternoons at the university when I so enjoyed their presentations, and for a minute I felt young again.

We left Mexico City for Cancun but decided to go first to *Chichen Itza*, a well-preserved Mayan City in the Yucatan Peninsula. We were all interested in archaeology, especially in the El Castillo pyramid. It was 80 feet high with 91very narrow steps on each side. I thought for an instant I would climb to the top, but I quickly changed my mind. Gil and Joyce did climb the steps, but only Joyce went all the way to the top. While they climbed, Orazio and I went to see the *Juego de Pelota* (Ball Court) where an unusual ball game was played. There were two stone rings on opposite sides of the court. According to one of the guides there, the game was played with a hard rubber ball, and the team to score just once by passing the ball through one of the stone rings decorated with serpents was the winner. The losers were sacrificed. However, no one seemed to be exactly sure who was sacrificed although some guides that day said that only the captain was sacrificed. Orazio and I were told to stand at opposite ends of the court. Orazio whispered to me, and I could hear him. The acoustics were unbelievable.

Once we had toured Mexico City and *Chichen Itza*, we were ready to relax in Cancun. At that time Cancun was not completely developed, and not many tourists were there. As a resort, it was only about eight or nine years old. It had few hotels and almost no downtown. Near our hotel there were a several small shops that sold clothing and souvenirs. Both Gil and Orazio each bought a Mexican shirt, the *guayabera*, and Joyce and I bought some souvenirs. We really enjoyed just lying on the beach looking at the clear blue skies and the crystal water, and Orazio made friends with everyone he met. Leaving Mexico was sad for me. A part of my youth would always remain there. I was certain, however, I would never return.

As time went on, Orazio became connected again to Catania when he met two men who lived in Plantation who had once gone to elementary school with him. It was a chance meeting in a supermarket. I was at the bakery and he at the delicatessen. There were two women standing at the delicatessen speaking Italian and wondering about the quality of the Italian cold cuts. Orazio, who was also there buying a few Italian cold cuts, offered his opinion and asked where they were from. They were not from Catania, but their husbands were. All of a sudden I heard a yell. Orazio had found his friend Carmelo, and the two men were embracing in the aisle. They had not seen each other in years. World War II had interrupted their friendship. We met Carmelo's wife Angela and her sister Rita and later that day Rita's husband Franco, who also knew Orazio from earlier times. We all bonded, and Orazio felt as though a bit of Catania was now with him. The years we spent together as friends were filled with unforgettable occasions of great conversations, laughter, and exchanging dinner invitations. Franco and Angela have since passed away, but Carmelo, Rita, and I are still "family." All of us at that time made repeat trips to Italy because we all had family there.

On a trip in 1980, Orazio and I decided that Stephen and Susan should come with us. While we had no trouble from New York to the London airport, arriving on time and having a two-hour layover, we almost missed our flight to Rome. I never thought I would be targeted at random to have the contents of my purse searched thoroughly by a Customs agent. I was asked to go to a separate table and remove all items from my rather large purse. I had totally forgotten about a small leather case in my purse that held a Chemical Mace spray. I had purchased it for self-defense after a woman had been raped on the college campus following a night class. Once a week I taught a Science Fiction and the Supernatural class from 7:00 to 10:00 p.m. I never used the mace, but I felt secure just having it with me. Not that day, however.

The Letters

The moment the spray fell out of my purse, I was asked to step behind the table. My purse was confiscated. The agent called two police officers, and I was seated behind the counter in a wooden chair with an officer on each side of me. Scotland Yard was called. I tried to explain that I had forgotten the spray and the reason for it being in my purse, but no one would listen. I was told, "Please be quiet." Meanwhile, other passengers coming through the line were whispering and pointing to me. I expected that reaction from them, but not from Orazio and our children, who just laughed and said, "Mom's in trouble." I felt like a criminal. Even with the long layover, I was afraid that we would miss our flight to Rome. Twice Scotland Yard was called, but no one came, no one spoke to me, and no one else's purse was checked.

I told one of the agents that he could have the spray. I again tried to explain why I had it, but I was ignored. Finally someone from Scotland Yard telephoned, and one of the agents spoke to the agent, whoever he was. The agent asked me to speak to the caller. I was asked some questions, explaining once more why I had purchased the mace spray. I was then told to give the phone to the Customs agent who spoke for a few minutes. With very little time left to board our flight to Rome, the agent took the spray leaving me the leather case, returned my purse and its contents, and I was finally released. I was very embarrassed because some passengers were still gossiping. I could hear their remarks, wondering what I had done. Even worse was the fact that my children were still laughing.

We expected to fly directly to Rome, but there were engine problems and we went to Greenland. We were there in customs for about an hour while the plane was repaired. There was no water available for the passengers and no air conditioning in the room. We were not permitted to leave customs except to use a single rest room that was available. Fortunately, once we boarded the plane again, the trip to Rome was uneventful.

Once more family and friends crowded the arrival gate at the airport in Catania, and everyone heard that "Mom almost went to jail." Again a feast was held at the home of one of our intimate friends, Antonio Maffei, who had just had a book published of Sicilian poetry written in the Catanese dialect. One of Antonio's daughters had married one of our nephews, but Antonio and Orazio were friends even before that marriage. Stephen and Susan were able to meet all of their cousins as well as the children of our friends. I missed not seeing Mamma Elvira and two of her sisters. Only Zia Giovanina remained. She was the historian of the family, and I enjoyed spending many hours talking with her. However, the dinner at Antonio's house became unpleasant for me. I was meeting Donato, Orazio's brother, for the first time. During the meal he said to Orazio, "I was in dry dock in Tampa for six weeks a few years ago, but you didn't know. I did not want to telephone you." I replied, "Why not. We are only five hours away by car? Why didn't you telephone? We would have been happy to see you. You could have stayed with us in Plantation." I was shocked to hear him say, "I vowed never to go to an American woman's home." Orazio and I had been married for nearly twenty years by this time. What was he thinking? He added, "I know American women. They get up in the morning and have a large glass of whiskey and soda, and they drink all day."

I couldn't believe what I was hearing. Suddenly his brother Giovanni and Antonio stood up and defended me. Italians are notorious for arguing, standing up and shouting. Donato never stopped. He continued, "American women don't cook. They just open cans. They're always shopping alone. They spend money. They go to bars." I answered, "Have you ever been in an American's home?" He said, "I know American women. I see them at all of the ports." Now Orazio was on his feet. "They only women you know are in the bars at the docks. I know you. If you didn't want to come to my home, I would have come to see you. We haven't seen each other in more than twenty years. Not since we met in New York before I got married." At that point I left the dining room and went outside. I was crying. Antonio followed me and tried to explain that many Italians had stereotypical images of American women, and Donato knew little about American families. The argument had ended, and Antonio urged me to return to the dining room. When I did, Donato apologized to me, but the tone of what was supposed to be a happy evening had become a solemn occasion. As the days went on Donato warmed up to me, and the evening we had dinner at his home, he had accepted me as one of the family.

A highlight of the trip was the marriage of Melita, Antonio's daughter, and Rosario. Susan had chosen to stay with Donatella, the youngest daughter of Antonio, at the home of the Maffei's in Mt. Etna and join in helping Melita plan events of the wedding. Antonio decided that the reception would be held outside of his home. He hired designers to erect a tent to cover the entire expansive backyard and hired the entire staff of a restaurant to provide dinner at his home for the reception. Long tables that had been rented were decorated and placed inside the home so that the wedding gifts could be displayed. Since we were unaware that there was to be a wedding before we left our home, we bought a ceramic casserole that Melita had wanted and attached a note: "When we return to the United States, we will send you a set of stainless steel tableware, service for 12 with all the serving pieces." She admired the set we had sent her sister Maria and our nephew Lino, when they married, that was not available in Italy at that time.

There were no wedding showers given at that time. It was not part of the Sicilian tradition. However, Antonio and his wife bought the couple the furniture for the bedroom along with all of the silk linens for the bed. According to tradition, several days before the wedding, the young girls, friends and cousins of Melita and Rosario, were selected to make up the bed for the young couple. Until that night, no one other than Melita's parents had seen the bedroom set or the linens. However, the girls always planned a prank. Sometimes they would shorten the sheet or place flower petals on the bottom sheet. Once the bed was made, the door was opened and the young couple along with the two immediate families who were celebrating went into the room to admire the parents' gift. Toasts were made and once more food was served.

The morning of the wedding, all of the guests gathered outside of the church, waiting for the bride and groom to make their appearance. The bride and groom entered the church first followed by the ring bearer and the six children who served as flower girls. Then the parents followed along with the all of the guests. The mass was very long, and at one point Diletta, one of the flower girls sitting on the step around the altar yawned and said, "*Basta, Ssignore Papa.*" (Enough, Mr. Pope.") The ring bearer was standing next to the couple holding the pillow with the rings. Just as the groom tried to pick up the bride's gold ring to place on her finger, we heard the sound of the ring fall to the marble floor and roll down the long aisle. Fortunately, it rolled past Orazio who followed it to the end of the aisle. He picked it up and ran to the altar as the guests in the church applauded. The reception lasted until midnight, and never had I attended such a celebration. There was a never-ending supply of Italian food and desserts. The orchestra played both Sicilian folk songs and popular songs. Of course, many of the guests joined in dancing the *Tarantella*, the Neapolitan dance, and even the children danced with each other.

Two weeks later, Orazio and I began to make plans. We wanted to travel extensively with Stephen and Susan throughout Catania and Sicily as well as the major cities of Italy. We visited all of the places in Sicily that were considered tourist attractions: Etna, Syracuse, Taormina, Palermo. We were invited to spend four days in Augusta where cousins had a large villa, whose backyard was the Ionia Sea. We wanted to visit Grotte, the birthplace of my father. On our trip there we stopped in Bagheria, about eight miles from Palermo. Orazio had a friend there who had worked with him in Milwaukee, and he wanted to see him. Unfortunately, Vincenzo was away on vacation. We decided to stay, do a bit of sightseeing, and have dinner in that town. We had no idea that there was a Sicilian festival for the Virgin Mary that day. There were vendors of all types. Among them were those selling food, ceramic figurines, hats, costumes, oil paintings, and leather goods. There were also games to play. A choir of children standing on a stage was entertaining everyone, and we stopped to listen to them sing. Later there was a procession of men carrying a statue of the Virgin as one by one people pinned liras on the robe of the Virgin.

By the time we made our way to the restaurant that had been recommended, it was late, and the owner told us that he did not believe he had enough food for all of the entrees listed on the menu. I was the last to order and all that was available was spaghetti with olive oil and garlic. There were eight of us in our party because my nephew Lino also came with his wife and two children. I found Sicily to be beautiful. The land was filled with olive trees, grape vines, orange and lemon trees. The grapes were so large that they reminded me of small plums.

Grotte was a small town in Sicily near Agrigento, where the well-preserved Roman ruins are located. We stopped there to tour the ruins on the road to Grotte, where my four grandparents lived before coming to America, between the years of 1903 and 1908.

My father, who was seven years old when he came to America, still remembered the plaza where there was a church on all four corners, and he often spoke of them. They were there just as he described them to me.

We were surprised to meet by accident a great nephew of my maternal grandmother. He remembered that my grandmother was his godmother, and he was baptized shortly after he was born because my grandmother and her sister were leaving Grotte for America. Leonardo's father was my grandmother's brother. I might never have known he was related but he resembled my grandmother; and when he said his name was Leonardo Buscemi, I told him my grandmother's maiden name was Maria Buscemi. He then realized that she was his godmother, and her sister Carmella was his aunt. He told us that nearly all of the immediate families of my four grandparents had died, but a few had moved to France. He took us on a tour through the town, showing us the type of home my great grandparents and grandparents must have lived in. One house was furnished as it might have been in the nineteenth century. There was just one large room. A double bed was at one end of the room with two trundle beds stuffed with straw underneath it. On one side of the large bed was a baby's hammock hanging from the ceiling. There was a fireplace with several large kettles hanging from a metal rod. The table in the center of the room was a wooden one with a bench on each side. The only other item was a trunk, which we were told held clothing. About six steps down from that room was a dirt room where the animals lived. It was just as my dad had described it. I always wondered why my father never wanted to return to his birthplace, but now I understood. He had told us that his grandfather had owned a sulfur mine but lost it because he was a spendthrift. On payday he would go to a bar and say, "Drinks and food for everyone." By the time he arrived home, he had spent most of his money. My father could remember only a life of hardship.

The Letters

We returned to Catania, planning to tour Italy so that Stephen and Susan could visit the major cities. One of our earliest stops was the Amalfi Coast, near Salerno. It is one of the most beautiful and scenic coasts in Italy. Orazio had been there several times before we married, but I had never been there on any of our other trips. We took a short tour through the town of Amalfi, enjoying the view there. There are two other small towns nearby, Ravello and Postiano, but it was getting late, and we did not visit them until the next day. We needed to find a hotel, but most of them were booked. We did find one. It was located on the sea, but we noticed that it had not been landscaped because it had just been built and had just opened for tourists. We were able to get a first-rate room overlooking the Amalfi Coast. The sight was splendid because it was located on the sea. No food was available, however, because the restaurant was still not officially open for guests. We decided to drive along the coast to a hotel with a restaurant that was recommended to us by the personnel at our hotel. We ate dinner at a table facing the sea. Although I no longer remember the names of the two hotels, as I looked around, I was aware that the Amalfi Coast was a famous resort area frequented by many of the young affluent and elite Europeans.

We left the Amalfi Coast and went to Naples and Pompeii. Orazio and I had been there before, but this was the first trip for Stephen and Susan. We noticed that a new area was just being excavated. During that excavation, a family, now turned to stone, had been uncovered, and we were among the first tourists to view them. They looked as though they were sleeping. I recalled that on our first trip I was prohibited from entering one of the buildings because orgies were held there, and the interior walls of that building had paintings of those activities, but I noticed Asian women were permitted to go in. I begged the guide to be allowed to go inside, but it was not until Orazio gave one of the guides at the door a bit of money that I was allowed in. I really was shocked.

276

We skipped that building when Susan and Stephen were with us. Besides they were busy reading the inscriptions on the walls, some telling where a prostitute lived. We spent the day there before moving on to Rome. Stephen and I toured the city mornings and afternoons. I was anxious for Stephen to see as much as possible. Susan and Orazio went shopping because Susan wanted to buy a pair of leather boots, but we all did go to the Fountain of Trevi to leave some coins and to the Coliseum, which Susan did enjoy.

We left Rome for Pisa. Susan was the only one to climb the Tower of Pisa, stopping at every level to shout and wave to us. Orazio, as usual, fed the pigeons, and Stephen, the family photographer, spent much of his time taking pictures of the city, the historical monuments, and the vendors with their brightly painted stalls. I just wandered among the stalls and bought a book. I wasn't anxious to see Florence again, but this time Florence was totally different. It was clean, void of all the hippies on the bridge, and we all really enjoyed touring the city. I saw it with different eyes this time. Our visits to the cities were short, no more than a day and a half for each one. Because Venice was the site of a world conference that summer, the city had cleaned all of the canals. We toured the Murano factory, and this time Susan was given a small horse that had been made by one of the glass blowers during the demonstration. Our final destination was Milan where we had just enough time to get to the airport for our trip back to the United States.

Losing My Hero

However, nothing would shatter my life as the unexpected death of my father on October 17, 1984. He had a heart attack in 1968, but never had another one. We all assumed that he was well despite the fact that he had angina due to an inadequate supply of blood to the heart muscle, but obviously he wasn't. He never complained and was always active. He retired once for a year, and finding retirement not to his liking, he entered the field of real estate, later to become owner and president of Coastal Realty in Ft. Lauderdale. He had little formal education although he was brilliant. When he took classes for his Real Estate license at Broward Community College, he made the highest grade in the class, 99 percent. Here was a man who never played sports but never missed a television sports event. He and my mom watched baseball, football, tennis, and golf events.

I had gone to a conference in Tampa, Florida, and before I left, I visited him at the hospital where he was scheduled to have a procedure where a catheter would be inserted into the heart through a vein in his leg. When I returned two days later, I telephoned him at the hospital. He asked who had won the Pro Golf Association's (PGA) tournament. I checked our copy of the *Miami Herald* to tell him that Lee Trevino, the Mexican-American golf pro, had won. He wanted Trevino to win. I promised him that I would visit him the next day, but he mentioned that he was coming home about 9:30 in the morning. He never came home. Orazio and my mom did go at the appointed hour, but he was in a coma. Because my brother Buddy and his wife, Mary, were on the road driving to Florida for a vacation, they were unaware of our dad's condition.

Mary Ellen Cipolla Grasso

I drove to his home to put a note on the front door. *We are at the Plantation General Hospital. Meet us there. Connie and Dom are flying in from Milwaukee. Orazio will go to the airport this afternoon.* The day was all a blur. I returned to the hospital, sat in the family room, and wept quietly. I had a strong bond with my father. Connie and Dom had arrived with Orazio, and within the next hour Buddy and Mary were also there.

We never thought of him as being old. He was just 82, a husband, a dad, and a grandpa. For us he was the model of a young immigrant who came to the United States early in the 1900's, and he exemplified the best qualities of an American. His attitude towards work was unparalleled for he began working at age fourteen. He married young, and his concern was always for our mother. Near the end of his life, he fought death because he felt that no one could care for her as he did. Above all else, he loved his family, and anyone who ever met him knew his children and grandchildren intimately without ever having met them. It gave him great pride to name each child and his or her profession. Once he was asked why he had never taken a vacation to Italy or seen the wonders of America, for we were all convinced that he had subordinated his own desires to please his family. But that was not so. He said, "I never wanted to travel to Italy. You don't understand. I just wanted to see my children grow up and be happy."

As I sat in the waiting room, I wondered. How do we measure the success of a man? Is it by the wealth he accumulates in his life? Is it by the number of people who know him? Is it by his social and political affiliations? If so, then many men would never achieve success. Instead we measure the man in terms of the size of his heart, by his consideration of others, by his understanding and compassion, and by his love he demonstrates to his family. We also measure him by the love his family generates toward him. He was a strong, determined man, and his love for life was unexcelled. It will be with loving memory that we-his wife, his children, his grandchildren, his sisters, his nephews and nieces, and his friends- will always pay tribute to him. Several of my cousins have always said, "Were it not for Uncle Steve, we would have been desolate."

I prayed for a miracle, but there would be none. He lived long enough for his family to say goodbye. I couldn't. I stood by the bed as tears washed my face. My siblings and my mother were composed. I loved him so. He was my rock. My brothers Buddy and Ron and I made the entire funeral arrangements, and I thought I would be composed by the time the viewing was held; I simply fell apart as Orazio walked me into the funeral home. No one could console me. All I could say was, "I'll never forget you, Dad," and I haven't. Every time I see a picture of a deer running free in the woods, every time I see a rabbit hopping across the road I remember his love of hunting. When I see the United States flag at the polling site, I remember that he knew voting was a privilege, for he never missed voting in an election. Every time I see a high school or hear a high school bell ring or I pass the campus of a college, I remember him, for education to him was of prime importance. I remember him each time the announcer says, "Play ball" or "Round One," for he loved sports and never missed a high school football game. When a mazurka is played, and I see someone dance to the tune, I remember him dancing spontaneously in the kitchen alone or with Susan. He didn't need a dance floor. He just enjoyed dancing. Each time I see a father with a child on his shoulders, I remember when I was a child how he would put me on his shoulders so I could see the parade better or watch the Fourth of July fireworks. I always remember him a few days before Thanksgiving coming into my kitchen carrying a twenty-five pound turkey for me to cook or carrying ten pounds of Italian sausage for Christmas Eve to be grilled when we returned from Midnight Eve Mass. He loved holidays, and the more guests I invited, the happier he was..

A New Challenge

Susan returned to Italy in 1987 first to visit family in Catania and then to attend the University of Perugia. However, shortly after she arrived in Perugia, her appendix burst, and she never even started the summer term there. She had rented a room in a private home with two other students. The owner of the home had gone on vacation, but her son, Piero was there to manage his mother's affairs. We received a telephone call late one evening from Piero who told us that Susan was in the hospital. He explained that hospital personnel needed permission from her professor to operate. The professor had met with the students earlier that day, but he refused to give them his address or telephone number. He told the class that he would meet the students in the morning. We were helpless. I telephoned the president of the university in Florida to ask him if he had the information. He didn't. He told us that the parents should have an itinerary with all the information. We had never received one. Orazio and I were frantic. We telephoned Piero who told us that he knew where most of the professors lived and he would try to find him.

I telephoned the president once more, this time threatening that if he didn't find a way to contact his professor, the university was looking at a possible lawsuit. It was now two o'clock in the morning in Italy. Fortunately, Piero found the professor who was able to contact a surgeon who was ready to go on vacation with his wife. The surgeon's wife telephoned Orazio who said her husband was in surgery with Susan. There was not an anesthesiologist available on such short notice, but one of the nurses who was familiar with the procedure and had assisted one of the anesthetists several times volunteered to administer the anesthesia for the surgery. At 9:00 p.m. in Italy the surgeon telephoned Orazio, who received the call at 3:00 a.m., giving Orazio a complete report and assuring him that the operation went well. He told Orazio that they had to lift some of her intestines to "wash" them with a special medication. He planned to postpone his vacation until he felt comfortable leaving her with his assistant.

We had no way of contacting Susan. We did learn that she was operated wearing her blouse. There was no time to prepare her. Furthermore, hospital gowns were not available at that time. Out of desperation, Orazio telephoned the hospital several days later to ask the receptionist if he could speak with Susan. Little we did we know that there was no telephone available near her room. She had to walk down three flights of stairs because patients were not permitted to use the elevators.

During those years Italy had socialized medicine. If Susan wanted juice, the family had to provide it. Fortunately two American tourists heard about "the American student in the hospital." They went to visit her and brought several magazines for her to read. They asked her what they could do to help. She had no money with her, and she asked if they could get her some juice, which they did. Orazio and I were grateful for their compassion. Later an Italian serviceman, who heard about her, visited her daily, knowing she did not have family in Perugia. Piero brought one of his mother's nightgowns for her to wear as well as a cup and utensils for her to use since none were provided by the hospital. It was not uncommon for members of the family to provide additional food for patients since the food was limited. How fortunate we were to have Piero who kept in contact with Orazio.

When Susan was released from the hospital, she found that she couldn't take care of herself. Not all of the drainage tubes had as yet been removed. Once she had returned to the house where she lived, it was difficult for her to purchase food since students were either in class or on field trips although she did manage once to buy a dressed chicken that she prepared. We telephoned her nearly every day, but after nearly a week, she told us that she was leaving Perugia for Rome and coming home. We insisted she stay a few more days, but she said she couldn't. She got as far as Rome and fainted in the airport. Personnel advised her to remain in Rome and not continue the flight to New York. She insisted on leaving, and a young serviceman hearing the conversation came to her aid. He helped walk her to the plane and took care of her luggage.

Meanwhile we had no contact with her for hours. Her boyfriend, Joe, who eventually became her husband, went to the Miami airport to meet her. When he arrived there, he discovered she had missed the flight from New York to Miami. He telephoned us to tell us that he would stay at the airport until she arrived, and we three waited and waited and waited. When she finally arrived home, she was still quite ill. I noticed that the incision was very long: one side of her abdomen to the other. The stitches had not been removed, and the bandages were stained with blood. But she was home and safe. Nevertheless, she regretted that she hadn't attended the university in Perugia.

Orazio and I made several other trips to Italy, but I almost lost him during one episode in 1995. He woke up in the middle of the night, about 2 a.m. unable to breathe. I wasn't sure what was wrong, but I telephoned Gino to help me. I had telephoned a hospital in Catania, but I was told that the Emergency Room did not open until 8 a.m. and whoever was first in line was treated first. My nephew Giovanni, an EMT, came when my sister-in-law Fina telephoned him. But he was of little help. Finally, I telephoned the Sigonella Naval Air Station, about 50 kilometers or 32 miles from Catania. I had taken Stephen there in 1968 and in 1979 when he was very ill, and out of desperation, I telephoned the base. I was told that Orazio must have congestion heart failure, and if I could get an ambulance, they would take care of him. Gino tried several companies before finding one. There was, however, another problem. We had to take Orazio down the elevator with a kitchen chair because the elevator was too small for a cot. I ran up five flights of stairs to get a blanket because one was not available in the ambulance.

The attendant, an eighteen-year-old girl, did not have accessible an oxygen mask, just the nose tubes, and other than the blood pressure cuff monitor, there was no other medical equipment available. I also learned that the driver, also eighteen years old, had no emergency medical training. Since the gurney was only a canvas cot, I had to hold Orazio up so he could breathe. I sat on the wheel cover. Elvira and Pippo, pretending they were our children, sat on the floor because there were no benches. As Italian citizens they did not have a pass to enter the base. Gino drove his own car and followed us. At one point, we had to stop for about fifteen or more minutes for several farmers trying to drive a large herd of uncooperative goats across the road. I kept yelling at the goats as if they could understand or hear me.

When we arrived at the emergency room, a doctor and two male nurses were waiting outside with a gurney and an IV. They rushed him to a room and asked me to wait in the family waiting room. Shortly after, one of the officers accompanied me to the room where Orazio lay. He was speaking gibberish, a mixture of Italian, English, and Sicilian. The doctor told me that Orazio's blood pressure had dropped, and he was critical. The doctor needed the phone number of Orazio's American cardiologist. The news was grim. I was told to return to the waiting room. The administrator of the ER offered us orange juice, coffee, and biscuits.

The well-equipped treatment room astonished Gino, as well as all of the attention we were given by the personnel who offered us breakfast and treated us with compassion. She was aware that my niece and one of my nephews were not my children. It was obvious because they only spoke Italian, but she asked no questions. I confirmed her suspicion when I asked the administrator to please open the ambulance so my niece and nephews could see it. They were amazed by all of the equipment inside and later said, "Is this because this is an American naval base? You don't have ambulances like this for everyone, do you?" I told them that we did.

Eventually when Orazio was stabilized, we left the hospital. The cardiologist scheduled a private nurse to remain with Orazio, but I left with a heavy heart. He was always afraid of losing me, but I was terrified of losing the love of my life. The next morning Gino drove us to the base and explained at the gate that I didn't have a license to drive in Italy and he was serving as his uncle's interpreter. He had documentation with him and left a business card, giving the guard permission to call his boss for a reference. Gino was an administrator at the airport. Orazio had survived the night and was improving. I did not telephone Stephen or Susan. What could they do? Little did I know that they had their own crisis. Five days later Orazio was released from the hospital. I was given a bill for $6,000.00, which I promised to pay when I returned to America. Orazio was now well, and there was no reason to tell them about Orazio's congestive heart failure when Susan telephoned us and asked us for our return flight plans. We expected our daughter, Susan, Joe, and their three-year-old son Ford to meet us at the airport, but that was not to be. Only Joe arrived with his sister and her husband. I was surprised to see Dianne and Frank and greeted them warmly. Theirs was a solemn greeting.

We got our luggage, placed it in the van, and before leaving, Joe said, "Do you want the good news or the bad news first?"

The Letters

"What's the bad news?"

"We're going to Hollywood, Florida. Ford is at Joe DiMaggio Children's Hospital."

I'm thinking, "car accident, broken limb, pneumonia." I looked at Joe, "What's the good news? Are we picking him up there?"

"No. It's leukemia, but the prognosis is very good."

I didn't say another word. I was stunned. When we arrived at the hospital, Joe's parents, Euva and Jim, were there. I just hugged Euva, and we both cried. He was just three years old. I walked to his room where Susan was waiting for us. We all had to wear masks. I didn't bother to tell her about her dad. It now seemed trivial since he had recovered. Finances were a problem for Susan and Joe since their health insurance covered only eighty percent of the expenses. Orazio and I had not spent much money in Italy because family and friends insisted on entertaining us. We gave Susan and Joe whatever we had remaining, about $4,000. The following day, I sent a $200.00 payment to the financial administrator, an Italian, at the Sigonella Naval Station in Sicily. He was the one I had spoken with before Orazio was released. I wrote a letter and explained our situation, asking that we be permitted to pay monthly. Shortly after, I received a letter from him thanking us for the payment. He inquired about Orazio's health and hoped our grandson would soon be well. The administrator also wrote, "Consider the bill paid."

I recall a day that Ford wanted to leave his room. He was crying and just wanted to go out in the hall to see the murals on the walls. Euva and I were there and asked his doctor if he could. We bundled him, put a mask on him, and sat him in the wagon provided for children. As we wheeled him through the halls, he kept saying, "Take me where the elevators are. I want to go where the elevators are." It seemed like a strange request, but we took him there. I thought he wanted to see the guard who sat there and checked the visitors' passes. Tony knew most of the children and often kept new trinkets for them. He gave Ford a Matchbox car. We were ready to go back to his room, but he wanted to stay near the elevators. He said, "I just want to see the people and hear the elevator bell." Euva and I sat on the bench nearby, and in minutes Ford gave a sigh and fell asleep.

When Ford was in remission, I was his sitter for a month so that his parents could return to work. He still could not walk, an effect of the illness, but he used a scooter his paternal grandfather made for him. I recall a movie we were watching, *The Lion King*, and he suddenly said, "I'm brave like Simba." I couldn't agree more. I am indebted to the *Love Jen Fund* that still helps parents with emergency financial assistance as well as recreational assistance: a well-equipped playroom for the children being treated in the Division of Pediatric Oncology. I spent many hours there playing with the children. It wasn't always convenient for parents to be there. They worked or had other children at home to care for. Since I always enjoyed volunteering, I decided to spend my summer vacation helping the nurses who were assigned there. When Ford was in remission, he returned to his preschool, but there were days that he had to return to the hospital for additional treatment. It seemed to me that I spent a lot of time either in emergency rooms or in hospital rooms. But never did I believe there was more to come.

Just the Two of Us

Through that decade we kept in contact with the family in Italy through letters, photographs, and telephone calls. Nephews and nieces got married and had children. Orazio's brother Donato died of lung cancer at 64 years of age, a few years after he retired, and Gianni, who always loved the American advertisements, especially the "Sales," died nine or ten months after visiting us. Stephen and Lisa, Stephen's wife, and Susan and Joe, now married, gave us our first grandsons: Brenton, Kyle, and Ford. Those were joyful years spent with family and friends. Four of our friends, Guy and Marie Protano and Franco and Toni D'Avanzo introduced us to the Miami Cinematheque that became our favorite art theater patronized by aficionados of foreign films. While I no longer remember the name of the film that dealt with the early years of Mussolini's regime, I do remember scenes of Italian soldiers parading and singing. Suddenly Orazio joined in. My trying to hush him was useless. As he continued singing, patrons joined him in a rousing chorus of marches. I was embarrassed, but no one else seemed to be.

We never went home without first going to the most famous Cuban restaurant: *Versailles*, located in Little Havana in 1971 for the Cuban exiles. The striking decor featured floor to ceiling mirrors, giving the appearance of a much larger restaurant. *Versailles* was an impressive symbol of the Cuban culture and social style, featuring the best of Cuban cuisine. The aroma of Cuban coffee and food permeated the restaurant as we entered. The sounds of laughter and conversations filled the room, and among those who knew each other there were hugs and kisses when they greeted each other. Orazio loved the atmosphere because it reminded him of Italy: everyone speaking at one time. Besides we had already become fast friends with several Cuban families who lived in Plantation or Ft. Lauderdale.

Orazio and I were once again just a couple. It was only the two of us, and it felt strange not having to plan vacations centered on our children such as The Land of Oz Theme Park in the town of Beech Mountain, North Carolina. Here tourists could experience the cyclone in Kansas that struck Dorothy's house then walk along the yellow brick road visiting all of the characters: Dorothy, the Cowardly Lion, the Tin Woodsman, the Witch of the West. The Walk ended at Emerald City where visitors met the Wizard before returning to the entrance once again. The trip was by a colorful balloon or a bus. I chose the bus because of my fear of heights even though the park guides assured me that it was an "artificial" balloon, just a park ride, on a modified ski lift that gave the riders a view of the beautiful Boone mountain scenery as well as an entire view of the park.

We visited the restored Colonial Williamsburg, Virginia, the largest British colony in the Eighteenth Century. Like a living museum, it featured tradesmen and domestic craftsmen portrayed by men, women, and children who lived in the town. They wore period costumes and gave visitors an historic view of the town. At lunchtime we went to a restaurant and ate the typical food of the day: a thick slice of warm homemade bread and a bowl of thick soup. Before ending the trip, we knew there were always souvenirs to buy. There were Busch Gardens, St. Augustine, Gettysburg, Washington, D.C., and Philadelphia to explore as well as the Islands of Key West. Orazio was fascinated by every aspect of America and wanted his children to experience the sights and sounds of historical America. In truth he was the one who wanted to have all of those experiences.

The Letters

Today, I often wonder how much our young children remember of those vacations.

At the time never did I believe that an unexpected bolt of light-ning would soon shatter our world that we knew.

The Beginning of the End

Now alone, we planned to fulfill one of our dreams. Our plan was to travel west, as far as California, visiting family along the way and touring historical sites and famous cities we had often talked about but never visited. We had an itinerary and a set of maps marked with places of interest. The ones we always planned to tour. The day before we left, Susan, Joe, and Ford came to visit and to say "Goodbye." Our luggage was packed, and Joe helped Orazio put a few items in the van. Suddenly Susan said, "Mom, I wish you weren't taking this trip."

"Why? Uncle Bob will take care of Grandma. He lives less than an hour away. You don't have to worry about her."

"I know. It's not Grandma. I just feel that you shouldn't go. I worry about you and Dad. You're both getting older."

"Good grief! Silly girl, I haven't even planned to retire yet. We'll be fine."

The first leg of the trip was uneventful. We stopped the first evening in Tallahassee, the state Capitol of Florida. We left Tallahassee the following day, stopping first at Denny's buffet for breakfast. I wanted scramble eggs, but I had to wait about fifteen minutes for the new batch to be made. Orazio was impatient and wanted to leave. I wished I had just selected something else for breakfast. When we left Denny's, we began traveling west on Route 10. In the left lane an eighteen-wheeler truck began sprouting oil on our windshield. We couldn't see the road. The truck, slowing down, pulled to the right and stopped. Orazio decided to stop to see if her could help the driver with a tube of adhesive he had in his van that he believed could be used to seal the metal oil tube.

"Don't leave," I said as he began searching for the adhesive in the back of the van. "The driver can telephone for help." My plea fell on deaf ears. If anyone needed help, Orazio was sure to volunteer. I remained in the car, looking out the back window. As he walked to the truck, I saw from the window what I thought was another eighteen-wheeler truck whiz by. He was hit so hard that his body was thrown into the air and then dropped on the pavement. I saw his shoes and eyeglasses blow away as I ran outside of the van. Orazio had crawled under the driver's side of the truck. He was now unconscious.

Like a fool I ran into the highway flagging the traffic, trying to get the drivers to move to the left. As the truck driver called 911, a driver in a red pick-up truck stopped. He had no idea I had seen the accident. I was in shock. I kneeled down beside Orazio. Blood was flowing from his head, his right arm, and his left leg. A couple had parked ahead of our van a few yards away. They were driving a mobile home about 34 or 36 feet long and were the ones that had hit him. Two police cars came. The female police officer wanted me to get into her car because of the heat. I refused. Those who stopped at the scene pulled Orazio out from under the truck and laid him on the side of the road. I ran to our van to get the window sunscreens to fan him. He was moaning and sweating profusely. I just stood there. No one asked me any questions, not even the police or the paramedic who said Orazio was critical.

"We have to move him to the hospital in Dothan, Alabama. It's about fifty miles from here." He looked at me. "You have to follow us in your van."

I had never driven the van that was new, and I wasn't sure in my state of mind I could. I have no recollection of ever driving there, but obviously I did. Orazio was rushed into one of the emergency rooms. I was sent out. A few minutes later a nurse asked me to go into the room where Orazio was lying. He was moaning and babbling in Italian. The doctor was sitting in a chair frustrated. "I have no idea what he is saying. How can I help him?"

I looked at the doctor and wanted to shout, **"Help him! Just look at him! Look at his condition**! Instead I said, "He's an Italian national. He has resorted to his primary language. What do you want to know? I'll translate for you." Orazio was slipping in and out of consciousness. I feared the worst. Meanwhile, two other doctors came into the room. I remained with them for about forty-five minutes, and they asked me questions and answered mine. I could see that his right arm had the most damage, extending from his shoulder to his hand. "Can you save the arm? Will he be able to use it?" They were most compassionate. "We'll do everything we can to save it. You need first to go to Admissions to sign some permission papers."

I first telephoned Stephen, who was a paramedic and a firefighter, minimizing the situation. I didn't want him to worry. When I went to Admissions, I was told that I could not leave the packed van in the hospital parking lot. It could not be protected. I needed a motel and asked the clerk if she could recommend one.

"You're going to have a difficult time finding a room. There is a convention in the city, and I doubt if there are any rooms available."

However, she did give me the names of three that were nearby. I was so distraught. These were the days when no cell phones were available. If I left, how could anyone get in touch with me? I knew that Orazio would first have diagnostic tests taken before having surgery. I just had to take a chance. There was no one to help me. At the last motel I went to, I was told that they had only one room left, but it had no air conditioning, and the room was extremely hot. It was July, and the temperature was in the 80's. I didn't care. I wasn't going to complain. I reserved the room because I planned to stay that night at the hospital with Orazio. The van was packed. I knew I had to put everything into the room. Nothing could be left in the van. No sooner had I started to put the luggage into the room that a thunderstorm came from nowhere. I was soaked. Clothes hanging from a rod in the van became wet even though I had tried to cover them with an umbrella. I was frightened, still in shock. I made trip after trip. When I had finished, I immediately telephoned the hospital to give Admissions the phone number of the motel. I first took a shower and dressed and then hung the wet clothes from the van on the shower curtain rod. I then returned to the hospital.

I no sooner entered the hospital when I heard, "Mrs. Grasso, please come to the family room on the first floor. It is urgent." I thought of the worst scenario. I felt faint, but then I hadn't eaten since breakfast, and it was now early evening. A young man rushed into the family room with some forms. "We're so sorry, but the permission forms you signed for the surgery were for the left arm, not the right one. The surgeon realized there was an error. The right arm is the damaged one. Your husband is in surgery, but the form must be corrected." I signed the new form, and with that, he walked out of the room. I never saw him again.

It was hours before one of the surgeons spoke with me. Orazio's arm was not amputated. It was repaired, but there was no guarantee that the nerves would recover. He needed stitches on his head and forehead. His leg had compound fractures. He was now in the recovery room. I realized that I was hungry and decided to go to the cafeteria. I hurried to Orazio's room and found that he was just returning from the recovery room. Brian, his nurse, was getting him settled. I was sitting in a chair waiting for Brian to complete taking Orazio's vitals. Brian just looked at me.

"I assume you are his wife, but I don't understand you."

"What don't you understand?"

"You're a strange wife. You're just sitting here calmly. Most women would be crying."

"I don't have time to cry. I have no family here. No one understands what he is saying, and I have to translate. Somebody has to be in control. I don't have the luxury of crying."

For the first week I stayed in the hospital, only returning to the motel to shower and change clothes. His condition was listed as "serious." I paid for a meal plan that delivered meals to me in Orazio's room. I had to be there to help the nurses and other hospital personnel understand what he was saying in Italian and what they were saying to him. He had slipped back to his native language. The following week Stephen came to Dothan to visit, and we made plans with the doctor to move him to Ft. Lauderdale when he was discharged from the hospital, which was three weeks later. There was a small commuter plane from Dothan to transport him to a landing field near the Atlanta airport, but the plane only had steps. There was no way Orazio could walk. Hospital personnel wheeled him on the tarmac and carried him up the stairway and into the plane. Meanwhile, Stephen had chartered a private ambulance plane with a male nurse and the pilot to take us from the small airport in Dothan to another one near the Atlanta airport. The cost was $3,000.00 payable in advance. Our vacation money was used for unexpected expenses.

Firemen met us at the private airport to transfer us to the airport in Atlanta. I needed to buy another ticket because Orazio needed two front row seats. Passengers who held tickets for those seats were very accommodating and switched seats with us. Once more paramedics from the Lauderhill Fire Department met us at the Ft. Lauderdale airport to transport us to the rehabilitation hospital in Sunrise. Once Orazio was settled Stephen drove me home. I was physically, mentally, and emotionally exhausted. It was only after I had showered and was alone in bed that I cried.

Orazio insisted on leaving the hospital two weeks later. He was supposed to be there for at least a month. I rented a hospital bed and moved it into our family room. A pulley was installed so that he could raise himself with his left arm. I had to return to work, but a nurse came every morning at six o'clock to bathe him. The agency required that I be there and that the bathroom door be left open. I prepared breakfast for him and a light lunch. Carmelo came every day, not only to serve him his lunch but also to stay with him until I came home about two-thirty in the afternoon. At six in the evening another nurse came to change his bandages and take his vital signs. I gave him a toy school bell to ring during the night should he need help.

Days became weeks, and weeks became months before he was able to sleep in is own bed. He still needed the pulley, but he could now get up and walk to the bathroom. Many a night I got swatted with the brace on his right arm as he tried to turn in bed. The months then became two years. Orazio underwent seven surgeries at the Cleveland Clinic in Ft. Lauderdale to restore some movement to his arm. But that was never to be. More devastating was the fact that there was a court trial a couple of years after the accident, two months before Orazio died, but we lost the case. We never knew why, but when I discussed the case with my brother Ron, he mentioned that juries sometimes are anxious to leave, and ours came to a verdict in fewer than ten minutes. Furthermore, the defense attorney was a "shark." Ours was not. We were not suing for millions of dollars, only to recuperate money for medical expenses.

Family and friends visited as usual as I tried to reconstruct our world, but I couldn't put all the pieces together. Our last trip to Italy was in 1997. Orazio and I spent three weeks in Catania once more visiting family and friends that remained and usual places. Santa and Rena invited us to Taormina for dinner in a private restaurant. The interior reminded me of ancient architecture. Somehow I knew we would never return to Italy. This time only Gino met us at the airport. I stood waiting for the baggage to be sent on the carousel. I missed seeing the familiar faces from the years before. After Gianni's death, Fina moved in with Tita, and we would be staying with them in Catania. Usually they lived in Fina's villa in Tre Castagna, during the summer, but they did not that summer because neither of them drove or owned a car. The young nieces and nephews of the family had summer villas or had moved out of the city to the suburban areas. Instead of the many colorful summer cabanas on the Ionian Sea, there were permanent villas built on the water in nearby cities. Orazio's brother Giovanni had built his summer home on the mountains, and we enjoyed once more spending a weekend there.

Remembering Life with Orazio

Now only our nieces and nephews and their families remain in Catania. Donato was the first of the Grasso brothers to die. He was just 64 years old. Then, shortly after, Lino died after having a kidney stone removed. Some years later Gino died suddenly, possibly of a heart attack while he was sleeping. Sadness enveloped me when I heard that Fina died and that Pippa had Alzheimer's. Fina had needed a valve replacement for many years, but it was denied her. I had just spoken with her days before. She was heartbroken at the loss of her two beloved sons. Now, I miss talking with all of them by telephone. Giovanni was the last of the brothers to pass away, and I miss the many telephone conversations we shared. I still correspond with our nieces and nephews and with friends of ours still living in Catania: Santi Di Stefano, the internationally known pianist virtuoso who was once a child prodigy, and his wife, Rena, a ballerina. Through Facebook, my children have connected with some of their cousins. Recently a great niece, Giovanni's daughter Ombretta, spent two holidays here, Thanksgiving and Christmas, when she attended the University of North Carolina, and the cousins became acquainted once more. A year or so later she spent her honeymon in the United States with her husband, Erico, and they both came to Florida to visit. Aldo and Erika's daughter, Daniela, who spent a year with us when she was young, along with her husband Florian and her son, Florian, Jr. also visited. Oh, how Orazio would have enjoyed himself being with them!

Orazio loved to travel and especially enjoyed cruises. We went on many. On one cruise, he won an award dancing the tango, not with me, of course; I never could dance the tango. I still have the prize, a ceramic reproduction of the smokestack of *The Flavia*. Our Christmas parties are still remembered by the younger generations who were just children at that time. We never had fewer than thirty-five guests. If we had a handyman who had just completed a week's work, Orazio invited his wife and him. Most of the neighbors were invited. The children and I usually began to make the traditional Christmas cookies in October and store them in the freezer. *Pizzelles*, the Italian waffle cookie, was a favorite of everyone. I kept the traditional Italian Christmas Eve dinner: seven fishes and spaghetti with clam sauce as well as a turkey and a ham for the non Italians, and several guests brought a covered dish. Orazio grilled homemade Italian sausage after midnight. Orazio's culinary specialty was octopus, usually thirty pounds of it. He cooked the octopus in a large cauldron on a special gas grill on the patio and then covered the cauldron with a heavy blanket when it was cooked. I have never been able to duplicate the lemon, wine, garlic, Italian seasoning, and parsley salad dressing for it. The dessert was always *cannoli*, the Sicilian pastry filled with sweet ricotta.

Orazio was a man who loved life and lived it passionately. He may have lived only 73 years, but he lived life to the fullest. He was unique – a man caught between two worlds. He loved America and was proud he was an American, but his roots stretched across the Atlantic Ocean to Sicily. He made his own direct line to Italy, calling his relatives and friends there on a regular basis. No friend, no second or even third cousin was omitted even though he might not have seen them for forty years.

Could I ever forget some of his antics? On one of our trips to Italy I urged him to take our family to visit the mausoleum where his mother was placed before we left for the United States. He called the cemetery and was told that the cemetery was open Monday, Wednesday, and Friday, but the mausoleum was closed on those days. The mausoleum was open Tuesday and Thursday, but the cemetery was closed except for funerals and visitors. However, he learned that there was a funeral on Monday. Family members were given a small flag at the gate so they could enter for the interment. Orazio decided we would become a member of the family. As we entered the cemetery with our flag waving from an antenna, all cars except ours turned to the right. We went left. No one stopped us, and we went directly to the mausoleum where a gardener opened the mausoleum for us after Orazio tipped him a few American dollars. I never could understand the rule, but Orazio just made his own visitation rule.

When we moved to Plantation, he immediately began to leave his mark. He offered help to everyone in the neighborhood; his price was a cup of coffee. He would say, "You gotta coffee ready?" and the neighbors always did. He never met a stranger. Everyone was his friend. As far as he was concerned, visiting hours were as early at 7:30 in the morning and as late as midnight.

Orazio also served as self-appointed mayor of Ninth Street in Plantation Park and a self-appointed advisor of many in Broward Community College's Central Campus's English Department where I served as department head. He knew the administrators of the college on a first name basis, many times having lunch with them, and knowing Orazio, they probably also received a bit of advice from him. Upon entering an Italian restaurant in the greater Ft. Lauderdale area, Orazio would head straight for the kitchen and tell his "friend," the chef what he wanted to eat because he never looked at a menu. Orazio believed menus were basic guidelines for other patrons. He never met a dish of pasta he didn't like, but *Fruta de Mare* (Fruit of the Sea) was his favorite.

He amused children and adults as well by tapping his stomach to find a hollow sound so that he could eat a bit more. He considered himself a four-star chef often overseeing any meal prepared in his home or in the homes of his friends. Those close to him knew a much guarded secret: his culinary talents did not extend beyond making an excellent octopus hot salad, grilling alligator tails, making a good cup of espresso coffee, and frying eggs. Espresso was his choice of beverage, and Stromboli Pizzeria or Bar Roma was high on his list, but he always had to have a double serving of espresso.

He was the only "musician" known for playing his own customized instruments – two china saucers, two crystal ashtrays, or two aluminum or wooden coasters. Once invited to a friend's home for dinner, he picked up two of her "no longer available" expensive coasters and began serenading the guests. In his exuberance he broke both plates, but, of course, the hostess forgave him. Orazio was passionate about all Italian music and fancied himself a singer equal to Pavarotti. Those of us who rode with him in his van knew he was tone deaf. While he never used the car horn in traffic, he did flash the car lights for anyone who was in his way. If the driver didn't move fast enough, he swerved into another lane. Speed limits were only for the faint of heart.

Nothing was permitted to break in his home. Orazio repaired it. He was a genius with his hands. He didn't believe in waste. Orazio himself was repaired and patched as the result of the many surgeries he had. He always said, "Columbus discovered America, and I discovered the hospitals." The kitchen table was his domain. He sat there to read the morning papers, eat his meals, and entertain guests. No living or family room was comfortable enough. Besides, the telephone hung on the wall behind him, making it easier to chat with relatives and friends.

The Letters

The term of endearment that Orazio used for anyone was *giufa,* loosely translated as "a clumsy oaf." Even until his death, former youth soccer players or friends who met him at the Broward Mall or in the Publix Supermarket were greeted by that name. When he retired, he was a familiar figure in Publix – shorts, shirt, and red suspenders. He knew all of the employees from managers to baggers. Publix was his social club. Any child caught crying there, he would say to them, "Oh, Pavarotti, what beautiful music." Most of the time they would stop crying and just look at him in amazement.

He loved to travel, and when the children were young, we always planned a family vacation. Above all else he loved his family, and he would never consider going on a vacation without his children. One of his favorite vacations was a cruise, and we took a few. Just before he died we had planned two: Greece and Alaska, but we never got to finalize those plans.

Losing Orazio

Unfortunately, I lost Orazio on May 29, 1998. I had taken him on Sunday to the Emergency Room with a strep throat, and he was supposed to be home on Tuesday. He wasn't. He suffered congestive heart failure and died after two weeks. His death devastated me, but I wanted his funeral to be a celebration of his life. He was well known in the city, having served on the Advisory Board for Parks and Recreation. I asked the funeral director to provide a large urn of coffee and a large tray of biscotti for visitors. I supplied a selection of romantic Italian ballads and joyous Neapolitan music to be played during visitation hours. I had scrapbooks of the soccer players from the soccer club he and a friend began. I placed the books on tables in the entrance room. The boys he had coached were then young men attending college or working. His grandsons drew crayon pictures because he always drew pictures of trucks, airplanes, and cars with them; and the boys placed their drawings with him. His oldest grandson asked the funeral director if his grandfather could be cremated with a jar of instant espresso coffee, his favorite choice of beverage. He was surrounded with many framed pictures of his life during happier times: working at the church fair, opening clams that he had helped collect and selling them; cutting his wedding cake; playing with his grandsons; and helping Stephen and Susan hang their Christmas stockings. He adored his children and me. I always knew from his first letters to me that family came first.

At one point during the evening visitation his friends began to tell anecdotes. There were many. One of his friends told about the evening we went to eat at the Rustic Inn, a restaurant that featured all-you-can-eat garlic crab legs. Usually Orazio ordered the crabs, but that particular evening he was undecided. He watched the waiters carry dishes to other patrons. Finally, he saw an entrée that was served to a man sitting just behind him, within arm's reach. He turned to the patron and said, "Can I taste your dish?" The man replied, "Sure." Orazio took his bread and butter plate and put a forkful of the entrée on the plate. "Umm, that's good." I said, "Orazio, you shouldn't do that." With a puzzled look on his face, he answered, "He didn't say, 'No'." He must have liked the pasta with clams because it was the entrée he ordered. He was just being Orazio.

With his passion being soccer, he was looking forward to seeing the world cup series. No doubt he now has the best seat in the house, screaming *giufa* at the players who may not make the plays he feels they should have and screaming at the referees who make the wrong call. No doubt he is also organizing a cherub soccer club because he loved coaching the youngest players. To Orazio, everything was "phenomena!"

I have never removed my wedding band. It is part of my life, and I never want to forget anything, not even his temper that was like a volcano, hot and quick, but it was over in minutes, and then immediately after, it was *Gioia*, his pet name for me, but he always called me, *Mariella*. One of the sympathy cards I received is typical of the many others sent to me. This one was sent to me by one of my colleagues and his wife, Roy and Joan Yater:

> *It takes a long time to get used to the loss*
> *of someone we love,*
> *But it is important to remember*
> *That when people die they leave*
> *Something very special behind—*
> *Orazio's many visits to the English Department*

Mary Ellen Cipolla Grasso

Were special occasions for all of us.
His infectious good humor, gestures, smile --
Even his broken English--made us forget
Our problems for a while. We cannot fathom
Your grief, but be assured, we survivors
Who knew him will miss him greatly.

Rereading Orazio's letters made me realize how fortunate I was to have met and married him. Ray, Memo, and Pedro claimed they loved me, but Orazio cherished and treasured me. Did we have a perfect marriage? I don't believe anyone does. We disagreed, but we settled our differences when we were alone in our bedroom. We compromised. Marriage for us was not a win-lose game. If we made an error in judgment, we always forgave one another. Above all else, we respected and loved each other unconditionally.

At my retirement party, just three weeks before he died, Orazio told the story of the time he decided to play "macho man." We had disagreed about something I no longer remembered. Neither did he. It probably wasn't important enough. He announced loud-ly, "I'm leaving." He started to pack two large suitcases. I helped him. "Do you need some towels? What about other linens? Do you want your pillow? What shirts do you want?" When he fin-ished packing, he set the suitcases at the entrance. He looked at them and then at me. He opened the door, looked outside, and sighed, "It's too cold tonight. I'll leave in the morning. Okay?" "Fine," I replied.

The suitcases remained there for a week or more. Life went on as usual. We visited friends, went to a movie, and watched television. We even slept in the same bed. I prepared dinner as usual. We never discussed the suitcases. After a week, Orazio unpacked his suitcases and never packed them again, except for vacations. At the end of his story, he told everyone at the reunion, "I'm a lucky,

lucky man. She is my jewel, my angel." I couldn't believe that at a reception for me, two days later at the Board of Trustees' meeting, he repeated the story. A few of the Board members and many of the administrators knew both of us, and they just howled with laughter. Orazio just smiled and shrugged his shoulders.

The years without him have been very difficult for me. When I left our home in Plantation a year later with a "For Sale" sign in the yard, I sat in my car parked on the circular driveway and cried. How could I leave the home that held so many memorable years? All I could say was, "Orazio, why did you leave me? I am so lonely without you." I did move, building a home we both had selected in Gainesville, Florida, across the yard from our daughter and her family. I still have the contract that he signed for the lot we had purchased. Of all the moves we made, this was the most difficult. We had always planned to leave Plantation and move to a smaller city with less traffic when I retired, but this time it was different. Orazio would not be with me.

I miss him. I miss hearing him breathe while sleeping next to me. I miss hearing his fast steps walking down the long ceramic tile floors in our hallway. He wore plastic sandals that he always modified, even before they were fashionable. I miss his spontaneity, the smell of espresso coffee brewing in the kitchen. I miss the warmth of his body next to mine on those cold nights when I could never get warm enough, and I couldn't fall asleep if he were not near me. I miss not being able to reach over to the other side of the king-sized bed to trace the outline of his face and kiss him goodnight one more time.

I miss the fact that I never knew who was coming to dinner or the times friends and we would combine our dinners for an evening of laughter and interesting conversation. I miss cooking for him. He always complimented me. Every dinner for him was "the best" I ever made. I miss sitting across from him at the kitchen table on weekends, having breakfast and reading the two morning newspapers: the *Miami Herald* and the *Sun Sentinel* and then discussing the articles we had read and how they differed.

I miss the bouquets of gladiolas he bought and arranged in a vase for me for no special reason. I miss the Valentine Day's cards always written, "To my angel wife," not "Mary Ellen" and the messages of love written inside all of the greeting cards he sent me through the years. He never signed his cards just Tuo Orazio. He signed them, *Ti amo per tutta la vita. Di cuore, Orazio.* I found a greeting card recently that I had saved in a photo album, but I don't know what happened to all of the others.

I have no idea what makes relationships work. I do believe that much has changed when it comes to lasting relationships between men and women. Have couples compromised more than they have wanted or have they failed to compromise? Are men and women still seeking that elusive "perfect" companion, husband, or wife? Do long-term relationships make a marriage more successful? In my case the long-term relationships never got to that point. What factors enter into the successful relationships, the failed ones?

With Orazio, I have a lifetime of marvelous years to remember, not just moments. I was once in love with Ray, Memo, and Pedro, but they were incapable of giving me unconditional love and sharing their lives with me. Orazio and I were soul mates and shared an unbelievable chemistry. We complemented each other in spite of our differences. We loved and respected one another. He didn't demand sex before marriage to learn if I would be a suitable wife. As he once wrote me, he had had a lot of women, a lot of sex, but never love. He was looking for love. No other man could have given me a lifetime of such incredible experiences.

The Letters

He brought his family and friends who lived in Italy into my life, making it richer and more colorful. Our marriage was a series of magical adventures with those we met for a day, a month, or a year, and for those who came into our lives and never left. The magic in my life still continues through our extended families, our friends, and, especially through our children and their spouses: Susan and Joe, Stephen and Lisa, and our remarkable grandsons, Brenton, Kyle, Ford, and Tucker. Brenton is now married to Grayce, and their daughter, my first great granddaughter, Abygale Jane, has now joined the family.

Could any woman have asked for more?

Epilogue

I am old now. And wise. When I am fortunate enough to sit with girls just beginning their journey through life or with women who have given up because they have not found the life they dreamed of, I want to tell them, "Just live---live! Your best life will find you." Mine did, and now I live to tell about it. I made naïve decisions and enjoyed reckless adventures. I loved and lost. I learned. I lived my life with passion and curiosity. I was lucky to meet a man who was attracted to the real me, and we forged ahead together leaving a huge wake behind us, enjoying every passionate moment.

Music was so much a part of our life, and even today should I hear the song *A Haunted Heart*, with lyrics by Howard Dietz and music by Arthur Schwartz, sung I want to return to those wonderful days.

> *In the night though we're apart*
> *There's a ghost of you within my haunted heart*
> *Ghost of you my last romance*
> *Lips that laughed, eyes that danced.*
> *Haunted heart won't let me be.*
> *Dreams repeat a sweet but lonely song to me.*
> *Dreams are dust. It's you who must*
> *Belong to me and thrill my haunted heart.*
> *Be still my haunted heart.*

So you see, it all worked out exactly as it was supposed to. I often hear people say they wish they could go back and relive their life knowing what they know now. I don't want to do that because I think everything happens just the way it should. Fate determines the outcome, and I wouldn't want to mess with that. Perhaps, Fate dreams bigger than all of us.

I'm not saying it was easy finding happiness. I learned the sadness of a broken heart, well--many broken hearts. I felt betrayed and discarded. I felt yearning, and I felt foolish. I second-guessed myself, berated myself, and although they never said a word, I probably worried my parents. But I just kept going, no matter what happened. Ultimately, I realized that I was in control of my destiny, and I better live life to the fullest. As I found out, no one really has control of his or her life. Fate is in charge. Even as I was supposedly controlling my life and forging ahead to greet new experiences, destiny came in the form of a fearless Italian national opera-singing man who, after spotting me from afar, wrapped his love around me like a great big octopus and wouldn't let me go. I didn't struggle for long because I soon realized he had my exuberance, matched my desire for living fully, and, of course, there is safety in numbers. So off we went together. I experienced the whole spectrum of emotions that a rich life offers, him by my side. I was gloriously happy and never bored because, I suppose, I had met my match, and he met his.

We lived a life together full of strangers who became friends, neighbors who became family, and a new and delicious experience presented itself every day. I never knew what to expect, but I better be ready. If not, I would have been lost in the whirlwind passion of my bigger than life Italian immigrant husband. I was so touched and ultimately very grateful that he picked *me* to accompany him on his grand adventures.

I haven't decided if the world is more dangerous now or if we are just more tentative about jumping in front of life and taking control of the journey. Back then, in the "olden days" as my grandsons call it, I wasn't afraid of traveling alone to third world countries, meeting new people, or eating strange food. It was these experiences that made me ready for my ultimate journey.

Appendix - Coming to America

Although my mother was born in America, my father was born in Grotte, a small town near Agrigento, Sicily. His paternal grandfather, Stefano Cipolla, and his grandmother, Antonia Garretto, had five children: Pietro (my grandfather), Calogerio (Uncle Charlie), and Uncle Angelo who immigrated to America; but my aunts, Maria Angela and Giusepina, remained in Italy. As a child Giusepina had fallen from a donkey and had broken her back. She became a hunchback, never married, and was the last member of the family to die. I learned that fact in 1980 when Orazio and our children visited Grotte. I always wondered why my grandfather had blue eyes and red hair, as did his sister Maria Angela, called Marangela. Many of the members of the extended Cipolla family were blondes or redheads with blue eyes. I was born a blonde with blue eyes that turned green when I was two years old. Now my eyes are bluer than they were green. My father had hazel eyes and light brown hair. His brother Peter was a redhead, but his sisters were blondes, and only one had brown eyes. All of the members of the family were fair complexioned.

Years later when a cousin began to trace the ancestry of the Cipolla family, I learned that according to the records of the year 1161, the Cipolla name originated in Sweden. In the year 1276, Ubaldo Cipolla resided in Verona, North Italy, with the title of "Nobil of Capua" because he had loaned money to King Carmine I, D'angio. The family then spread to the city of Oversea of the Naploitan State, moving in 1500 to Sicily. One of the men of the Cipolla family first became the Baron of Sciarra (a comedian in the theater) and later given the title Count Palatino under Emperor Frederick III. Unfortunately, my cousin died before he could continue his research, and no one persisted in tracing the ancestry between the 1500's and the 1800's. Still when I was young, I used to believe that if I placed a horned hat on my grandfather, he could be a Viking.

My father's paternal grandfather, Stefano, owned a sulfur mine in Grotte, but he was a terrible businessman and provider for his family. On paydays, he seldom arrived home with money. Instead, he would invite his friends to a bar and restaurant with the usual cry, "Food and drink for everyone." As a result, he lost the mine, and his son Pietro, who no longer had a job, decided to go to America with his two brothers, Charles and Angelo because they had heard that America was the land of opportunity. Pietro moved his wife, Maria *Concetta* (pronounced Conchetta), and his two children Stefano (Stephen) and Antonia into his parents' home in Grotte. A few years earlier they had lost a two-year-old daughter, also named Antonia. My father was about five and a half years old when his dad left for America; his sister was nearly a year old.

Life was difficult. After the mine closed, the family became poor. To supplement the family's income, my father's grandmother planted a garden, raised chickens, sold the eggs, and raised a few goats for milk and cheese. Most of their meals consisted of the vegetables grown in the garden, olives, cheese, bread, and homemade noodles. Whatever his grandmother made selling eggs was spent on other products such as lard, flour, and occasionally some sausage. A chicken was killed and cooked when it was either too old or no longer producing eggs, but a single chicken had to feed a family of seven, sometimes for two meals, the noon-day and evening meals.

The Letters

On a trip to Grotte with my family many years later, I was able to see a few houses, displayed for tourists or the younger Italian generations, like the one my father lived in and told me about many times. It was a small one-room stone house. At one end of the room was a double (matrimonial) bed with two small trundle beds underneath it. The mattresses were stuffed with straw or hay, the pillows with feathers. A hammock suitable for a baby hung from the ceiling above the double bed. A fireplace was on one side of the room, and a large homemade picnic-style table with benches on each side was in the center of the room. Several wooded chests that held clothes, linens, and other small household items were at the far end of the room. Above the chests was a long shelf that held dishes, cups, utensils, kettles, and a few small jars of spices and dried herbs. A short stairway of about five steps led to the bottom dirt floor where the few animals were kept during the winter and at night such as a donkey, the goats, and the poultry.

Because of similar conditions, many Italians left their homeland in the early 1900's for America, many men leaving their wives and children behind until the men could find a job, rent a home, and save money. They brought nothing with them except a few clothes, a small amount of money, their culture, traditions, religion, their language, and their dreams of betterlives. My father remembers his father sending a small amount of money to support his wife and children, but his grandfather always managed to take a few dollars for himself. He persuaded Conchetta to remain in Sicily, believing his son would return to Grotte if she did not leave, but she was determined to go. Not only did she want a better life for her family, but also she heard the rumors that husbands whose wives did not follow them to America, simply remarried again without the benefit of a divorce, abandoning their families in Italy.

Mary Ellen Cipolla Grasso

My dad was excited to leave. He wanted to go to school. He had no opportunity to do so in Sicily. He remembered that his God-father, one of the richest men in town, invited all of his godsons who were leaving for America to a going-away dinner. I had heard the story many times because it had such an impact on my dad. When the first course was served, the boys just sat looking at it. First it was a small dish of spaghetti with bits of meat in it, not sausage. Then their Godfather's wife set a large platter of veal chops in the center of the table with a basket of hot bread rolls. The boys had never seen grilled chops and had never used a knife and fork to eat such food. It wasn't until the Godfather, realizing that the boys had never eaten veal chops, began eating that they imitated him. He told them about the wonders of America because he had been there. He told those young boys, "Go to school. Work hard. Be good Americans." My dad never forgot his advice.

When the day came that Conchetta and her two children were to leave Sicily, her father-in-law agreed to accompany them to Genoa although he had not resigned himself to their leaving. When they arrived at the dock, my grandmother remembered him pulling our red hair from his head and beard while screaming, "*Traditore! Traditore!*" (Traitor! Traitor!) Conchetta, who was just twenty-three years old, walked up the gangplank and into the ship with her two children and never looked back.

The Crossing

Like many other immigrants, Conchetta and her children crossed the Atlantic Ocean in steerage, the cheapest accommodations for passengers. My grandfather, whom we called Papa P, not Papa *Pietro*, told me that a ticket cost $25.00. My dad remembers playing with the other Italian children, but neither my dad nor my grandmother ever wanted to talk about the crossing in detail. It had been nearly a year and a half since Conchetta had seen her young husband and was worried that he would forget to meet her. On the other side of the ocean, he was worried that his unschooled wife would get lost and take the wrong train. All she had was a slip of paper that read "Rimersburg, Pennsylvania." Little did Pietro know that Conchetta spent most of her trip in quarantine with their daughter Antonia, who had chickenpox, a contagious disease for children traveling by steerage.

Stefano, who spoke no English, was taken from his mother and given to a young Polish boy, a teenager, who was told by one of the crew to take care of him. Stefano, who was just seven years old, had no idea what had happened to his mother and his sister until one of the Italians explained that his sister was ill and his mother had to take care of her in a special room so that he couldn't get sick too. Over the years I have wondered why he wasn't placed with one of the immigrants who spoke Italian, but he wasn't. While his companion, *Josep*, tried to entertain him and teach him a few Polish words, Stefano was very sad. He remembered that *Josep* would take off his shoes, socks, pants and shirt before washing him and putting him to bed. Every morning the boy brought him breakfast--warm milk and bread--but Stefano had to be encouraged to eat. As a result of that journey, after arriving in America, he never drank milk again. I can only imagine how frightened and sad he must have been, especially when the ship docked in New York, and he and other children had to wait until a doctor came on board to examine all those who had been quarantined so they could be certified "healthy" before being permitted to disembark.

Papa P was at the railroad station in Rimersburg, along with other men waiting for their wives with small children; a teenage son or nephew, traveling alone; a brother; an uncle; or a friend. At first Conchetta did not see her husband, but she could hear him, *"Conchetta, Conchetta! Stefano, Stefano!"* She started to cry as she ran towards him, relieved that she had finally found him, and she was home. She was in America.

Rimersburg

Their first home was a "company home," owned by the Acme Coal Mine Company, the largest mine in the area, attracting many Italian immigrants. The homes were rented to the miners, and rent was deducted from their wages. The relationship between the owners of the mine and the miners was one of owner and servant. Conchetta did not expect to find such poor conditions of the homes and the camp. Seldom was any home painted or repaired. Most homes had at least two bedrooms (a few had three) as well as a kitchen and a living room. An outhouse was behind the home. My grandparents had only two bedrooms. There was a back porch where the women washed their clothes in the winter and where the men washed themselves from the waist up after work before coming into the house. They removed their shirt and lowered their one-piece underwear to the waist and washed each other's backs and then hung their work shirts on pegs outside to be worn the next day because clothes were washed only once a week. There were pegs on a wall inside the doorway that held their "clean" shirts. The men and their families, exploited by the owners of the mines, had a harsh existence. No home had an indoor water pump, but there were outdoor communal water pumps for every so many homes, maybe six or eight, depending on the whim of the owners. Miners were paid with *scrip*, a credit voucher that could be used only in the Company Store. It could not be exchanged for cash.

As a result, miners could never save money. Furniture, kerosene lamps, clothing, and food had to be purchased at the notorious Company Store. If you needed a doctor, he was provided by the company store, and his fee was deducted from the miner's wages. Conchetta recalled that on one visit to the store she was told that her kerosene lamp was too old, and she needed a new one. She refused to purchase a new one because the old one still worked. By the next morning the lamp was found broken, and she was forced to buy a new lamp. Sometimes shirts hanging on an outside peg went missing or torn, and they had to be replaced. No one expressed the conditions of the mining camps better than Tennessee Ernie Ford, who in 1946 recorded *Sixteen Tons*. The first four lines are well known:

> *Sixteen Tons and what do you get,*
> *Another day older and deeper in debt.*
> *Saint Peter, don't you call me, 'cause I can't go.*
> *I owe my soul to the Company Store.*

The relationship between the owner of the mine and the miners was always one of owner and servant, even in death. I learned of an incident involving Great Uncle Angelo, Papa P's youngest brother, choosing not to leave the mining camp in Rimersburg and move when his brother Pietro did. Angelo continued working the morning shift, from seven o'clock in the morning until late afternoon. Just before eleven o'clock one day, he had finished dynamiting a coal vein, and while doing so, he was pelted by the blast. Miners worked in pairs, "buddies," and they looked after each other. At the Acme Mine many of the men were known as *paesanos*, men who came from the same region in Italy. That day many men who were also working in the morning shift saw the accident, and several men ran to the crew boss for help. Uncle Angelo at that time was still breathing and able to talk with the other miners. The men were told by the crew boss to continue working until the shift ended. No help came. During those hours Uncle Angelo lay on the cold damp ground, complaining that he was very cold. He wanted water and some food, but the men were not permitted to leave their work. There is no doubt that the superintendent was afraid that the *paesanos* would leave their work to carry Uncle Angelo out of the mine, and they would lose time. When the shift was over, the men were allowed to take Angelo out of the mine, but my twenty-six-year-old uncle was dead. His young wife was told of the accident. At the same time she was told that Angelo had to be buried that evening before sunset. The hidden agenda, the men knew, was that the superintendent feared the men would not report the next day for the morning shift if they had to go to a funeral.

Many mining companies had their own cemeteries, another way to control services and deduct money from the miners' wages. Meanwhile, Pietro had not only received a telegram from the coal company learning of his brother's death and the unusual early burial, but also another one from his sister-in-law who was despondent over the early burial. Could Pietro help her? Desperate to delay the burial, Pietro and Stefano rushed to the courthouse to ask the judge to delay the burial. The judge telegrammed orders to the Acme Coal Company, giving Pietro a copy of the order stating that Angelo could not be buried until his family from out-of-town could be there for the funeral. Since a car was not available at that time. Pietro and Stefano hired a driver who had a wagon drawn by a team of two horses. They rode all night, arriving at sunrise. At the burial site, the superintendent lifted the lid of the wooden coffin and said, "See. This is your brother. You can say a prayer before he's buried." Filled with grief and being exhausted, Pietro just bowed his head and cried. No clergy was there to say a few words. Finally, one of the miner's at the site said, "*Angelo, ritorna con Dio.*" I'm certain that Uncle Angelo did return to God. As for the miners, the superintendent made sure that they did not miss that morning shift. Pietro went to his sister-in-law's home for several hours to mourn with her and his very young niece but not before going to the Company Store. I never learned what happened to Uncle Angelo's family; only that his widow and her daughter went to live with her parents who also had immigrated to America.

Although there was a labor organization in 1890, it was not until 1933 that the United Mine Workers (UMW) began to spread throughout the United States under the leadership of John L. Lewis, who had become President of the United Mine Workers of America (UMWA) in 1919 serving until 1960. The UMWA fought for justice, fair wages paid in cash, not *scrip*, better working conditions with benefits, the freedom to live or shop wherever a miner wished. The UMWA became one of the most powerful labor organizations in the country, and my father considered Lewis to be a courageous leader. However, my father's family did not reap any of the UMWA's benefits because my grandmother, Mama Conchetta, found a way to leave those harsh mining camps.

Other than the fact that Stefano (now registered in the public school as *Steve*) was finally attending the elementary school, Mama Conchetta at first believed that there was no opportunity ever to leave the camp to have a better life for her family. Then she saw a way to earn cash when some young unmarried miners were hired. They were not eligible to rent a company home, but they could live with relatives or a family friend and negotiate rent. Since the mining company did not deduct rent from their pay, they had more available cash. However, they did buy their own food from the Company Store. Conchetta decided to take in several boarders who paid an agreed amount of money for lodging. They were responsible to buy their own food and other essentials from the Company Store. Because the house had only two bedrooms, the men had to share one. Since they worked different shifts there were always one or two cots available. Conchetta was no different from any of the other women who took in boarders. Now she had to bake bread every day instead of every other day, not only for her family but also for the boarders. However, each of the men bought his own meat, cheese, or fish, spaghetti, and tomatoes for the sauce, giving Conchetta special instructions of how each wanted his sauce to be made. Instead of following their instructions, she told me she made one big pot of sauce and then divided it into the individual pots they had given her. She would add the meat, sausage, or poultry; serve their dinners; and they never knew the difference. They provided the food for their lunches, and she packed their buckets. Sometimes she would add a piece of "Johnny cake," which was just sweetened baked bread dough she made for her family.

The boarders did pay her for doing their laundry. Also, Steve earned a few pennies each day by washing the men's backs when they came home from the mine. He gave the money to his mother, and she saved every penny. A growing boy, Steve remembers that he was always hungry since his mother cut back on the grocery bill buying only the essentials. Knowing the situation, the boarders would leave a bit of bread and dinner for him. As the men left the kitchen to go outside, they would say to him, "I'm too full. I can't eat anymore." He remembers that when they left the room, he would walk around the table, sopping up the bits of bread in the dishes that many times had a piece of chicken or sausage in it. He once said to me, "The plates were so clean when I finished that they looked as though they had been washed." Still, he thought he was lucky. He attended the Rimersburg Grade School, completing sixth grade, not unusual for immigrant children during the early 1900's to have even fewer than six years of schooling or none at all. In 1914, not yet fourteen years of age, Steve went to work in the mine with his father and a cousin.

In those days the miners were paid only for the railroad cars filled with coal that came out of the mine. The men worked, essentially, two days without pay. The first day was used to make holes for the sticks of dynamite that were placed into the holes in order to break the veins of coal that could run eight feet to seventy or ninety feet deep. On the second day, the men shoveled smaller pieces of coal from the veins in the wall to the bed of the floor and began to fill the railroad car. The third day they continued to shovel the coal into a railroad car to fill it. Steve, wanting to help his father and uncle, who worked side-by-side in the mine on the same shift, would go to work before his shift, dynamite the holes and break up the coal for both of them so they were able to begin shoveling the coal into the car. I once asked him, "Dad, how could you do all that?"

"I was young and strong, and I had to help them."

Because there was no Catholic church in Rimersburg until 1941, Steve could not attend Mass or "Sunday School" to prepare him for First Holy Communion or Confirmation. Meanwhile, during those early years, his mother was able to save enough money so they could leave. She still kept boarders, but now both her husband and son were working. Their plan was to go to Rochester, New York, where Pietro's brother Charlie had settled, but Pietro decided instead in 1919 to move to Arnold, Pennsylvania, where he was told that the mine there did have a Company Store, but it was not mandatory for the miners to purchase everything there or live in a company home. The only drawback was that Pietro wasn't familiar with the town. He wrote to his friend, *Vincenzo Antonio Puglisi* (Vincent Anthony), whom he personally knew lived in Arnold. They had been close friends and neighbors in Grotte before coming to America. Antonio, as he was called, was happy to invite his long-time friend with his family, a son, and three daughters: *Antonia, Francesca,* and *Angelina.* They planned to stay less than a month or until Pietro could find a job and a home. Antonio had come to the United States June 6, 1903. His wife had the same name as Pietro's: *Maria Concetta.* Maria, as she was called, arrived in America one year later on June 6,,1904, with two sons. Michele (Michael) called Mike, who was seven, and Leonardo (Leonard), who was five. Arriving in Pennsylvania, she was so excited to see her husband that while running to meet him at the railroad station she fell on the railroad tracks and broke her leg.

From 1904 to 1919, Antonio's family, including his parents, *Michele* and *Maria Grazia*, lived in many small towns in Pennsylvania, moving to find a perfect town, and the family grew to ten children, seven boys and three girls. Antonio's goal was to have a grocery store with a butcher shop where his sons could work. Shortly after 1919, he had achieved that goal. He hated mining coal, as did his son Leonard, called Banard, who worked one week in the mine before quitting his job and working as a butcher. The Cipollas lived with the Puglisi family for a little more that a month. Neither Antonio nor his wife, however, thought that these long-time friends would become their life-long relatives.

The Elopement

Steve, who was not twenty years old, immediately began working at the local coal mine along with his father, but Pietro had other intentions, and working in the mine and renting a home was not part of his long-term plan. Hadn't he once heard about the many opportunities in America? The streets may not have been paved with gold, but he knew he could achieve his dream. Doing so would just take time.

Meanwhile the two families bonded. Antonia (now called by her nickname, Anthony) and Grace, the oldest Puglisi girl, shared household duties and cared for the younger children. The wives, Maria and Conchetta, cooked, washed laundry, ironed, and repaired the clothing that always seemed to need repaired. When the older boys wore out the foot of their socks, the foot was cut off and the remainder was sewn into tube socks for the younger boys. Nothing was wasted.

My mother, Grace Puglisi, was the oldest girl in a family of eight brothers, three older than she and five younger, as well as two younger sisters. She had less than a happy childhood, one filled with much responsibility. Because it was customary at that time to name children after grandparents, if one child died, the name was given to the next newborn of the same sex. Thus, she was given the same name as her infant sister who died in Italy when she was nearly two years of age.

A gifted student, my mother wanted to complete high school. If she had, she could have taught in the elementary school, according to the superintendent of the school she attended. However, her mother was pregnant again and felt she needed Grace's help. The superintendent came to Grace's home to beg her parents not to withdraw her, but my mother was withdrawn from school after sixth grade with a promise to the superintendent that she would return a year later. That never happened. Her childhood was gone. Instead she was given many household tasks such as cleaning the house, helping with the laundry, especially ironing all of the clothes, and taking care of the younger children. She was even denied taking free piano lessons from a neighbor because she had "no time."

There was a player piano in the house, and the young people spent their evenings playing the many music rolls and singing along with the printed lyrics on the rolls. It wasn't long before twenty-year-old Mike became interested in Anthony, not yet, sixteen years old; and no one thought Steve's teasing of Grace, just fourteen years of age, was more than boys being boys. Grace avoided Steve, believing him to be arrogant and spoiled. She was delighted when his family finally moved, not realizing that Anthony and Mike, who had fallen in love, were to be married on October 6, 1920. Now Steve would always be around since Mike and Anthony lived in the cottage behind the Puglisi home. Anthony began to deliver love notes from her brother, Steve, to Grace, which she initially ignored. But then, coming home from the mine, Steve was so lovesick that he would forget to turn off the light on his miner's helmet as he deliberately took the longer path just to pass her home. After a while, Grace found herself standing by the parlor window just to see him walk by.

Pietro had purchased an apartment building with an attached small grocery store. As fate would have it, the building was across the street from a butcher shop and grocery store that the Puglisi family had, and the two families were closer than ever. In the

meantime, Anthony began to deliver notes betwen Grace and
Steve hiding them under a rock, near the freshwater spring on
Woodmont Avenue, several blocks away from their homes. Because Anthony no longer wanted to be involved in the clandestine
affair, Grace began to go to the spring more than once a day to
get the cool fresh water for her family and to leave a note for
Steve. No one suspected her motives, except Anthony. Grace always left a note for Steve hidden under the same rock, but she always destroyed his notes before returning home. Although Grace
and Steve were never at the spring together, they, too, had fallen
in love. Still Grace knew her parents, especially her mother, would
be opposed to a marriage to anyone because she was only fifteen,
and she needed Grace at home. But Grace didn't know that her
father had promised her to his friend's son, Joseph, when the men
were childhood friends in Grotte.

It was now December 1921, and Steve and Grace agreed to elope
on December 7. His last note to her read, "If you don't marry
me, I will kill myself." Years later I asked my dad if he would have
killed himself. He simply said, "Of course not! I wasn't a fool.
I knew your mother would elope with me if I threatened her."
Grace told Anthony about their plans and begged Anthony to
keep their secret, and Anthony promised that she would help her
mother-in-law with the chores that Grace did. Steve hired a taxi
to leave at ten o'clock that night, but Grace had trouble leaving. It
was getting late, and her parents insisted they all go to bed. Need-
ing an excuse to stay up, she told her parents that she wanted to
scrub the floor after her brothers came home rather than wash it
in the morning because her brothers always tracked in mud. She
scrubbed slowly on her hands and knees, waiting for her parents
to go to bed and hoping her brothers wouldn't come home.

Finally, she was able to sneak away. Grace left by the back door,
which faced the alley. She carried her shoes and a small bag and

ran across the snowy yard in stocking feet to Steve, who was waiting for her. As she was running, the family dog chained in the
back yard began barking. They were almost caught. She could
hear a yell, "Anthony, why is the dog barking? I'm going to check
outside." Grace's heart was racing, but she heard Anthony reply,
"Oh, Mike, it must be a cat. Go back to sleep." Steve was waiting
in the taxi, parked in the alley behind the barn, with a bouquet of
flowers and a box of candy. Grace was so excited to see Steve that
she never noticed until much later that she had put her shoes on
the wrong feet. Their plan was to stop at the home of a Justice of
the Peace between Arnold and Pittsburgh and then spend their
honeymoon in a Pittsburgh Hotel.

The next morning when Grace and Steve were found missing,
Antonio and Maria went to talk with Pietro and Conchetta, who
told Antonio they suspected that the couple might have eloped
because Steve had given his dad his entire last paycheck he had
earned as a single man, something he had never done before. Until 1999, neither I, nor my siblings, ever understood why the two
families had feuded during our parents' marriage. We assumed,
however, that my mother's parents were angry because they were
sure that Papa P and Mama Conchetta knew of the planned
elopement, feigned surprise and anger, but accommodated the
young couple by having a two-room apartment available for them
when they returned. Papa Anto, as we called him, felt sure the
young couple would not have eloped if the Cipollas had not made
the apartment available for the young couple. Steve had asked
Grace's father permission to marry Grace when she became sixteen, but he had refused. He told Steve, "I have other plans for
her." He no longer permitted Grace to have contact with Steve
unless it was a family event, determined that she would marry his
childhood friend's son.

Mary Ellen Cipolla Grasso

For sixty-three years we celebrated my parents' anniversary on December 7. On their 50th Anniversary my brother Buddy and his wife Mary gave them a special oak plaque with the *Praying Hands* and the dates engraved on a gold plate: *1921 to 1971.*

When Orazio died, and I was moving to Gainesville, my mother planned to live with me. Connie, Bob, Ron, and I, along with several grandchildren, came to her home to take whatever furniture or household items she did not want. Buddy, a Magistrate, had died in 1991, leaving Ron, an attorney for the Department of Agriculture in Washington, D. C., to read through all of the documents that had been filed away. He walked into the dining room where we all were sitting, holding what looked like a marriage certificate.

"Guess what! Mom and Dad weren't married on December 7. They were married on January 23, 1922."

We thought that was impossible, but the church's marriage certificate, the only one Ron found, read, "January 23, 1922." We looked at each other and started to laugh. Suddenly, hearing all our laughter, our mom walked into the room, snatched the document from Ron's hand, and said, "Give me that. You're not supposed to read it." We couldn't contain our laughter. We knew what had happened. She was some modern mother we had, out of sync with her generation. I must have inherited that trait from her. Finally, she sat down and told us the story. She and our dad did have every intention of getting married by a Justice of the Peace that night. At that time, many a Justice of the Peace married couples in their homes, but none were available so late at night, nearly midnight. Our dad convinced our mom that since they were in trouble anyway, they might as well enjoy the honeymoon. They just continued on their way to Pittsburgh to stay at the hotel where he had reserved a room.

The Letters

When they returned home after a week, they could not present proof of a valid signed marriage license to their parents. It would have been a scandal in that small town, not only a disgrace for the parents and their Italian families but also humiliation for the young couple. Relatives and neighbors knew they had eloped and were legally married and asked when there would be a celebration. The actual events were hushed up, but their parents began to tell everyone who asked, including the relatives, that they didn't consider it a marriage because a priest had not married the couple in a Catholic Church, mandatory for Italian immigrants.

Thus, a charade began. First Antonio and Pietro spoke with the parish priest, Reverend Nicola Fusco (the late Monsignor Nicola Fusco), a friend who had lived in Antonio's home when he was first sent to begin St. Peter Catholic Church. After speaking to Fr. Fusco, they then spoke with a Notary whom they knew and who agreed to issue a new license. The original outdated one, never validated, supposedly was lost and a new one had to be issued at least three days before January 23. Steve and Grace were married on January 23, 1922, in the church, and a small reception was held in the Puglisi home for relatives and close friends. Other than their parents, the priest, and the Notary, no one else ever knew the truth, not evening the siblings. Steve and Grace's secret was kept until 1999. Connie and I still have the only two remaining gifts from their wedding. Connie has the cut class oil and vinegar cruets, and I have the matching relish dish as a reminder of their marriage.

The Early Years

Adjacent to my Cipolla grandparents' grocery store with their apartment behind the store and above it, my family lived rent-free in the first floor apartment—a railroad type four room apartment with one room leading into another like railroad cars: the living room, bedroom, dining room with a sleeper sofa, and kitchen. Buddy was four and Concetta (nicknamed Etta) was three. They always enjoyed being at our grandparents' home because our teenaged Aunt Angie played with them. On the day of my birth they were at home. Our mother, knowing that she was in labor, told them she was sick, and they were to go to Grandma's for the day and tell her that "Mama is sick, and she had called the doctor." Aunt Angie stayed with them, but Mama Conchetta, along with Aunt Frances, the older teenager, went next door to wait for Dr. Frank Pessolano.

Meanwhile Aunt Frances went into the kitchen to boil a large kettle of water. When the doctor arrived, Mama Conchetta served as the unofficial midwife to assist him. It was a very difficult birth, and Mama Conchetta was told I was dead. I was simply set aside on the bed by the doctor who began to care for my twenty-year-old mother who had a blood clot blocking a deep vein and was having trouble breathing. Mama Conchetta refused to accept a "dead" granddaughter. She ran into the kitchen and filled a basin of hot water from the stove, instructing Aunt Frances, who was in the kitchen, to fill another basin with cold water and ice. Because we did not have an icebox, she had to run to their store next door to get a chunk of ice from the icebox there. When she returned, Mama Conchetta had me in the hot water, rubbing my body. She immediately began plunging me from the hot one to the icy cold one. Suddenly, I gasped for air and began kicking and screaming. I guess I had no intention of dying, at least not that day.

Dr. Pessolano obviously had little experience with phlebitis, a deep vein thrombosis caused by a blood clot blocking the vein in her left leg because he advised my mother that her left leg should be amputated. My mother refused to follow Dr. Pessolano's advice. She now had three children: a four year old, a three year old, and a newborn. No medication was prescribed, but the doctor insisted she remain in bed for at least six weeks. During those weeks he visited her at home, perhaps only three or four times, leaving my grandmother to care for both my mother and me. Dr. Pessolano had a reputation of leaving his patients after surgery, even those in the hospital, and would sometimes go on vacation, leaving patients only in charge of a nurse. Some patients died from his lack of care after an appendectomy, including a nineteen-year-old who lived next door to my parents. Still, the Italian immigrants continued to have Dr. Pessolano as their doctor because many could not speak English, and he could communicate with them. Besides, since he could speak Italian, they trusted him.

Mama Conchetta and my two aunts became the official baby sitters, housekeepers, and cooks. Wanting to get ahead, my father worked two jobs. Besides working as a miner, he sold fruits and vegetables early in the morning. When he started peddling, he needed to buy a truck to carry all of the produce. He had never driven a vehicle, but he was sure he could. All he needed was the book of instructions.

I listened with amazement years later when he said, "I purchased the truck, put the booklet of instructions behind the steering wheel, leaned it against the windshield, and drove home. There weren't a lot of cars on the roads, and I drove slowly. During my spare time, I practiced driving until I could drive all over town and even to Pittsburgh where the produce was." He was now ready to become a huckster.

To buy the freshest fruits and vegetables, he would leave home long before dawn to drive to the wholesale markets in Pittsburgh, located about eighteen miles south of Arnold. Returning home earlier than that other peddlers, he would make his rounds in the neighborhoods, selling produce to customers. Then he went to work in the coal mine. He was only able to be with his wife and children on the weekends. He must have been both emotionally and physically exhausted. Because my mother could not produce milk, she was unable to nurse me. My aunts fed me evaporated milk diluted with water and three months later a Uneeda Biscuit soaked in warm milk or sugar water. The biscuit, created in 1899 by Nabisco (the National Baking Company), was the first pre-packaged soda cracker. It replaced soda crackers that were stored in large barrels purchased by the bagfuls, and the crackers were more sanitary. Since there was no baby food in jars for sale, my grandmother cooked and pureed fruit. As I became older, she cooked and pureed vegetables from the garden, mixing them with beef or chicken broth and cooked *pastina*, a pasta made especially for babies. At times she would mix an egg into the cooked *pastina*. My mother was then able to feed me while she sat on a chair.

Unfortunately, my mother's affected vein was permanently damaged, and the condition worsened. Trying to take care of us, cook, and do light housekeeping, she hobbled with her left leg bent on a chair, using the chair as a walker until she could walk without it. My aunts helped take care of me until I was four months old, but I always believed they did so because they escaped chores at their home. Other than to wear elastic stockings, there seemed to be no permanent cure for my mother, but she never again had Dr. Pessolano care for any of us. Our new family doctor was the young Dr. Robert Johnson who was able to treat her phlebitis so she could walk without pain. Although she was advised not to have more children; she had two more after me: Robert Stephen named after both the doctor and our dad, and Ronald David, named after a character in a novel she had read.

Every evening my mother, who loved books, spent time reading to us. First, it was fairy tales, then books written for children, and finally novels suitable for older children such as *Treasure Island* and *Kidnapped* by Robert Louis Stevenson. Stopping at the most exciting parts, she left us hungry for more. We begged her to continue, but she always made us wait for another day. During that time, we children would discuss the book, trying to decide what would happen next.

Despite that fact that she had only a sixth grade education, my mother became a remarkable woman and mother. Her salvation was the love of reading. During her life she just didn't read books, magazines, and daily newspapers; she devoured them. Subscriptions to the *Book of the Month club, Reader's Digest,* and *Ladies Home Journal* delighted her. Later in life, she read my *Time, Newsweek,* and *Life* magazines when she visited my home even though she was considered legally blind. Although she had lost the vision in her right eye following cataract surgery, she still read every day. No audio book was suitable for her even though I urged her to listen to one I had brought home from the library.

"I'm not blind," she'd say, "I just can't see from one eye."

I recall one of the books I had bought her was one she considered a "dirty, sexy book." She reprimanded me, saying that I had given her a "really dirty book."

"Oh, I'm sorry," I said. I'll donate it to the Friends of the Library."

Without hesitation, she replied, "No! I'm going to read it again."

I had no answer. I just smiled. When she was nearly ninety-five years old, she had trouble reading and understanding what she had read. She was living with me then and had just begun reading a book she had received as a Christmas gift. She read for about ten minutes before closing the book. Holding the book in her arms, close to her, she said, "Why did God do this to me?" I asked, "Do what?" She answered, "Not letting me read again." I turned my head quickly because I didn't want her to see that I had tears in my eyes.

The Maverick

Although my father was born in Italy, I was not reared in a stereo-typical Italian family. One of five children, I was the middle child. The oldest, Buddy, originally named Peter, was four years older that I. He got his nickname the second day he was born when my father announced to the miners he was working with that he and his wife had a son. Someone said, "Now you have your own "buddy," and the name remained. His legal name automatically became Buddy P. Cipolla. He went to school and World War II as Buddy, married, became a Magistrate (a Judge of the Lower Court), and died as Buddy. Connie was three years older than I, but because she started first grade before she was five years old (no public kindergarten existed then) we were light years apart. All summer she had insisted that she wanted to go to school, and because my mother claimed that Connie's birth certificate had been burned in a fire, which we did experience, Connie was registered for first grade only on my mother's word. There were two younger brothers: Bob was four years younger than I, and Ron was nine years younger.

My father left mining when I was two years old, and in a few years became president of his own trucking company, hauling coal to residential homes. As the years went on he began to haul coal to factories such as ALCOA (Aluminum Company of America), Gulf Research, American Window Glass Company, and others as well as office and retail buildings. My mother was busy serving as his secretary, taking telephone orders, scheduling the truck drivers, handling their time sheets, and receiving their signed receipts

Mary Ellen Cipolla Grasso

at the end of each day. She had household help as assisting my dad took up much of her time.

At home we spoke no Italian except when my grandparents or other elderly relatives or friends visited. My father spoke fluent English without an accent. Buddy was the only grandchild who spoke fluent Italian. As the first grandchild, he spent many hours with our Cipolla grandparents and his aunts and learned the language. Papa P never mastered English, but three afternoons a week, Mama Conchetta went to the elementary school to study English. I still see her with her clean, crisp housedress, carrying her books, meeting her neighborhood classmates, and walking to school with them. She was the one who dealt with the salesmen, not Papa P. Connie understood the language and spoke a little Italian, but I, at four years of age, could do neither. Since we lived next door to our grandparents, every night before bedtime we went there for a half hour. Mama Conchetta told us bedtime stories before out returning home, but the rule was that we could stay up and hear them if we understood the language. When she finished the story, we had to tell her what it was about. I couldn't so I had to go home and go to bed early. I began to realize that if I wanted the same privilege, I needed to learn the language. As a result, I started to connect articles with their Italian names when my grandparents spoke. While I couldn't speak it, I did understand it.

Most of our meals were considered "American" rather than Italian. We did have some traditional dishes such as lasagna, minestrone, lentils, baked chicken with vegetables, and spaghetti with sauce. During the early years of our parents' marriage, they rented an apartment from a woman of English descent. She taught our mother many different recipes such as baked ham with raisin sauce, candied yams, potato salad with mayonnaise rather than olive oil, French toast, grilled cheese sandwiches, stuffed pork chops, and cranberry sauce.

I was eight years old when I began to cook. My mother had become ill, and she decided I, rather than Connie, would stay home from school to help care for her and cook a simple dinner. She felt that since I was in elementary school, I could easily make up the schoolwork I would miss. I was to make marinara sauce for spaghetti. Our home then was a three-story colonial-type house. The bottom floor was a finished basement with a combination kitchen, family room, and laundry on one side. Many Italian hones had two kitchens. One was also on the first floor. The other side of the basement had a bathroom and a shower, a furnace, coal cellar, and fruit cellar (a cold room where the dozens of jars of canned fruits and vegetables were stored), and clothes lines to hang the wet laundry during the winter months or when it rained.

I would forget some of the instructions and have to run up three flights of stairs to ask, "What else, Mom?" I stood on a wooden chair to stir the ingredients, proud that I could cook. When it came time to fill the large pot with water, I telephoned a neighbor, Mrs. Vivola, to help me carry it to the stove. As the spaghetti boiled, I tasted it to make sure I didn't overcook it. Once of twice I got stung with the boiling water, but I didn't mind. Mrs. Vivola returned in time to drain the pasta, but I stirred the sauce in it. Connie had set the table and sliced the loaf of bread, and we both served dinner. My parents told me, "It's delicious." I'm not sure it really was, but no one complained, and they complimented me on my efforts.

When my youngest brother, Ron, was two years old, my mother couldn't handle him, four other children, and the business. She simply said, "He's all yours." I was eleven years old, and I raised him. Everything was "Mallen" since he couldn't pronounce "Mary

Ellen" when he was a toddler. I bathed him, potty trained him, read to him, and put him to bed; and when he was older, took him to the movies every Saturday. I helped him with his homework until he graduated from high school. I remember many times at one o'clock in the morning when he would awaken me to check his English essay. When he got hurt, he would run to me, "Mallen, I fell down." When he eloped with Ruth after they both had graduated from Bucknell University, he telephoned me. "Mary Ellen, I just got married. Can you send me $350.00 from my bank account?"

"Married!" I yelled. "You just registered for Dickinson Law School. Have you told Dad?"

"No, but you tell Mom and Dad. You know how to break the news."

That wasn't an easy task. When they did plan to come home for their first visit a few weeks later, our dad, still very angry, refused to welcome them.

I recall my mother shaking her finger at him and saying, "Steve, you know what we did. Just behave when they walk in. Be civil."

I thought it was because they, too, had eloped or that Ron still had to complete law school. My dad soon had a change of heart and told my mom to go out and buy them whatever household items they needed to begin marriage. I opened my Hope Chest and gave them half of everything that I had saved. It was 1958, and I had no desire of ever getting married.

Many years later Ron said to me, "When I think of Mom, I think of you as my mother." In all fairness to our mom during that time, she also took care of three nieces and a nephew everyday because Anthony and Frances worked. Frances, who had lived in Niagara Falls, New York, was a widow at twenty-one. Uncle Joe died of tuberculosis, leaving her with a two-year-old daughter and a son who was twenty-one days old. Frances returned home to live in Arnold in one of her parents' apartments. Anthony, whose husband was not living with her at the time, had two daughters who also stayed with us during the day. My Mom never had fewer than eight children to care for at our home. Still, I had a lot of responsibility.

I was capable at thirteen of getting an entire New Years' dinner prepared including roasting a twenty-five pound turkey because my mom had become ill with the flu on New Year's Eve. My parents had invited out-of-town relatives, and my mom did not want to cancel the dinner. I always helped her in the kitchen and was delighted to take charge. It was a challenge, fun for me. At five o'clock in the morning I woke up eager to get started. Fortunately the pies had been baked the day before and stored in the cold cellar along with the cranberry sauce. The turkey was in cold water ready to be stuffed and baked. How difficult could that be? It wasn't, but I was exhausted at the end of the dinner. Connie had made plans to meet her girlfriends that afternoon, expecting someone else to clear the table, put the remainder of the food away, and wash all the dishes, the roaster, and the pots and pans. The guests did clear the table and put the leftover food in the refrigerator, but Connie, despite her plans and one look from our dad, had to wash and dry the dishes.

Early Childhood

Although I seldom played with my sister, my childhood was very happy. Connie and I were very different. I never remember her playing with dolls or paper doll cut outs or reading books. On the other hand, I spent hours reading; playing with those booklets of paper dolls that cost ten cents and featured Shirley Temple, Princess Elizabeth and Princess Margaret, or the Dionne quintuplets from Canada; dressing the dolls in their changes of clothing and imagining scenes they could enact. Buddy was gifted at designing many different board games that we three played together. But we didn't need always to play together. Living in neighboring apartment building or near relatives' homes, we always had cousins or friends to play with after school, on weekends, or during vacations. The boys made kites, played with cards and marbles, or just roamed in the nearby woods picking berries or dandelions when they weren't climbing trees. The girls had sticks of chalk for hopscotch, jump ropes, and a set of jacks, a game played with a small rubber ball and ten jacks, metal pieces with points shaped like a star. The player picked up the jacks in combinations from one to ten jacks all at once without dropping any jacks or bouncing the ball twice. At first, my friends were cousins or children of Italian immigrants. Buddy's friends were also cousins and neighborhood boys. Connie's were cousins and classmates, but usually not children of Italian immigrants.

I wasn't always the obedient child. I had a mind of my own, once terrifying my entire extended family when I left home without permission one Sunday in search of St. Peter's Church. My mother, who was frequently ill, had just come home from the hospital.

The Letters

Buddy and Connie were going to Mass and Sunday school, and our dad gave them a few coins to put into the collection box. I wanted to go with them, but because I was not quite three years old, I was not permitted to go with them. Instead my dad gave me a few pennies to buy some penny candy at Papa P's store. I still wanted to go to church. When they left, I started walking down Drey Street, passing the playground and crossing the railroad tracks. I recognized the American Window Glass Company to my right and assumed I was going in the right direction. At the next intersection, I turned left. I had no idea where I was going, but I knew I was somewhere downtown as I had been there several times window-shopping with my mom. Suddenly nothing looked familiar. I kept walking, but after a while I became so tired that I stopped to rest, sitting on a step to the entrance of a closed store. In those days all stores were closed on Sundays. I must have walked more than a mile.

Finally, a girl stopped. According to her, I was crying.

"Where are you going? Do you live around here?"

Though my tears, I said, "I'm going to church. Take me to church. My brother and sister are there."

Since I didn't know the name of the church, she took me to hers, the Greek Orthodox Church in New Kensington, a neighboring city, not Arnold where I lived. After the service she took me to the New Kensington Police Department. In the interim, not finding me at home or at my grandparents' store, my father became concerned. Had I gone to Aunt Mary and Uncle Banard's home to play with Marie (nicknamed Tootsie)? I hadn't. He checked other relatives who lived nearby. I didn't seem to be anywhere. By this time aunts, uncles, and friends who had cars quickly began searching for me, asking people walking on the sidewalk if they had seen a little blonde girl around three years old wandering around. One pedestrian claimed he had seen a little blond girl wearing a pink sweater near the Allegheny River. The description was accurate. My father became frantic. He telephoned the Arnold Police Department. They had no report of a lost girl or a drowning.

Of course, they hadn't seen me. I was miles away in New Kensington being entertained by the police who were trying to get information from me. It seemed that when they asked me what my name was or where I lived, I would say, "You don't know me. You can't find my house." They asked, "What's your daddy's name?" Sitting on the desk wearing one of their caps and eating a lollipop that they had given me, I answered, "You don't know my daddy." It wasn't until one of the officers decided to check with the Arnold Police Department that they were able to identify me. It never occurred to them that this small, feisty, no-longer-crying child had walked nearly two miles from home.

My dad rushed to get me only to find me entertaining the police who were laughing with all my chatter. Not knowing whether to hug or spank me, my dad scooped me up in his arms, thanked the police, whom he knew, and silently drove off. He didn't spank me, but the relatives who had now gathered in my mom's bedroom reprimanded me. "You're a naughty girl. Why did you run away? Why didn't you give the police your daddy's name? Look how sick your mommy is! You need to be spanked!" I just crawled up on the bed, lay down beside my mom, and cried, "I just wanted to go to church." No one hugged me, held me, or kissed me. Exhausted I fell asleep, holding on to my mom's nightgown. I expected to be punished the next day. Instead, my dad bought me a beautiful child's tea set of rose-colored glass dishes with cups and saucers, a sugar bowl, a creamer, and a teapot. My cousin Vincie was there at our home the next day visiting me. He played all afternoon with me with the tea set that I still have.

School Days

I knew that when I was six years old, I would be scheduled for a tonsillectomy before registering for first grade. Children in those days had their tonsils removed before entering first grade. School always started after Labor Day, the first Monday in September and ended the day before Memorial Day. Since children did not go to the hospital for minor surgery, my tonsils were removed in Dr. Johnson's office. After surgery, my father wrapped me up in his coat jacket, put me in my mother's arms, and drove home. I still slept in an iron-framed crib, large enough for a six year old. When I opened my eyes later that day, I saw my dad in the bedroom with a friend, a carpenter, whom he had hired to make me a beautiful wooden cradle for my dolls. He had put one of my dolls in the cradle and was rocking it.

"Wake up, honey. Mama has something for you to drink. Look at your dolly in the cradle. She's sick, too."

All I could say was, "My throat hurts. It's beautiful, but I want to sleep."

My father and I always had a special bond, and I loved him dearly. Yet, unlike my siblings, there is only one photograph before I was two years old, and it is with my father. I am nine months old seated on the hood of a Pontiac, my dad's first car. He is standing beside me smiling. There is only one other photo of me as a child, taken during the Depression by a door-to-door photographer. I'm two years old, and I am sitting in a child's rocking chair.

I was soon well, looking forward to entering first grade. When my mother and I went to the elementary school, named The Leishman Avenue Building after the avenue where it was located, I was excited to learn that I would be in Miss Steffey's class, one of three first grade classes, and everyone loved Miss Steffey. The other two schools were The Victoria Avenue Building and the Orchard Avenue Building for the Junior and Senior High School classes. Before World War II began, there were no married women teaching in the schools I attended. I remember Miss Daisy Culp, who taught for 49 nine years before retiring, and Miss Frieda Cook, who taught for 38 years. I was teaching in the high school when both retired. It was not uncommon in those days for female teacher not to marry, but to have a lifetime career as teachers. However, once the male teachers were drafted for the war, married women were hired to replace them.

I don't remember any African-American students attending the Arnold Schools in those days. Most African-American families lived in New Kensington, the city Arnold had seceded from in 1895. Before going to school, I was not really aware that anti-immigration prejudices existed among some of the teachers. My parents entertained people of all nationalities or religious beliefs. At one time some Catholic priests believed it was not proper to entertain divorced couples, but my family did. It wasn't until third grade, just before Thanksgiving Day, that I realized prejudices against Italian immigrants did exist.

School was to be dismissed early on Wednesday, the day before the holiday. There, perhaps, fifteen minutes remaining before the dismissal bell rang, Miss Wallis was just filling up time by talking about the first Thanksgiving Day and by asking who was going to have a traditional Thanksgiving Day dinner with a turkey. I, along with a few others, raised my hand. I heard, "Put your hand down, Mary Ellen. You're not having turkey."

The Letters

I insisted I was, "My dad bought a live turkey. It's in our back-yard. The neighbor next door is going to chop off its head."

"No," she replied. "Italians don't have turkey for Thanksgiving or any of the other traditional American foods."

I stood up. I was angry and started to yell. "We do, too. My mother is making cranberry sauce, corn, stuffing, and candied sweet potatoes."

"Sit down, Mary Ellen, we all know Italians have chickens or capons, not turkey."

The dismissal bell rang, saving me from another outrage, and we all filed out of the classroom. Feeling embarrassed, I started to cry, but the worst was yet to come. Walking along with me, down the alley, was my friend Yolanda, trying to console me.

"Don't cry, Mary Ellen. You know Italians don't eat turkey or that other food."

Two years later, when I was in fifth grade, there was another episode. I always had one or two pencils with me for school, tucked in my book bag. After all, Mama Conchetta always made sure we grandchildren had a new pencil from her store when we only had a stub of a pencil left. For some reason I had not packed my pencils that morning in my book bag. Perhaps, after completing my homework, I left them on the kitchen table. Miss Radaker, who always had a small box of pencil stubs on her desk, gave other students a pencil from the box if they had forgotten theirs. It was the first class of the day.

I raised my hand that morning. "May I borrow a pencil from the box? I forgot mine." I expected her to say. "Yes, but walk quietly."

Mary Ellen Cipolla Grasso

Instead, she yelled. "You Italians are always forgetting something. You're never prepared for class. You never seem to have a pencil."

I flew into a rage. "You always give Betty, Jean, Shirley, or Marilyn one. Why not me?"

Miss Radaker continued, "You Italians are all alike. All you eat is spaghetti with garlic."

I don't remember what I said, but I was livid. What did food have to do with a pencil? I became uncontrollable. Miss Radaker instructed a student to get the principal, who came with the school nurse. When they walked into the room, I was still raging. I knew the principal, Miss Jay, and the nurse personally because I had been selected as an office girl that took notes to teachers and collected the attendance sheets for that hour of class rather than being assigned to a Study Hall to begin to do homework. The nurse managed to take me to her office. I don't know whether or not my mother became involved, but Miss Rhodes never opposed me again, not even when I began teaching in that school after graduating from college, and she became Mrs. Fitzgerald.

I was surprised to have a problem with a teacher in a public school. Weren't they supposed to be models of trust and honesty? Weren't we taught to respect them? I did have some excellent teachers. Miss Florence Ford, who taught Grammar and English and American Literature, was a wonderful teacher. Obviously, not all fit that pattern. Take, for instance, the marching band director, Glen Davis, who also taught music. He was young and very handsome, and many girls had a crush on him, including me. I had written lyrics to a football song, and I asked him to check it. Did he think it was good enough to be played at our high school football games? I remember the first two lines:

347

The Letters

You do the playing; we'll cheer you on.
Don't be delaying, victory will dawn.

He checked all of the lyrics and suggested that I change one of the words: *dawn* to *don*, defined as "to take on." I preferred the word I had used, but because he was the teacher, I assumed he knew better so I agreed to change the word.

The first time the song was introduced to the students at a pep rally, I was given credit for the lyrics, but that was the last time. It was my senior year, and I graduated at the end of the term. I left for college and had no reason to return to Arnold High School. However, I happened to be home when I was persuaded to attend a band concert at the school. My song was played following an announcement by the principal: "The band will now play our popular football song thanks to Mr. Davis who wrote the lyrics." I sat in disbelief. The next morning I wrote a letter to the principal, setting the record straight, but Mr. Davis's name was never removed from the sheet music, and I lost all respect for him.

During the elementary and high school years, the girl friends I had always played with were no longer permitted to play with me after my family moved up the hill on Drey Street, just three blocks away from our old neighborhood. I never knew why until years later. My father had built a large home for the times, along with two large garages to house the trucks for his growing trucking business and the family car. The home had a ceramic tile lavender and mint green bathroom, a clothes chute on each of two floors for us to throw the dirty laundry down to a cage in the laundry room. I once heard my dad say that the home alone cost $8,000, which was expensive in that town for 1935. According to realtors, a new 6-room home cost slightly below $4,000 and a good used home between $3,000 and $2,500. Fourteen years later my gross salary as a teacher was only $2,000 a year.

My father was a well-known businessman, but he never forgot his Sicilian friends. While he was a member of the Elks Club, the Moose Lodge, the Eagles, and later the first President of the Arnold Lions Club, he also belonged to the Grotessi Club, whose founding members had immigrated from Grotte. He was now president of the Cipolla Fuel Company, a coal mine that he and his two partners had purchased. One partner was Irish Catholic and the other was Jewish. My parents made no distinction among people and judged them by their character, not their nationality or religious beliefs. Besides, I'm certain that if out ancestry were known, there might have been people who held prejudices and who might have avoided us. Papa Anto had a Jewish Great Great Grandfather, a young boy who traveled with a Jewish peddler throughout Sicily. I never knew his name, but I remember Papa Anto and his sister Grace always had arguments because she didn't want the relationship known. Papa Anto always told us that the young boy fell in love with a Sicilian girl from the Puglisi family and chose to remain in Grotte and marry her, and, I suppose, he became Catholic.

On the other hand, Mama Conchetta's father, from the Cimino family, was an ordained priest who left the church after saying his first Mass. It was customary among Italians for the oldest son to become a priest and the oldest daughter, a nun. When Jiacomo (James) was a teenager, he had a girlfriend, Francesca, and he was very much in love with her, but he had to enter the seminary. The day he held his first Mass, his parents said to him. "I have good news for you that will make you very happy. Your brother is going to marry Francesca. She will be your sister." Still in love with Francesca, a few nights later he left his clerical robes in his room and eloped with her. Unfortunately, it was a very tragic marriage. In her late thirties or early forties, she had a massive stroke and became paralyzed, spending the remainder of her life on a cot in the kitchen. Jiacomo's brothers, all farmers, would give their brother a plot of land, donkeys, goats, and chickens. The land dried up, the animals died, and his brothers would give him a new piece of land and more animals, but it was always the same outcome. What was strange was that when his brothers took the dried up land back, it became fertile again producing many new crops.

In a letter to his daughter, he once wrote that God was punishing him for leaving the church, and he regretted his actions. Some years later, Papa P received a letter with the envelope bordered in black, signifying a death. He put it away, sure that his mother-in-law had died. He told my father that he would give it to Mama Conchetta at a later date. After all, she was always expecting to receive such news and even prayed that her mother would no longer have to suffer. Death would be a blessing. She herself had already lost four children, the last being three-year-old Peter, who died of strep throat. Grief was unbearable for her when Papa P finally opened the letter. Her beloved father had died at age 54 of a massive coronary while working in the fields.

It was 1939, and my life had already changed. I belonged to Girl Scouts, going to Day Camp in the summer by riding my bicycle to the camp. Although I had received the bicycle for my eleventh birthday, I shared it with Connie. I had a scooter, and the bicycle and scooter were passed down to Bobby and Ronnie. All of us had roller skates, but Buddy had ice skates. The younger boys had a sled and wagon. When Buddy was 18, he got a new Plymouth to drive that cost about $500.00. I didn't realize how different we were from our childhood immigrant friends until some years later when I was riding a bus with one of them. I asked Anto-niette why she was never allowed to play with me or join some of the clubs at school after we had moved. She said, "My parents thought you would be a bad influence on me because they couldn't afford some of the activities your parents could." I never thought I was different, except when it came to my relationships with my siblings.

Connie and I were never close as sisters when we were young. The only thing we had in common was that we both sang. She was an alto and I was a lyric soprano. We often sang duets while we washed and dried the dishes. She won first prize, a wristwatch, in an amateur hour contest, and she sang on the radio. When I was nine, I was cast in the school musical, *Babes in Toyland*, playing the roll of a black-faced doll with pig tales. I sang *Dinah* and received the biggest applause of the night. When there was a testimonial banquet or a political fundraiser, I was asked to sing *The Star Spangled Banner*. I was also asked to join the Senior High School A Cappella Choir while I was still in ninth grade, the last year of junior high school.

During World War II when movie stars traveled around the country to sell war bonds, I was always selected to open the program by singing the National Anthem. At one fundraiser, Hollywood actor Robert Preston was the celebrity. We sat on stage next to each other. I was probably fifteen. He asked me where the piano and my accompanist were. I said, "I don't have either." He looked at me. "You're not going to sing cold, are you?" He meant, "Without accompaniment."

"Of course I am," I replied. "I always do."

When I had finished, I sat down again. Astonished, he looked at me, shrugged his shoulders, and said, "I guess you *can* sing cold."

I became involved in school activities, but I never seemed to fit in with my generation, not like Connie did. Named Princess of her class, she was charismatic and began dating early. We didn't even resemble each other as teenagers. She was thin. I was overweight.

She had a knack for styling her hair. I did not. She was very social, attending all of the school dances, and dated early. I did not. I was elected president of Girl Reserves, a service club sponsored by the YWCA. We collected products donated by retail stores and families for the servicemen, packed shoe boxes of the items and sent the boxes to the servicemen overseas.

Our father treated Connie and me differently. He was stricter with her than with her. I had more freedom but more responsibility. When Ron was six years old, the doctor detected a hurt murmur and suggested that our mom take him to Florida for the winter. She left in November, and Connie and I were in charge. At age fifteen I was given the responsibility of paying all bills and going grocery shopping. All utility bills were paid in cash at the bank. Groceries were also paid in cash. Since Connie was attending Commercial College and working as the secretary at the Cipolla Fuel Company, I had to start dinner if she were late. We did have a woman six days a week who cleaned the house and did all the laundry, and Mama Conchetta would check on us once a day as we were preparing dinner.

Our dad loved chocolate covered marshmallow cookies, and one day in my haste after shopping, I just shoved the package in a cabinet along with other items. He rushed into the house for a snack as he was repairing a truck in the garage with one of his drivers. He reached into the cabinet to grab some cookies.

"Mary Ellen, what kind of cookies did you buy?"

"The ones you always like. Why?"

He opened his hand. He had reached for the dog biscuits instead. He was still chewing and swallowing when I said, "Those are Duke's." He then threw away the rest of the dog treats he had in his hand and washed out his mouth with water. We were expecting him to explode with anger, but he just shook his head and said, "No wonder they tasted dry." I handed him the package of marshmallow cookies. "I'm sorry, Dad. I was in a hurry." I never did that again. Duke's treats were put on a shelf in the laundry room, and Dad never said another word about my mistake. If dinner wasn't exactly right, he would just say, "You'll do better the next time, girls."

Connie, Bob, and I never forgot another incident during those months our mother and brother Ronnie were in Florida. We were just finishing dinner, and Dad began telling us the story of Charlemagne, the founder of the first empire after Rome fell. He was very animated. Suddenly, he stood up, leaned over the table swinging an imaginary sword over his head, slashing some imaginary enemy warrior, and said, "And Charlemagne came charging down the road fighting." At the same moment he accidentally hit the nearly empty basked of sliced Italian bread and the platter with the remainder of the roast beef and vegetables. They went flying off the table and onto the floor. For a moment, we didn't say a word, but he said, "All right, girls, just pick it up." The dish didn't break, and miraculously the food stayed on the platter, and bread remained in the basket. Only the floor was dirty where the gravy had splattered on the tile. Connie, Bob, and I burst into laughter, putting the basket and platter back on the table. Someone said, "Hey, Dad, that was great!" Then he also began to laugh, "Well, anyway, Charlemagne won."

I don't ever remember going to a movie or *Jacob's Ice Cream Parlor* with Connie. We went our separate ways. We were both involved in several activities at school but not at the same time: *The Broadcaster*, the school newspaper; the National Honor Society; the choir; and the theater. I saw the injustice of some of the school rules and tried to change them. One of them was the fact that boys were able to substitute classes for required ones, and the girls weren't. The school had three tracts: Academic (college prep), Commercial (secretarial and bookkeeping), and Vocational (automobile repair and mechanics). In tenth grade I was scheduled to take the required biology class since I was in the Academic tract, but I refused. I couldn't think of dissecting a frog. We had to take only one science course, and I planned to take chemistry before I graduated. I went to the principal to ask if there was another class I could substitute for biology. There wasn't, at least that's what he said. However, there was one for vocational students, printing, but only boys were permitted to register for the class. I discovered it could be used for an elective, but I still needed a written approval from the principal, which he finally gave me. I enjoyed every class although some of the boys would scramble or spill the letters and symbols in my chase, a rectangular-shaped frame used to lock in print. I had to put all the letters and symbols in the proper slot before using the press. They also would leave me to clean the press when they had used it. It was a rule: if you use the press, you clean it, but the teacher never interfered. Nevertheless, I learned a lot about printing that I would use later.

The following year I became aware of another problem. First, the winters in Pennsylvania were very cold, and girls were not permitted to wear slacks to class. Students in high school no longer wore snowsuit pants under a skirt or dress to class as they did when they were younger. Junior and senior high school students had to change buildings, walking up a steep incline, known as Rankin Street, and then climb up one hundred steps to the Orchard Avenue Building to take classes in home economics, chemistry, biology, Latin, printing, and the mandatory vocational classes, known as shop, for the junior high school boys. Many girls fell down the icy steps or slipped on the sidewalks, bruising their knees and embarrassing themselves when their coats and skirts flew up to their waists. I spoke with a few girls about wearing jeans and flannel shirts or sweaters, and about eight of us did. According to the superintendent, it was not suitable attire, and we were to be given a zero for every day we attended class wearing those clothes. Regardless of what our grade average was, at that rate, we would all fail. Needless to say, we stopped after a week. We never would have ever guessed that years later jeans would become appropriate attire for all public school students.

Top: Rafela Scifo, Pippo Grimaldi, Orazio, and Ombretta Scifo standing in front of a souvenir shop in Mt. Etna.

Bottom: Guests at the wedding reception for Susan and Joe included Stephen's former baby sitter, Marie Rizzo and her husband, Dick, Connie, Gil and Joyce Puissegur. Gil and Joyce vacationed in Mexico with Orazio and me.

Top: Standing on the beach of the Ionia Sea with Orazio are nieces and nephews with their children: Maria, Tancredi, Gino, Velia, Simona, and Loredana.

Below: Visiting family on one occasion we stayed with Lino and his family: Diletta, Tancredi, Donato, and Maria.

Top: The Twenty-fifth Wedding Anniversary of Pippo and Elvira. With them are aslo her sister and bother-in-law, Vito and Giovanna Scifo.

Bottom: Mary Ellen, Fina, Tita, and Gianni on a cruise to the Bahamas. Gianni bought two laterns and then converted them as hanging lamps for this home in Catania.

Left: Galloping on grandson Brenton's hobby horse, "Thunder," while visiting us for six weeks in Florida: Tita, Fina, and Gianni.

Bottom: Meeting our Grandmother Maria's nephew in Grotte, Sicily. Leonardo Bucemi with Susan, Orazio and me

Right: The wedding of Gino's daughter Simona: Loredana, her son Antonio, Gino, Simona, and Velia.

Bottom: Connie and Ernest Goggio in Marmaris, Turkey.

Top: Cruising for Mom's 80th birthday party in 1992 with Ron, Orazio, Mary and Buddy.

Left: Stephen, Lisa, Kyle, and Brenton

Top: Professor Mary DiStefano Diaz at my home in Gainesville, Florida March 2007.

Left: Youngest brother, Ron and his wife Ruth.

Right: Visiting Bob and Sandi in Port Charlotte, Florida.

Top: Having a reunion in 2005 in Pennsylvania and remembering our adventurous trips to Mexico: Jerry, Mary Ellen, and Dorothy.

Bottom: Steve and Grace's Golden Wedding Anniversary in 1971. Front Row: Stephen and Susan. Second Row: Jay, Connie, Mom, Dad, Mary Ellen, Lisa. Third Row: Dom, Mary, Buddy, Ron, Bob, and Orazio.

Top: Our parents 60th Wedding Anniversary. Mom and Dad, Mary Ellen, Buddy, Connie, Ron and Bob. Dom died in 1978 of a sudden heart attack.

Right: Our first family portrait was taken in 1930. Our parents were Matron of Honor and Best Man for the wedding of Lena and Tony Lamendola. Connie was seven, I was three, and Buddy was eight. Connie and I were given some coins to hold.

364

Right: Grace's baptism April 1907. She was three months old. Left to right: Mike, Papa Antonio with Joe on his lap, Mama Maria with Grace, and Leonard (Banard).

Mary Celen   3 yrs

Left: The "runaway" who got lost trying to find Mt. St. Peter Church.

Left: Mike and Anthony's wedding portrait.

Bottom: I'm panning for gold July 27, 2006 by separating the gold from the bag of dirt and gravel at Gold Dredge No. 8 in Fairbanks, Alaska. It was the trip Orazio and I planned three times but could never take together.

Top: Each year there was a birthday picnic at Scanga's Farm for Papa Anto and the extended Cipolla and Puglisi families. Papa Anto and Papa P were caught in a deep coversation.

Bottom: Mama Maria and Mama Concetta (Conchetta) loved nothing more than watching the youngsters' activities during the birthday celebration

The World War 2 Years

For high school students, the bombing of Pearl Harbor and the start of World War II had a profound effect on out lives. Not only did we ever forget the announcement on the radio on December 7, 1941, but also, the special meeting Superintendent H. L. Holste called to announce that a recent graduate, George Leslie, was among the first serviceman killed in Pearl Harbor. I didn't know him well, but Connie did. All field trips were cancelled, and as the draft began, we lost most of our young male teachers. For the first time, married women were hired to teach, and a few former female teachers came out of retirement. As the war continued, students who turned eighteen seemed to be drafted immediately. It was not unusual when I was a senior to learn some mornings that one of our classmates had voluntary joined the service and left for training. I still remember that cold morning, standing at the railroad station with my family, watching Buddy go off to war. He was deferred twice because he was working for the government by driving a coal truck to fulfill the government contracts the Cipolla Fuel Company held.

The older men, no longer of draft age, became Air Raid Wardens, and I, along with other teenagers who were at least thirteen years old, became Junior Air Raid Cadets. On nights when the city had a blackout as part of an air raid drill, our job was to walk with the warden, making sure that every home was completely dark. There could be no visible lights, and shades and curtains should be drawn. If there was a violation, we knocked on the door or rang the bell, reminding residents of the drill and the law while the warden we were assigned to accompany stood on the sidewalk. On my first night, I wanted to be sure I followed orders, but I didn't know this warden had a warped sense of humor. That evening I was unaware of his motive. I adjusted my helmet and armband and checked to make sure my flashlight had batteries that worked. Suddenly, the warden ordered me to check a house that he noticed did not have all the shades drawn. One on the second floor the shade was partially drawn, but there was no light coming from the window. Nevertheless, he ordered me to knock on the door until the owner responded. I must have been on the porch fifteen or twenty minutes.

I shouted, "No one's home."

"You just keep knocking," he urged me.

Finally the owner came to the door. He noticed that his friend Frank was standing on the sidewalk. He was visibly angry. "Frank, don't you have anything better to do?" Frank just laughed. "You go to bed too early." The joke was too subtle for me. I was among those young naïve girls who had been sheltered by their parents. As the war continued, more of our young men were killed. Once a week before classes began there was a short assembly in the auditorium. Students who had lost a father, a brother, a grandfather, or uncle pinned a large gold star on a ceiling-high blue banner that was lowered by a rope. There was never a dry eye.

One day during a social studies class, we were feeling especially sad, and we began complaining to our teacher, Mr. Milton Klein: gasoline was rationed, food was rationed, field trips were cancelled, and the newspaper articles and radio reports made us feel hopeless and depressed. Could we do anything? Mr. Klein suggested that we plan an informal dinner dance, perhaps at the school. I don't know how I got involved in planning the event, but I became chairman of the committee. We collected money from all those in the junior class who wanted to attend. The committee decided on a spaghetti dinner, and my friend Lucille and I volunteered our mothers who were to make the meat sauce and cook the spaghetti.

But we had another problem. Where could we hold this dinner? We had an idea. Why couldn't we hold it in the Orchard Avenue Building? We could use the kitchen for the home economics classes and use the hallway for the dinner. We were sure we could borrow tables and folding chairs from one of the men's clubs. We thought it was a brilliant idea, but the administration didn't. "No!" Mr. Berkey told me. "The school must be closed when classes end. A spaghetti dinner is not part of the school's curriculum, such as a concert or a play." We had planned a budget for the food and beverages, leaving us with only five dollars. How could we rent a social hall? The committee wanted to drop the idea, but a couple of us didn't want to give it up, especially me. Students were going to bring a portable phonograph and the records. One of the bakeries agreed to give us a discount for the bread. I just needed to find a place. Finally, I went to the Italian American Social hall (IAES). They had a large social hall with a large kitchen that was perfect. Well, not quite. There was a bar at the end of the room, and that's how the club made its money, not on five-dollar rentals. I spoke with the president of the club who was willing to rent the room at our price, but the bar had to stay open. However, he agreed to screen the bar from the hall. I knew that the men could use the back door from the alley that led to the bar, but we could still see the men coming into the bar. We wrote invitations to the members of the School Board, to our social science teacher, and to several other teachers who, learning of our efforts, volunteered to serve as chaperones. We had parents sign permission slips.

The two mothers who were to cook enlisted advice from the women who generally cooked for banquets and testimonial dinners at the IAES, and one of them volunteered to help our mothers that day. All three women started early in the morning making the sauce, and several men from the IAES set up the tables and chairs which the club provided as well as donating a roll of white paper to be used as table cloths. Although ice water was served at the tables, with money from the tickets sold we were able to provide a bottle of Coca-Cola or lemonade for all guests. A beverage distributing company in town who learned of our dinner dance gave us a discount. Food was served buffet style, and many mothers sent dessert: cakes, pies, and cookies. Before dinner, I noticed that the members of the School Board had gathered together and were talking. I paid little attention until the dancing started. The chairman, Pete Giuliani, took me aside for a talk with the Board.

"Mary Ellen, why didn't you have the dinner at school? Why here with a bar?"

"I tried, but we weren't allowed to use the school."

I gave him the reasons. I noticed that he was angry, leaving me to speak with the other members who remarked about how well the students were dressed, how well they behaved, and how they were obviously enjoying the music while dancing. The members of the Board may have been angry about the locale, but for the students it was a night they could all have a bit of happiness.

Two days later, I was called into the principal's office for my insolence. I had been told, "No!" I explained politely that it was not a school function. It was held out of school with the parents' permission, and no students or guests had access to the bar. That same evening Mr. Giuliani telephoned me to congratulate me and the other students for planning such a wonderful event. I caught my breath when he added, "Wait a couple months and then ask to use the Orchard Avenue Building for another dinner dance." I begged, "I'm in enough trouble." He kept insisting, and I agreed to his plan. Much to my surprise Principal Berkey gave us permission to have another dinner. In the hall adjacent to the home economics kitchen, we served a wonderful ham dinner that more mothers had volunteered to prepare. This time the school administration and a few more teachers attended. That was the last dinner dance we had, but we weren't finished. Other seemingly wild suggestions would come later.

The War Effort

Many of the organizations at school began to find projects to help the war effort. Girl Reserves continued to pack empty shoe-boxes for service men. Many students collected toothbrushes, toothpaste, stationery, hard candy from residents, and wool socks and scarves that women of the town had knitted, as well as other items that were requested by the Army to help with the project. With permission, I printed cards in the print shop with the names of the officers of the club, never realizing that many years later, it would come back to me in a very unusual way. It happened in 1953. Margie and I had been shopping in Pittsburgh, and she suggested that we have lunch at a unique restaurant that catered to women and featured waitresses who read tea leaves. Margie's suggestion sounded like fun, and we were eager to see what the tea leaves would reveal about us. We entered the restaurant, scanned the menu, and ordered. A cup of tea with leaves inside was served during lunch. We finished our lunch, and one of the women came to our table to read the leaves in the teacup. Margie was first. She kept nodding her head so I assumed the reading was favorable. I was next, and the first thing the reader said was, "I see you are a nurse." I shook my head. "No, I teach school." The reading went on. Suddenly she said, "I see a leather gift coming to you from India." I answered, "India? I don't think so. I don't know anyone overseas, especially from India." Margie and I left the restaurant after the readings were over, laughing all the way to the parking lot.

I had forgotten all about that reading, but several months later, I did receive a package from India. I was sure it was a mistake. I opened the package, and there was a beautiful leather purse inside. I opened the purse to find a letter and a snapshot of an American soldier inside. He wrote that during World War II he had never received a box of any kind in the mail, and he was surprised that he had received one from a high school club in Pennsylvania. He kept the card that had been enclosed in the box, promising himself that he would find my address and someday send a gift. He had written to the high school several times before the principal sent him my address. He had placed the card in the envelope to assure me that his explanation was authentic. I wrote to him and thanked him, but I never heard from him again. How strange that a simple gesture to an American G. I., who must have been feeling very lonely and forgotten during those dreadful years, should fulfill a promise he had made to himself many years before.

Still, the Girl Reserves was not the only organization to help with the war effort. Other clubs planned fundraisers such as "Movie Nights for Students." Proceeds from those events were donated to the war effort. We collected cans, oil, aluminum, and scrap metal. I regret that we did not have high school yearbooks during the war to record our efforts. All we had were group pictures taken with our home room teacher. Yet, with all of these activities, once classes were over, students had little to do after school except to go to *Jacob's Ice Cream Parlor* or *Frank and Mead's Grill* where for a quarter or less we could buy a burger or a cheese burger and a soft drink. It was during those years that I learned to drink coffee without sugar, since sugar was rationed. We were all issued a War Ration Book by the government with our name, address, age, sex, weight, and height, and our occupation on the front cover. The book was valuable, and if anyone lost his, a new one would not be issued because residents were required to present the old book, which was numbered, in order to apply for a new one. Many items were rationed: shoes, meat, cheese, coffee, butter, oil, nylons, and many other items we were accustomed to buying without stamps. I still have Book No. 4 that has 192 stamps remaining; however, more than one stamp was always needed for an item. Some items needed 10 or 20 stamps.

Even with all these activities, I never seemed to fit in with the high school social crowd—not like Connie had. She married Dom Perino at nineteen and moved to Milwaukee a year later. No matter how self-reliant I was, I always felt self-conscious, always shy among a group of people I didn't know. I wasn't pretty enough or thin enough. I had no sense of style. My nose, broken as a child, left me nearly without a profile. The accident happened when I was eight years old. Connie, sliding down the banister rail of the basement staircase, said, "Look, I can slide down the railing while I'm sitting by holding the banister behind me." I replied, "I'll bet I can do it without holding on." That was a tremendous mistake. I went flying down, falling and smashing my nose on the cement floor. My mother rushed me to the doctor, but he assured her that I really hadn't broken it, and it would heal, but it never did. As years went by, I had trouble breathing. There were no plastic surgeons available until after World War II, and all a doctor could do was remove all the broken cartilage from my nose so I could breathe. The doctor wanted to put a plate inside my nose to frame it, but I refused. My nose was now flat, and for many years, people would ask me, "What happened to your nose?" I always replied, "I fell." I seldom attended social activities. If I wasn't reading, I was working on some new project, like an after school program.

Some of the students realized that if a student didn't play in the band or orchestra, wasn't an athlete or cheerleader, or wasn't cast in a school play, there wasn't much to do after school. Even if someone had a driver's license, gasoline was rationed: four gallons a week for residents. Although my father had a government contract and a gasoline pump was installed near the garages for the truck drivers, there were safe guards. The owner had to account for every gallon of gas. Women began to work as the men were drafted, and mothers were no longer at home after school to supervise their children. A few of us realized that teenagers needed an after-school program. There was a solution. The school had two small gymnasiums for classes: one for boys and one for girls. In addition, there was a large auditorium that lay dormant after school. Why, we thought, couldn't a shuffleboard game be painted on the floor? The auditorium floor was just painted cement. The shuffleboard could always be painted over, if necessary. Surely, the school could afford to buy the equipment. Why couldn't the gyms be opened, one for dancing and socializing and the other for volleyball, basketball, or board games such as Monopoly, checkers or chess. Why couldn't boys and girls play together? We took the plan to the principal who agreed to it as long as two teachers volunteered to chaperone, and students would be responsible for all of the equipment, gathering it and giving it to the custodian for safe keeping. Teachers usually remained in their classrooms grading papers but did wander in and out of their classrooms to monitor students. No one misbehaved, and former students, who came home from camp before being deployed, would also spend an afternoon with us. I especially remember David Holste, one of the superintendent's sons. We chatted for some time. He mentioned that he had little basic training but was ready to go. America had just entered the European war, but that was the last time I would ever see David or talk with him.

During the war, my family always waited anxiously for a letter from Buddy. As long as a telegram didn't arrive, we knew he was safe. It was on one particular day, however, when the telephone rang. I answered it. It was Mrs. Permutico, asking to speak with my mom. She was cheerful, so I didn't expect bad news. I handed the phone to n mother, who kept shouting. "No! No!" All of a sudden, she fainted. I didn't know what to do. I picked up the phone lying on the floor. "What's wrong?"

"I'm trying to tell your mother that my son, Victor, was on a hospital plane with your brother. Your brother's face was completely bandaged, but Victor read the tag on Buddy's uniform: "Pvt. Buddy P. Cipolla."

My mother now recovered was lying on the floor. I yelled for my dad, who was in the garage. He came running into the house. It was chaos. I tried to explain that Buddy hadn't been killed; he was just wounded. My dad immediately called Mr. Holste, Chairman of the local Red Cross, who came immediately to our home. My parents didn't know why there had been no telegram, but Mr. Holste discovered that Buddy had the telegram stopped, but he didn't know how that was possible. I shall never forget that Mr. Holste, sitting in our living room consoling my parents, already had one critically injured son, Bob, in a hospital overseas and would soon learn that he would lose his younger son, David, a month after the first one had died. Unlike Bob, David had never seen action. He was shot standing on a sidewalk.

Days later, my parents received a letter from a chaplain in an English hospital. Buddy was in a psychiatric ward. Unfortunately, he happened to see his face when the bandages were removed by using a small mirror he had hidden away. This once handsome young man had part of the left side of his face blown off with a mortar shell during the Battle of the Bulge. Had he obeyed the lieutenant, who gave orders the night before, "When I say, *Advance*, obey immediately," he would have been killed instantly. Instead, Buddy was kneeling behind a tree trunk, and as an experienced game hunter, he looked around the trunk first before standing up. All night he lay bleeding and crying, in and out of consciousness. Twice he called for medics, but both times they were killed trying to reach him. Early the next morning, he was taken to a home of two elderly German women. Inside the house were German prisoners of war being held by American soldiers. One of the prisoners, a medic, offered to help him, but Buddy refused. However, he remembered that one of the women beat an egg, mixed it with wine, and gave it to him. She also tore some article of clothing and bandaged his face. He didn't understand a word she said, but later he always praised her for helping him. The next morning he, along with other wounded men, was flown to England. It was on that flight that Victor had seen him. In England, no plastic surgery was available, and the doctors just closed the wound, pulling, stretching together, and stitching the gap in his face, leaving his face disfigured.

He came home after a year in the English hospital, not wanting to speak to anyone, not wanting to hear any noise. Today it would be referred to as Traumatic Stress Disorder. It seemed as though there was no more medical help for him. When he asked for more help, the request was denied. His face would remain twisted. Because my father had connections with a Congressman, he was able to have Buddy transferred to a veteran's hospital in Philadelphia where plastic surgery was practiced. When my parents would visit him, he would say, "Don't cry for me. Cry for those pilots who are burned, for those who are blind, for all of the others who will never come home." The surgeons performed several plastic surgeries on Buddy, leaving him with only a badly scarred face. For months, I was the only one who could remove with tweezers the shards of shrapnel from his face. Years later, I said to my son, "Do you notice Uncle Buddy's scarred face? That was from the war." He said, "What scars, he looks fine to me." He only saw his uncle's smile, his great heart, and his love for his family and friends. I always called Buddy "Zeke," and I loved him. I had a special attachment with Buddy, which we had forged when I was still very young.

My father and I also shared that special bond, and I loved traveling with him, especially on the Sundays when our family went to Conneaut Lake, Pennsylvania's largest natural lake. The park had many rides, but I remember only the carousel and the picnic area. I was more fascinated by the lake with its many fish. We children would stand on the metal railing, peering into the water, as our father would call our attention to the very large fish swimming by in enormous schools. The fish were so large that I believed we could have touched them. He made the trip exciting as he did with any other event we attended.

Every year in May, usually from May 2 to May 4, the circus came to town. Our father made sure to clear his agenda for one of the days. He even took time off several days before the actual event to take us to the parade in town as the circus traveled from the railroad station to the campground to watch the tents being raised. But it was always the day of the circus that we anticipated. Before the actual event began, we fed peanuts to the elephants, looked at the lions and the monkeys in their cages, and saw some of the suitable-for-children sideshows: the magician and the man who swallowed swords. We were the venders' best customers, eating whatever was sold.

I can still hear my mother's voice. "Steve, the kids are going to get sick. No more cotton candy or soda. They already had a hot dog and ice cream, enough already." Her pleas fell on deaf ears.

"Leave them alone, Grace. They'll be fine. What's the worst that can happen?" It always did. One of us would vomit while walking home.

When I was fourteen, and Bob was ten, our dad took Bob and me on a three-week vacation to Gettysburg, Washington, D. C., Mt. Vernon, West Point, Annapolis, and other historical sites. Connie refused to go, and my mother remained at home. She felt that Ron was too young to enjoy such a trip. Dad hired guides at each site, adding to the information the guide gave us: "Look, kids! This was George Washington's house. Can you imagine that! The Civil War was fought here. Listen to the guide tell you about the battles." We got to attend a session of Congress when Representative William Kelly of Pittsburgh, a friend of my father's, escorted us to the chamber. Before I left his office, he autographed a copy of a law book and gave it to me. I became interested in politics, and my father began taking me to political fundraisers and testimonial banquets to honor outstanding men. He once tried to teach me how to shoot a hunting rifle so I could go hunting for small game with him, but I wasn't just gun-shy; I was terrified of guns.

Planning the Future

During my senior year in high school, my chemistry teacher began talking to the students about attending college. As few girls were going to nursing school. Others were applying to Bell Telephone to work as an operator. The girls in the Commercial tract were going into business as secretaries or bookkeepers. A coveted job was to get a secretarial job at ALCOA or other factories in New Kensington or at U.S. Steel in Pittsburgh. Families were still recovering from the Depression, and college was not only considered expensive but also unnecessary for girls, especially among immigrant girls. During one of the chemistry class, Mr. George McLaughin passed some brochures around the classroom, giving brief descriptions of various small colleges in Pennsylvania. My eye caught the one for Westminster, a co-education United Presbyterian College in New Wilmington, about 66 miles from Arnold. I wanted to enroll in the pre-law course, believing law was my destiny. I brought the brochures home to my parents, telling them I wanted to apply. Westminster was $375.00 a semester for tuition, room and board, increasing, however, to $425.00 my junior and senior years. Linens were provided to the students and laundered once a week at no extra charge. Cost didn't seem to be a problem for my parents, but they had other reservations.

My father made the mistake of discussing with his parents the possibility of my attending college. My grandparents were totally against his sending me, especially my grandfather. What was his son thinking of by sending his daughter away to a school with boys? If I was so intent on going to school, what was wrong with Mt. Mercy Academy in Pittsburgh, an all-girls' school? I could take the bus every day. My grandfather, seeking other advocates, began speaking to some of his friends. It wasn't long before friends began to make Sunday visits to our home. It was always the same.

"Steve, we hear you and Grace are planning to send Mary Ellen to college. We just want to give you a bit of advice. You still have two young boys at home, and Grace needs help to take care of them. Besides, Mary Ellen should begin to learn how to cook, do laundry, and take care of a household. It will be a waste of money. She'll just get married."

"Married! Married! With whom would I marry?" I thought, "I don't even date. I *already* know how to cook and take care of a house, and my brothers aren't toddlers, one is 14, and the other is 10. Why would I want to get married?" I knew many young wives with children, totally dependent on their husbands. That was not for me. I was determined to go to college.

Finally, my father signed the application, sent a check for the first semester, and my mother and I began to shop for school clothes in Pittsburgh. Although the city was only eighteen miles away, this started another argument with my grandfather. What was wrong with me? Why couldn't I have shopped in my hometown? Neither my mother nor I drove, and taking the bus upset Papa P. I did buy a few clothes in New Kensington, but the department stores in Pittsburgh had a larger selection. After I left for college, my father and grandfather did not speak for six weeks or until I came home for the first time. During the interval, the college would send out brief articles about students' activities to their hometown newspapers. One was about my becoming a member of the A Capella Choir, well known for its concerts at Protestant churches in nearby cities. It was during my first visit home that my father and Papa P reconciled.

Mary Ellen Cipolla Grasso

Coming from a small high school, I struggled at first with my assignments. My first day in English101 we were told to write an in-class essay on Ophelia, but I had never read Hamlet. At Arnold we were taught how to write letters, not essays. I turned in a nearly blank sheet of paper explaining my problem. Fortunately, all freshmen were assigned a counselor, whom we met with frequently. When I entered the counselor's office for the first time, I thought that Connie would have no trouble speaking with him, and the first words that tumbled out of my mouth were all about her. Then I said that I was not enamored by my pre-law course, realizing that I was in the wrong field, and my roommate and I were not compatible.

The counselor looked at me and said, "I'm sure you can do something your sister can't. Why don't we schedule an occupational interest test? I don't believe that law is right for you."

I took the test and returned to his office several days later for the results. "Journalism or English?" The counselor said. "I would say you belong in journalism."

"Journalism," I thought. "I don't want to work on a newspaper. I really want to sing."

Meanwhile, the counselor registered me for a one-credit journalism course for Term II, but I was obstinate. I asked the counselor if I could have a double major: journalism and English just in case I didn't do well in journalism. He agreed, but that meant I would have two majors and more credit hours. I liked English and worked hard in those classes. I didn't even want to try to like the journalism class, not even doing my best in class or meeting attendance requirements. I was sure I was barely passing the course before the end of the term when I overheard a conversation between Miss Nixon, my journalism professor and an English professor, Miss Charles who happened to know me.

I heard Miss Nixon say, "Do you know Miss Cipolla?"

"I do. I met her during the fall registration and told her that I remembered the editorials she had written for her school newspaper, The Broadcaster. I even suggested she take a journalism class."

"She thinks she can outwit me, but she can't. She's getting an A for the term, not a C-, which she earned. She belongs in journalism."

Professor Nixon was right. I flourished in the field when I entered it professionally a few years later. College allowed me the opportunity to become a Copy Editor for the Holcad, the school newspaper; Managing Editor for the literary magazine, Scrawl, for the spring semester one year; and selling and writing copy as a part time job for a local restaurant, as well as doing the layout of some of the advertisements for Argo, the college yearbook.

As a member of Radio Workshop, I wrote a radio script, a documentary of Ernie Pyle, the famous World War II correspondent who wrote vivid accounts of the way he trudged along in Europe and Japan with the foot soldiers. He never glorified war and took the readers of his newspaper articles to the battlefield along with the soldiers, detailing all of the action. He was killed in Japan in 1945, shortly before the war ended. A bullet from a machine gun shot by a Japanese soldier killed him instantly. He was only 45 years old. When his death was announced in the newspapers and on radio, everyone mourned his loss, especially the soldiers who considered him a hero. He had given them a voice during the war, their voice, not a correspondent's. Miss Nixon told me that a radio station asked permission to broadcast my script. Years later I used an article with permission from his book Brave Men describing his account of the Normandy Beach invasion in a college textbook I wrote for English 101 for freshmen whose assignment was to write a personal experience essay.

I earned an A in an editing class for having an article published with a byline on the front page of the local news section of a Pittsburgh daily. I had a good assignment, interviewing the artist commissioned to paint the portrait of Dr. Robert Galbreath, president of the college who was retiring. His portrait was to be placed in the college library. By the time I graduated, I realized I would never have been a good lawyer. I didn't have a passion for it.

By no means was I a student who followed all of the college rules. We were not permitted to attend the movies on Sunday, but I, along with two other friends, went to a movie in a nearby town only to find ourselves sitting next to the Dean of Women. We were sure we would be expelled, but we weren't. Girls had a curfew: 9:00 P.M. on school days. I was working on the yearbook, and the staff could work beyond the curfew. About ten o'clock one night everyone got hungry, and I was chosen to go to the Grill to purchase the staff's orders: burgers, fries, and beverages. As I collected the money from each of them, I thought about the curfew. "Am I going to get in trouble?" I asked. "Shouldn't one of you men go? You don't have a curfew." The editor assured me that none of the administrators would be out at that time. I walked into the Grill with my list and the money, and who was there? It was the Dean of Women with a friend. She looked at me and said, "Who's having a party?" I just stammered, "It's the Argo staff. We're working late. Everyone's hungry." Fortunately, I never heard anything more about that night.

The Letters

But I came close to being expelled when I disobeyed a serious rule. I had to have written permission from my parents to leave the college campus and go to another city, but my parents refused to give me permission. It was my sophomore year, and I roomed with five other girls. We had a suite—two dormitory rooms connected by a bathroom. One room had four girls, but mine held only two. A few of us were invited on a Sunday to go horseback riding at the home of one of our roommates. I had been there before horseback riding. This time, since there were six of us riding that day, all of the horses from the stable were out. I was asked to ride Major, the owner's horse, because I had some experience riding. All the western saddles were used, and I had to use the English saddle, which I had never used. The circle was ten miles. We had ridden five miles when Major and another horse, both leaders, decided to race, jumping over logs and hedges. I realized that the saddle was loose, and as I fell to the ground I braced myself with my left arm. The pain was unbearable. One of the stablemen riding with us stopped to help me.

He simply tightened the saddle and told me I would have to ride the last five miles even though we both realized I had broken my arm. There was no other way to get back to the house. Driving back to campus, my roommates and I realized that I had violated a rule, and I was afraid my father would blame the college. I would be expelled this time. My roommates and I decided on a plan. We lived on the second floor, and the carpet on the stairway steps was frayed and should have been replaced. One of the girls decided that I would fake a fall down the last few steps. As I lay on the floor with books scattered around me, the girls screamed for the housemother, who assumed I had fallen down the steps. She reported the accident saying, "Those stair treads need to be replaced before someone else falls." I was taken to the hospital after my eight o'clock class, which I was told to attend. I did have a broken arm, which was placed in a cast, and no one else ever knew the truth, not even my parents.

Since I was the first girl from the Cipolla and Puglisi families to graduate from college, my four grandparents decided to attend the graduation ceremony. Since Bob was graduating from high school the same year, my parents were planning to host a large barbecue celebration under the grape arbor in our backyard. During the barbecue, when I was receiving congratulations from the guests, I suddenly heard Papa P say, "Yes, her grandmother and I are very proud of her. After all, we were the ones that wanted her to go to college." I just looked at him and smiled at his lapse of memory.

Finding the Job and a Career

I wondered how others who left college or university were able to bridge the years from being a student to finding a career. I knew I would miss all the activities I was involved in at Westminster, especially Little Theater, where I had an opportunity to work backstage or act in a play. I will never forget the night I played Aunt Jenny in *I Remember Mama*. The scene called for me to be eating a slice of homemade bread with jelly while talking on the phone. Usually, since there was not a slice of thick homemade bread, properties toasted a slice of ordinary white bread so that I could handle it easily, but one of the crew forgot to toast the bread. The actor playing my sister was supposed to take the slice away from me and nibble on it, which she did, but at the end of the dialog, I was supposed to grab it back. All I could see was this slice of bread with jelly sail over the audience. Only a corner tip of the bread remained in my hand. As I tried to remain in character, the audience, roaring with laughter, followed the bread to see where it would land. It landed on a man's lap. At the end of the play he came backstage to speak with us. He had cleaned his trousers as best he could, but the director assured him that the Drama Department would reimburse him for professional cleaning. Fortunately, he saw humor in the accident. I was just embarrassed.

I could never forget when I was hypnotized during morning Chapel and was asked to make an announcement in a second grader's voice about a special event the college was sponsoring. There was laughter by the audience and applause, but I had no idea why I was standing. It wasn't until later that one of the students told me why.

Those college days were over. It was time to find a job. I was sure that if I first found a job, I could find the career. Connie wanted me to leave Arnold and look for a journalism job in Milwaukee. She was the first girl in the family to leave Arnold permanently. The day she left, our mom cried as though Connie were leaving for some distant part of the world. As Connie and Dom waved goodbye from the car, my dad assured our mom that a plane trip to Milwaukee would take fewer than two and a half hours. Now Connie's invitation to me didn't seem to be a problem. All during my college vacations, my mom would spend six weeks every summer visiting Connie and Dom. Carrying my portfolio and several resumes in a briefcase, I left for Milwaukee to find a job. I had high hopes, but after only two interviews, my dad telephoned me. "There's a teaching position open in the junior high school, and one of the school board members asked me if you were interested in applying for the position."

I had a Teaching Certificate from the State of Pennsylvania, and I had completed six weeks as a student teacher, receiving glowing references from both the journalism and English teachers since I had to teach in two disciplines as a double major. Since I knew that Mary, who was among my best friends, had already been hired to teach elementary school, I returned home to apply for the position. During the interview I was told that I would teach seventh grade grammar and literature. I was excited because in college English was always a favorite subject. The first semester always began the day after Labor Day. I don't remember an orientation only for new faculty, but all the teachers met with the superintendent and principal before classes began. I had my first taste of reality when I heard, "Miss Cipolla, your schedule has been changed. You will teach arithmetic and English and you will have a one-hour class in counseling." "Good grief!" I thought. "Arithmetic? I'm not ready to teach arithmetic."

Still the worst was yet to come as the principal continued. "One of your classes has all slow learners, ages 12 to 15. The two oldest boys have just come from Italy and know very little English, but they are not slow learners. You will have the class for arithmetic and English five days a week and the one-hour counseling class once a week."

I thought to myself, "Counseling for slow learners? I'm the one who needs counseling." I had hardly recovered from the news when I heard, "Oh, yes! Your class is in the junior high library, so you will act as the librarian for the year." I swallowed hard and thought, "What do I know about being a librarian? When would I do that?" I learned very quickly when I would do that: before classes began and after school. The library was just a regular class-room except that there were floor to ceiling bookshelves on two walls. The third wall was the blackboard, as it was called, and a wall of windows completed the room. As everyone filed out of the room after the meeting, one of the veteran teachers, my former eighth grade history teacher, stopped to talk with me. "If you need any help, ask me." Actually I didn't know what I'd need or what to say.

Perhaps I should have listened to the advice Dr. Davis had given me when I was still in college. He was my voice teacher who wanted me to give up college and pursue music in New York. He even had a voice coach ready for me. Dr. Davis drove me to Pittsburgh to audition before a music critic. I couldn't read music, but I was told I had an excellent voice. I remember that audition because it did change my life. The critic was in agreement with Dr. Davis. I should quit college and study music. I asked him, "When I return to Pittsburgh and give my first concert, will you give me a good review?" His answer made the decision for me. "The voice is like an instrument. It could fail you." I simply said, "I can't take that chance. I'll stay in college."

Now I was stunned and in a state of shock. The faculty meeting was over. Had I made the right decision to leave Milwaukee? We were given the rolls and instructions for the first day, which would be a short day, allowing us to introduce ourselves, distribute textbooks, and tablets and pencils (given once a month to all students), and write our classroom rules on the slate blackboard. Two of my classes were filled with those I considered excellent students: intelligent, motivated, and well behaved. They became a joy to teach. Fortunately I had them for both English and arithmetic.

On the other hand, the class of slow learners and those with behavioral problems was a challenge. Discipline was difficult. I had never seen a condom, but I was surprised to see my first one stuffed with cotton being passed around the room. All I could say was, "I'm leaving the room for a minute. Make it disappear." A few months later, I would strut down that aisle, pick up whatever was being passed around the room, and throw it into the wastebasket. If it was a note, I read it aloud, saying. "Ah! We have a short-story writer in the class." After the first note, I rarely saw notes being passed around.

There was no question that those students needed a counselor, but could I help them? One of the girls took the bathroom pass I had made and instead of going to the rest room, she went outside to solicit the young window washer who was washing my classroom windows. I had to leave class, issuing a warning about behaving, and run outside to retrieve her. When I returned to the classroom, the students were very quiet. That incident was the end of the bathroom passes and the beginning of a new respect for me. Yet there was always a new problem. One of the Italian immigrants, Tony, would punch a certain girl's shoulder every time he passed her for any reason, like going to the pencil sharpener. I was always reprimanding him. Then one day I had just stepped into the cloakroom to get some supplies stored in a cabinet there. I heard a desk being turned over and students yelling, "Miss Cipolla, Miss Cipolla." I ran out to find Tony and Evelyn fighting. Evelyn ran to her seat. Meanwhile, I grabbed Tony, put one arm behind him, and walked to the principal's office. Really angry, I declared, "Tony has a problem, and I can't seem to solve it. He's now your problem." I explained to the principal what had been going on inside and outside of class. He questioned Tony, "Why are you always hitting Evelyn? What has she done to you?" His answer wasn't one we expected. "Evertima I see her, it's likea fire in me. I lkea her, but she no likeame. So I puncha her. Thata way she looka ata me." Tony had a lot to learn about teenage infatuations and how to get a girl to like him.

Those problems were mild compared to the one that threatened my life. Like all cities or small towns, there are always boys who get into trouble, and Tony was among them. He had an older friend, Mario, who was about twenty years old and lived in a neighboring city. Tony and Mario began robbing drug stores and automobile garages. They stole tires or car radios from the garages and over-the-counter medical items as well as cosmetics and other items from the drug stores. There were articles in the newspaper, *The Daily Dispatch*, concerning these crimes and mentioning that the police were involved in solving the robberies. I knew Tony's parents, both who worked. Tony had spent the war years in Naples, Italy, living by his wits because he and his mother were unable to join his father in America once the war began. Tony no longer waned to associate himself with Mario, confided in me, and asked if I could help me. Could he walk me home every day and then stay with me until his mother came home. They lived just a block away on Woodbine Alley, and his mother could stop at my home to pick him up. I was happy to help him. He was an intelligent student and just needed guidance. I supervised him, making sure that he did all of his homework.

A short time later, Tony confessed to me that he had told Mario about our arrangement and that he had told me about their robberies. It was then that Mario planned to kill me because I knew too much, and he didn't trust teachers. I didn't know what to do. What I did do is write a letter and place it in an envelope, addressed this way: "To Be Opened Only in Case of Death." I shoved the letter in the back of the top center drawer of my desk at school in the event I was killed. I locked the drawer anytime I left the classroom. I was terrified. Mario was everywhere I seemed to be, but I made sure I was never alone. He would stand outside my first-floor window, on the grounds of the school. Sometimes he managed to be in the hallway near my classroom, but there were always too many teachers around. Nevertheless, I knew he had a gun, and I was always in a state of terror. I wasn't sure if he would kill me or if he was just threatening me. But I did know about his life in Italy during the war when the Germans occupied the country. My guardian angel must have been protecting me because Mario was finally arrested and held for criminal activities, including murder. Why did I think a letter shoved in the back of a drawer would be of any help? It wouldn't, but I didn't want Tony to be involved. That's why I didn't go to the police. I never told anyone, not even my parents, about my involvement.

By no means did teachers earn a lot of money in those days. My gross salary was $2,000.00 a year, but my net salary was $133.33 a month. The custom of the day in many homes was that adult children who worked gave their salary to their parents who then gave them a few dollars to spend. Some parents saved the remainder for their children, perhaps to give it to them when they married or bought a home. Other parents used it for the needs of the family. In my case, when I handed my first check to my father, he took it, looked at, and then returned it to me with this advice: "I don't want your money, but from this day on, you are on your own. This is your home. You don't need to pay rent, but don't ask me for a penny. You now pay all your bills: doctor, insurance, cosmetics, clothes, long distance telephone calls, entertainment, and anything else you want." When the telephone bill came, he would circle my calls, put the bill on my desk for payment the next day. He always found the money in an envelope on his desk the next morning. When I wanted to enter the University of Pittsburgh to begin work on my Master's Degree, I needed $75.00 to pay the tuition. I did borrow the money from him, but I paid him back within a month. He did buy my first car, a used 1940 Plymouth business coupe and the second one, a used 1950 four-door Ford sedan, but I paid for all repairs and gasoline. I was grateful. So much so, that I bought my parents a freezer, one of the first chest-styled ones. Neither my mom nor dad would use it and reprimanded me for spending so much money on them. But when hunting season came, I suggested that all of the game such as venison, duck, and rabbit could be stored in it for future use. Once the holidays were near my mom realized how useful the freezer was, and as years went by the freezer held a place in our home. Because my parents trusted and respected me, I wanted to do well as a teacher.

During that first year, I chaperoned the girls' bus for our out-of-town football games. The girls were the cheerleaders, the majorettes, and the female members of the band. I became friends with some of the younger teachers and began to socialize with them. I went to see a plastic surgeon in Pittsburgh about my nose. He agreed to operate on me saying, "You don't have to live with that nose. I'll give you a new one." I began to lose weight when I was put on thyroid medication and spent my Christmas vacation in the hospital having my nose rebuilt. It was major surgery, and it took nearly six months for the outside to heal and much longer for the inside since I had grafts of bone and cartilage. I couldn't chew or blow my nose. I had to be careful that I didn't bump my nose. I had my hair styled like the new Vidal Sassoon cut, bought a new wardrobe, and began to date. I finally made the transition from college. It was also during that time that Miss Nixon, my former journalism professor, telephoned me, asking me if I would be interested in a job in Oregon. Friends of hers, a minister and his wife, were seeking someone to work for a church as a public relations writer. I could rent a room from them. I turned the offer down, deciding to continue in the teaching field and complete the Master in Letters Degree. Several of the male teachers I knew also took classes on Saturday, and the men offered to drive me to the university. I had a minor in speech and intended to get a major in the field. I was able to earn enough speech credits during the spring and summer sessions to add that discipline to the teaching certificate.

I was hired the second year to teach ninth grade English and speech, a much better schedule than the one I had the year before. I was also asked to serve as advisor to the yearbook staff. However, I had one problem. I had the same principal as the year before when I was convinced that he always put barriers in front of me, but this year seemed to be different, that is, until the week of final examinations when he put another barrier up. He would prove me right. All teachers who wanted their final examinations typed by the secretary were to give them to her at least two weeks before finals. I complied, but the day I was to administer the finals, I received the handwritten final with a note from the principal: "There wasn't enough time to type your exam. Put it on the board." How could I write one hundred questions on the board? It was an impossible task. For the first class I reduced the number of questions, left some out, and substituted essay questions for the multiple choice ones. When the class left, I had to find a way to cover the questions so students who wouldn't take the test until the third hour didn't have access to them between classes. By the time the semester was over, I was burned out.

Timing must have been everything because Miss Nixon telephoned me again, "Mary Ellen, you belong in journalism. I've set up two interviews for you in Pittsburgh; One is at Heinz, and the other is at The Pittsburgh Motor Club. Make sure you keep them."

The Pittsburgh Motor Club

Both positions were for a public relations director. My first interview was at Heinz, which I thought went well, but after the interview, I realized I was not a good fit. I was not quite twenty-three years old, and I looked younger than my age. I had no experience, no work references in that field. Two days later I had an interview at The Pittsburgh Motor Club (today the American Automobile Association) with Bob, the man who would be my supervisor. A few days later I received a call. Bob offered me the job, and I accepted. Whoever heard of a teacher just giving a two-week notice in the middle of a semester and leaving to accept another very different type of job? I would be giving up a future pension and the possibility of tenure, giving me job security until I chose to retire, in exchange for only a slightly better salary, $2,400.00 a year. I would be working twelve months, not ten, but I had an opportunity to work in a field I would really enjoy. I wrote several letters of resignation: one to the chairman of the Board of Trustees, the superintendent, and the principal of the junior high school. Several days later, I received a telephone call from the chairman asking me if I were leaving because of the principal. Remembering the advice many older businessmen had given me, I said, "No." I knew never to burn a bridge behind me because I might one day want to cross it again.

The first morning I arrived at work, my immediate supervisor introduced me to the president, who had never interviewed me. He was also considered the editor of *The Pennsylvania Motorist*, the monthly newspaper. I was listed on the masthead as the managing editor. The president seemed cordial, asking me a few questions.

The Letters

Then Bob took me on a tour of all of the offices, introducing me to the other employees. I met the secretaries and bookkeepers first because their desks were just behind my glass-enclosed cubicle. The switchboard operator at the left entrance of the Motor Club showed me a panel that already had my name on it. There were arrows that pointed either IN or OUT, to indicate if a person was in the office. I was always to make sure that I used it. The panel was only for the president, the assistant to the president, Don, the underwriters, who would always visit clients out of the office, and me. To the left of the entrance were the offices of the underwriters. I met a few underwriters that day, but I was anxious to get started with my job. I had many duties.

Once a week I wrote a half-hour radio script: "Innovations in the Automotive Industry." My deadline to give the president the script was Tuesday morning at eight o'clock. Later that morning he would broadcast the program at one of the radio stations in Pittsburgh. I worked late many Monday evenings, making sure there were no errors concerning the innovations. I no sooner finished one script than I began the next broadcast, researching many current magazines about the automotive industry: information, at first, that was all new to me. My workday began at 7:30 a.m. when I called the Weather Bureau for the day's weather report. Since there were no computers or copy machines, I would type a notice and tack it on the bulletin boards for everyone to read. If a motorist called before the switchboard operator arrived, I took the call and gave the caller the report. I worked closely with the director of advertising, a man I seldom saw. We communicated by mail or telephone. I liked working with him. He sold the advertisements, but I was responsible for the layout and sometimes the copy.

It wasn't long before a Commissioner of Pittsburgh asked me to write a column for him once a week, titled *This Week in Pittsburgh*.

398

Mary Ellen Cipolla Grasso

I never met the commissioner personally, but he sent me a list of points he wanted me to cover, and I wrote the articles. Nonetheless, in the beginning I found that being a ghostwriter was a difficult task for me since I had to use his voice. He never complained, so I stopped worrying. Besides I rather enjoyed earning the extra money and reading the complimentary letters readers sent him that he sometimes shared with me.

I seemed to be surrounded by men and the politics of the day. The Motor Club became involved with the members of the Pennsylvania Grange who campaigned for various state and local agendas. Created originally by a group of rural farmers, the members of the Pennsylvania Grange wanted to improve the lives of those who farmed the rural areas. Among the Grange's efforts was a campaign for the regulation of the Pennsylvania Turnpike, known as The Big Truck Bill, limiting the size of trucks using the Turnpike by suggesting alternative routes. Don asked me to meet with a couple members of the Grange and then be responsible for the writing of editorials in the Motor Club's newspaper. I was scheduled to meet the men at a restaurant before dinner. When I arrived, they were sitting at the bar waiting for me. I assumed we would eat dinner and then begin to work on an outline. I was wrong. It took almost two hours before we began talking about the bill. They talked about everything but the bill. We worked for a week every evening deciding exactly what information was to be included in the editorials. Before the men left Pittsburgh, they did remark that they "didn't expect to be working with such a young girl."

I may have been young, but I quickly became educated by the men who published the Motor Club's newspaper. When I first began working with the printers, I was just ignored. There were rare times when I wanted to change an item or the location of a box that had already been placed on one of the layout pages. I

399

tried to ask questions. They turned their backs on me. If I wanted a headline moved, they just looked at me. Then I began to notice other clients. They didn't say, "Please" or "Could you?" When they spoke, they demanded attention. Curse words, some I would never use, were part of their everyday vocabulary. I decided to change my way of dealing with the printers. My vocabulary increased along with the tone and volume of my voice. It was astonishing how well those printers responded when I changed my approach, but I was getting tough, and I didn't like what was happening to me. Many times when I had lunch with a few of the writers for the Pittsburgh dailies, I noticed I was becoming "one of the boys." I even learned to lie. I had a friend who worked for a weekly for one of the nearby towns. He mentioned that he had heard that in a few days the mayor's office was going to break a news story that he thought was important. "Could we cover it together?" he asked. I told him I wasn't interested. Instead I returned to my office, called the mayor's office and made an appointment for an interview, which was granted. I got the story and a picture first, but I lost a friend. He never spoke to me again.

My supervisor, unfortunately, began to drink more. If the president wanted to reprimand me or another employee, he screamed at Bob instead. Many afternoons when Bob didn't return to the office after lunch, I would go searching for him at all the nearby bars and take him back to the office. I walked. He staggered. Some days he didn't come to work at all, but I always did, trying to cover for him. I enjoyed writing articles for tourists, suggesting places to vacation. I wrote a story about Hershey, Pennsylvania, suggesting a tour through the chocolate factory. I had taken the tour when I traveled there to research the area and conduct some interviews. Weeks later, the Hershey public relations department sent me a thank you letter and a carton of their special Fifty-fifty bars, fifty percent almonds and fifty percent chocolate. Those bars were never sold, only reserved as gifts. The Cranberry Association sent me a sterling silver cranberry serving spoon. Treasure Island, Florida, a newly developed resort area on the Gulf Coast, offered me a free one-week vacation. Real Estate companies, of course, were trying to entice potential buyers to move to Treasure Island, which was part of the Tampa Bay area. I never took the trip, however, because I lacked vacation time.

Still the working conditions did not improve, and I was beginning to become stressed. I felt sorry for Bob, but I couldn't help him. Problems began to escalate. I had been there a year, but I knew it was time for me to leave. I told no one about seeking another job, not even the women with whom I had become friends. I began to check the classified ads. I saw one for an editor for a weekly newspaper. The job was located in Millvale. I realized that I could drive instead of riding the bus an hour each way because of all the stops. Besides, I could park on the street, just outside the building, which also housed a taxi company, the printing press room, and three offices on the second floor: one was to be shared by the editors for two weekly newspapers. The other offices were designated for the publisher and the taxi company. I decided to apply for the position. I was hired on the spot to serve as editor of *The Catholic Observer*, a weekly for churches of the Pittsburgh Diocese. What the offices lacked in appearance, they made up for it by the friendliness of those who worked there. The salary was the same as the one I was receiving, but I worked only four days—Monday thru Thursday.

The Catholic Observer

I found that working on *The Observer*, as it was called, was much less stressful than the previous position I had held since I was responsible only for my behavior, but I was now writing or editing different types of articles. The articles from convents, monasteries, churches, and Catholic organizationswere sometimes mailed in or brought to the office. Usually they sent just notes or announcements, and I had to write the news articles. However, there were times when I had to leave the office and interview whoever was in charge of distributing the information. One of my responsibilities was to check the Legion of Decency each week to get the list of what movies were approved for viewing by Catholics. Once a year parishioners took a pledge not to see motion pictures or television shows rated as immoral and were not to attend the movie theaters that did not adhere to the Legion of Decency's ratings. There were times when I couldn't understand why a certain movie was banned. Sometimes it was just a scene, and sometimes it was an entire movie. According to the church, the ratings, which were quite strict, were supposed to encourage Hollywood to make more wholesome films. Today there is a Catholic Bishop's Legion of Decency moderate ratings list, but it has almost no impact on Catholics, Hollywood, or the television industry.

There were also articles sent from public relation offices such as those from Bishop Fulton J. Sheen's television broadcasts, *Life is Worth Living*. His radio and television broadcasts and newspaper articles were very popular throughout the nation, appealing to non Catholics as well as Catholics, and like many other people,

I seldom missed a program. Today Bishop Sheen is considered to be the first television preacher. I have no idea what happened to my autographed copy of one of his books.

Sometimes when the printers were late in getting the newspaper ready to be printed, or as they said, "to bed," I would help the printers set headlines and place linotyped articles in a chase. I still remembered from my high school class how to do those tasks. However, I wanted to help the linotype machine typists, who, using a keyboard, set the type on a metal slug that was the width of a column. I wanted one of the men to teach me how to do that, but I had no aptitude for that skill. Thursdays were the longest workdays because the paper had to be printed that night, ready for distribution to the churches the next morning. We worked so late one night that while driving home, I fell asleep at the wheel, drifting into the wall of the Pennsylvania State Penitentiary in Blawnox, not far from my home. Although the bumper of my car was resting against the wall, there was no damage to the car because my foot must have slipped off the accelerator. A police officer on a motorcycle stopped to assist me and decided to escort me home. I was surprised I didn't get a ticket, just a warning. On another occasion, despite all the coffee I had drunk and the two short naps I had, I was zigzagging all over Route 28 at six o'clock in the morning. I heard a siren and pulled over. The officer thought I was drunk and asked me to remove my sunglasses. When he saw my eyes outlined with heavy dark circles, he began questioning me. I explained that I was tired and sleepy after working all day and night. Once more I was escorted home. I wondered what the neighbors thought, but I was too sleepy to care.

Having a three-day weekend allowed me to become more active in organizations. I joined the Pittsburgh Regina Choir, and we cut a record to be sold in the Catholic Churches. Margie and I joined Grey Ladies, a branch of the Red Cross. With other Grey Ladies, we volunteered to teach dancing at a veteran's hospital to patients who had psychological problems and had forgotten how to dance. Most of those men, veterans of World War II, lived in open wards, and dancing was part of their occupational therapy. We taught the fox trot, the waltz, and the jitterbug. The men were not allowed to have matches, so we lit their cigarettes with a lighter we carried in a pocket of our uniforms. We also provided refreshments for them: cake, cookies, coffee, and lemonade. Two men, selected by one of the therapists who supervised us, would help us in the kitchen by making coffee in the 36-cup coffee urn. There were times when a therapist had to intervene should a patient get out of control while we were teaching a dance step. Every so often one of the men would say, "Oh, yeah! I remember." Everyone in the ballroom celebrated his efforts by applauding and hooting. We knew when that happened he was one more step toward his way to returning home.

During orientation, we were advised never to walk alone in the hallways, but one evening I left my purse and coat in one of the offices assigned to us. I didn't know the office had closed early. Without thinking, I started down an unfamiliar hallway that I was not aware led to the closed wards where the more emotionally distressed and violent men were housed. I realized I was trapped. I was at the end of the hall, facing the double doors of the locked wards. All of the other doors in the hallway had automatically closed behind me. I was sure I heard footsteps. Someone was walking behind me. I could barely breathe. He stood behind me for a minute. I just stood still in front of the double doors praying. Suddenly, I heard keys rattling, and I knew I was safe. It had to be one of the administrators because they were the only ones allowed to have keys. He said sternly, "Didn't you remember what we said in orientation?" I apologized, explaining that I needed to get my coat and purse. He had little sympathy for me. I had to be more careful. I should have asked one of the therapists to accompany me. Meanwhile, Margie was waiting in the parking lot wondering what had happened to me since I was gone for half an hour. She had locked her purse in the car.

In addition to volunteering at the Vet's hospital, Margie and I volunteered to work in the small café of the New Kensington General Hospital. We made sandwiches as well as hot dogs and grilled burgers; we heated soup and chili. We sold pastries, slices of cake or pies, made ice cream sundaes, banana splits, and milk shakes. I remember one of the doctors, a bit chubby, always ordered potato chips, a milk shake, and a pastry or candy bar. Then he would complain to me about his gaining weight. Finally, I said, "Fine. I won't serve those to you the next time you come in for lunch. You should plan on having a cup of soup and a sandwich." He just laughed, but that's what he ordered on his next visit.

During the time I worked at *The Observer*, I met Carol, who was hired as the editor of the *Millvale Weekly*. She was a bright, energetic woman with a wonderful sense of humor. We shared the office and became instant friends. Many of our days were filled with chatter and laughter, but we were focused and did get the newspapers published on time. We shared confidences, something I was never able to do with other women. I really enjoyed working in the journalism field, but there was always something missing in my life. It was as though I still had not found myself. Buddy took me to meetings of the Young Democrats, and I became involved in politics. Later I was named Young Miss Democrat of Westmoreland County. I met John Perry at the first meeting of the Young Democrats, and we began to date, but not exclusively. Sandy and I were still dating, and I enjoyed being with him. Meanwhile, I continued attending the University of Pittsburgh, planning to work on a doctorate.

As Young Miss Democrat of Westmoreland County, I attended political fundraisers, dressed in a formal gown, wearing a sash with my title on it. I was to make sure the wife of a politician was never alone as her husband walked around the room greeting and meeting various people. I made small talk, took her to the Powder Room, introduced her to local women she may not have known, and just kept her company. If she met a friend and began talking, I just stepped back a few feet. I remember being invited to work at a $100.00 a plate dinner in which the former President Harry Truman was the guest speaker. I sat eight feet from the President, who was standing on a platform with Secret Service men nearby. He was a dynamic speaker, receiving a standing ovation with a prolonged applause. I was supposed to be working, but I really wasn't needed that night. There was no small talk. The women were more interested in meeting President Truman.

My life seemed to be on track until I received a telephone call from Dr. Joseph Pallone, the principal of Arnold High School. "Mary Ellen, I am planning to schedule Spanish classes again. I've looked through your resume noticed that you had taken Spanish at college. The classes at the high school won't begin until the next school year, and we will offer only Spanish I. Do you think you can prepare yourself to teach Spanish I? You belong in the teaching field, and I want to hire you. You would teach two Spanish classes and three of English." I was shocked. I would need just six additional credits to add the discipline to my teaching certificate, but I needed many more to become proficient in the language. His intention was to add Spanish II and Spanish III during the next three years. I knew one thing about myself. I missed the interaction with students. In short, I missed teaching. Was Dr. Pallone right? Had I finally found my career? Was I fair in leaving *The Observer*? Would I enjoy teaching Spanish? Was I making the right career move? There were many sleepless nights before I could answer him.

Changing Careers: Changing My Life

There was no valid reason to leave *The Observer* except that I realized I belonged in the classroom. I had come full circle. I wanted to develop course curriculum, to make a difference in just one student's life. If I could do that I would consider myself successful. I decided to accept Dr. Pallone's offer. During the summer, I took six additional credits of Spanish, enough to be certified by the state to teach Spanish. During the fall semester I continued taking courses at the University of Pittsburgh.

I dated John frequently, even planning to get married the following Valentine's Day. But as time went on I believed I was not the right woman for him. I knew the relationship had to end. All we had in common was the Young Democrats' Club. Graduating from college, earning both a Bachelor of Arts and a Masters of Letters and working in the journalism field had changed me. I became the independent intellectual. I discovered that my hobbies were different from those of other women that I knew. Jerry and I took golf lessons, bought a set of clubs, and joined a new golf club for young adults in Vandergrift, a nearby town. The golf course was only nine holes, but we had the opportunity of meeting a variety of people, some with college degrees and some without, but they had a wide set of interests: art, music, theater, current events, sports, and politics.

John and I were no longer dating, seldom even speaking to each other. I was the one who ended the relationship. I continued to pursue my interests: acting or working on the stage crew in the

The Letters

New Kensington Civic Theater, wanting to see operas, going to art galleries and museums, and reading all type of publications. I had to be true to myself. Margie, Jerry, and I joined the Junior Women's Club, and for the first time in a couple of years, I was no longer "tough" or considered to be "one of the boys." Buddy was angry with me and couldn't understand why I had ended the relationship with John. He knew John loved me, and he thought I loved him. He had introduced us at the first Young Democrats meeting, but there was no way I could explain to him why I was the wrong girl for John. Buddy couldn't understand that I had changed.

Everything about me seemed to change, even the styles of clothes I wore. I would find a dress or skirt I liked, but couldn't afford, in one of the fashion magazines. I would take the magazine to my uncle who copied and tailored several skirts for me designed by Chanel. At times I would order from a magazine a dress designed by Jonathan Logan. I also bought I Miller, uniquely designed dress shoes, expensive for the time, about $25.00, more than a third of my week's salary. My wardrobe consisted of clothes for work, for casual dating, and for formal occasions, evening gowns. My parents had bought me a fur coat as a college graduation gift, but several years later I purchase a tan cashmere coat that just caught my eye and a white coat for more formal affairs. I was truly out of sync with my generation in my town in the 1950's and 1960's. In short, I loved the fine arts: operas, concerts, Broadway plays and musicals, lectures, museums, and art galleries. I enjoyed traveling, playing golf, performing in the Civic Theater.

There is no way to compare the life of a young girl living in the small western towns of Pennsylvania at that time to the life of young women today. Times were very different. Although Pittsburgh was only eighteen miles south of Arnold and New Kensington, for many it was as though going to Pittsburgh was like traveling to a distant place. Those who worked in the city or attended the University of Pittsburgh, Carnegie Tech, Mt. Mercy, or other universities or colleges traveled to Pittsburgh, but many did not shop in Pittsburgh. Transportation was by bus or car, and riding or driving to the city took an hour. It was stop and go traffic until years later when a direct route was constructed. Leaving Arnold by bus, we traveled through New Kensington, Harmarville, Cheswick, Springdale, Oakmont, Millvale, and various suburbs of Pittsburgh. Few young women drove or owned cars. Few men and women had an opportunity to attend college or university. Many married at a young age, before reaching the age of twenty-five, including Connie who married when she was nineteen. Some believed that if you didn't marry by twenty-five, your chances of getting married were slim.

The dating ritual was very formal. The young man usually telephoned a girl several days before a date with specific plans for the evening. Relationships began in high school, in college, or at work. It could be the boy next door or one introduced by a relative or friend. I don't remember ever going to a bar with a group of girls, but men and women did go stag or with friends to dances during the Big Band era, having an opportunity to meet one another. Long distance phone calls were very expensive and were almost seldom made. So we all became very good letter writers. Sometimes the days revolved around the mailman when a special letter was expected.

There was a lot of prejudice against people of ethnic origins in those days. Misunderstandings and assumptions about what we were and what we weren't were prevalent in every part of my life growing up. Anti-communism was rampant after World War II, so many foreigners were suspect. Schools held "duck and cover" drills in response to the Soviet Union exploding its first atomic device in 1949, and we lived in fear. It was a way of life. Fear was incorporated into our daily life as everyone prepared for disaster: the possibility of an atom bomb. Throughout my childhood, I was full of life, and as an adult I expected a life that would allow me to live happily every after. I never realized, however, that receiving the first of many letters when I was planning a wedding would change my life.

Acknowledgements

It is those letters, remembrances of relationships from long ago, written by five men that became the catalyst for this book. It is a memoir, a detailed account of my life inspired by true events. The memoir is not only a love story, but also it is my life based on joy, deceit, and heartbreak that finally led me to unconditional love with an Italian national, my late husband, Orazio.

I was like any other young woman who attends an international university, seeking adventure but finding romance. It is a rare book that is product of one person. Rather it is a collection of others who have contributed to the completion of a product. This book could not have been completed without acknowledging those who walked in my life and never left while sharing with me those adventures in Mexico, leaving me with life-long memories: Patty DiSantis, Carol Kelly, Dorothy Marinucci, Geraldine (Jerry) Vairo, and Gil and Joyce Puissegur.

Thanks to my daughter, Susan Swails, Technical Editor, whose expertise in computers and editing, assisted me in completing the book; to those friends, Professor Mary DiStefano Diaz and Phyllis Luck, who read portions of the first draft and urged me to continue writing; to Roy and Joan Yater, who gave me permission to include their sympathy note in the text; to Editor Elizabeth Pagel-Hogan, who suggested editing changes, to April Urso, who designed the front and back covers of the book and edited the photos, and to Sherry Frazier, a Public Relations professional, who gave me encouragement.

Finally, thanks go to members of my family who supported me during the two-year writing period of several drafts.

WA